The Singing Book

The Singing Book

SECOND EDITION

MERIBETH DAYME

CYNTHIA VAUGHN

W. W. NORTON & COMPANY
NEW YORK LONDON

W. W. Norton & Company has been independent since its founding in 1923, when William Warder Norton and Margaret D. Herter Norton first published lectures delivered at the People's Institute, the adult education division of New York City's Cooper Union. The Nortons soon expanded their program beyond the Institute, publishing books by celebrated academics from America and abroad. By mid-century, the two major pillars of Norton's publishing program—trade books and college texts—were firmly established. In the 1950s, the Norton family transferred control of the company to its employees, and today—with a staff of 400 and a comparable number of trade, college, and professional titles published each year—W. W. Norton & Company stands as the largest and oldest publishing house owned wholly by its employees.

Printed in the United States of America
Second Edition

Manufacturing by Quebecor World—Eusey Division
Book design by Martin Lubin Graphic Design
Book composition and music typography by David Botwinik, Willow Graphics
Production Manager: Jane Searle

Cover illustration: André Masson. Street Singer. 1941. The Museum of Modern Art, New York, NY. Purchase (158.1942). Digital Image © The Museum of Modern Art/Licensed by SCALA/Art Resource, NY. © 2003 Artists Rights Society (ARS), New York/ADAGP, Paris.

Editor: Maribeth Payne
Managing Editor—College: Marian Johnson
Project Editor: Allison Courtney Fitch
Project Manager: Kim Yi

Library of Congress Cataloging-in-Publication Data

Dayme, Meribeth Bunch, date.

The singing book / Meribeth Dayme, Cynthia Vaughn. — 2nd ed.
p. cm.
Includes bibliographical references (p. □) and index.

ISBN 13: 978-0-393-93052-8 (pbk.)

1. Singing—Instruction and study. 2. Singing—Physiological aspects.
I. Vaughn, Cynthia. II. Title.

MT820.B86 2008

783—dc22 2007035541

W. W. Norton & Company, Inc., 500 Fifth Avenue, New York, N.Y. 10110
www.wwnorton.com

W. W. Norton & Company Ltd., Castle House,
75/76 Wells Street, London W1T 3QT

3 4 5 6 7 8 9 0

Contents

In addition to new songs from *The Singing Book*, Second Edition, the following traditional/art songs from the first edition remain available on the student website, **wwnorton.com/web/singing**

The Frog in the Bog (Canada)
Gaudeamus igitur (Germany)
Banana Boat Song (Day-O) (Jamaica)
Ego sum pauper (Latin)
Civil War Medley (America)
The Lark in the Clear Air (Ireland)
Westryn Wynde (England)
Paun I Kolo (Bosnia)
Ah! si mon moine voulait danser! (Canada)
Mi caballo blanco (Chile)
My Lord, What a Mornin'! (America)
Ombra mai fù (Handel 1685–1759)
Auf Flügeln des Gesanges (Mendelssohn 1809–1847)
Bitte (Franz 1815–1892)
Ici-bas (Fauré 1845–1924)
Gentle Annie (Foster 1826–1864)
Modern Major-General (Gilbert & Sullivan)

Welcome . . .

. . . TO THE SECOND EDITION OF *THE SINGING BOOK*

The first edition of *The Singing Book* has been so popular that we were reluctant to make drastic changes; however, we have been inspired by your suggestions and comments to make some important additions. New songs and arrangements have been added, a Singing IQ quiz now appears in the appendices, IPA and translations are now placed with each foreign-text song, and we have changed the design to make it more user-friendly.

Let's begin with what we have done with the songs.

NEW SONGS AND ONLINE BONUS SONGS

Twenty-eight new songs have been added to the repertoire. And, very importantly, the public domain arrangements or songs that have been deleted from the printed edition will still be available to you on the student website (wwnorton.com/web/singing) as bonus songs. For this second edition, we are particularly pleased that we have been able to secure the rights to recent songs from Josh Groban and others. A *Singing Book* exclusive is the first published arrangement of "Be Who You Were Born to Be" by Lucinda Drayton and Andrew Blisset of the popular British group Bliss.

Encouraged by your comments and suggestions, we have included the following in the new song section:

- More standard Italian songs, including a traditional arrangement of "Selve amiche" and a fresh new arrangement by Scarlett Antaloczy of "Star vicino"
- More optional duets and songs that lend themselves to male voices.
- Songs with outstanding and inspirational texts from great poets (William Shakespeare, William Butler Yeats, Robert Louis Stevenson) and contemporary sages (Lucinda Drayton), and more accompanied traditional and patriotic songs, including "The Star Spangled Banner," "O Canada!," and "America the Beautiful"
- Additional improvisations
- Listening suggestions including suggested artist recordings (many available as easy downloads from iTunes, Rhapsody, and other online sources)
- A new feature inspired by the popular Pandora website and the Music Genome Project: "If you like this song, take a look at ________"

Did we mention online bonus songs, including 17 songs from the first edition of *The Singing Book*? See wwnorton.com/web/singing for more information.

MORE NEW FEATURES OF THE SECOND EDITION

- We have added a fun section to the Appendices called What's Your Singing IQ? It is an interesting exercise for students to take this test at the beginning of their studies. It is strictly fun, and not official, yet it will give students an idea of the accuracy of some of their perceptions about singing. It furnishes the fuel for some lively discussion and discovery in classes and lessons.
- Additional and updated websites and online resources
- Revised IPA (International Phonetic Alphabet) for foreign-language songs

CHANGES IN ORGANIZATION

The IPA for each foreign-language song is now placed just before the song. We wanted you to have all the information in one place. However, we have kept our accessible "Sing First, Talk Later" approach. Part One is still a quick-start guide with enough information and technique to start you singing better "right out of the box." Part Two still contains a very wide variety of songs, from easy to moderately challenging; from folk and classical songs to jazz standards and contemporary songs. Part Three has been praised by many for its clarity and accuracy of information about the voice.

Finally, you will notice a new design that will help you identify the different parts of the book more easily—no more flipping through pages.

THINGS WE WANT TO EMPHASIZE

- The information in this book is the foundation for all styles of singing.
- Improvisation is an important tool for freeing the voice. While it may feel uncomfortable at first to "not have control," persist, because you will be a better singer for it.
- Once you have explored Part One's quick-start guide (The First Steps to Singing Easily), you'll be eager to learn more about How the Voice Works in the detailed chapters of Part Three. However, some students may not want to know more than the information in Part One at first. For that reason, we continue to keep it separate.

WHAT WE WOULDN'T DREAM OF CHANGING!

Both students and teachers loved the ease of use and the clarity of text in the first edition of *The Singing Book*. The *Finding out for yourself* sections gave everyone practical ways to learn about the voice.

We have made dozens of songs available on our student website (wwnorton.com/web/singing) that you can print out in any key.

Everyone applauded the variety, appeal, quality, and quantity of the songs and the accompaniments on the CDs—more than any student could sing in a single class. A collection of such wonderful music is a gift for life.

WHAT HAS BEEN SAID ABOUT THE BOOK

"It has a great variety of repertoire beautifully played on accompanying CDs, and has some of the best modern, science-based descriptions of vocal anatomy, physiology, and function I have ever read in such a book."

— Robert Edwin, *The Journal of Singing,* May/June 2006

"The strongest feature of *The Singing Book* is its matter-of-fact, egalitarian approach to the vocal art."

— Debra Greschner, *The Journal of Singing,* September/October 2004

"A refreshing approach to learning the art of singing. A wealth of useful information for performers, students, and teachers alike."

— Fred Hersch, *Western Michigan University*

"Thank you for the helpful variety of songs. I love that this text engages students' imagination and creativity."

— Dawn Hayes, *Simpson College*

"By far the best singing anthology available. The song selections are terrific."

— Eric Bronner, *Salve Regina University*

"The repertoire is broad and well balanced. I appreciate the inclusion of songs from other cultures. The most up-to-date and useful classroom singing text available."

— Henrietta Carter, *Golden West College*

"I'm thrilled with *The Singing Book* . . . clear, straightforward prose and the fact that you never talk down. It's an exceptional book—really well-written and well-presented."

— Valerie Walters, *Kennesaw State University*

"I love *The Singing Book*! The songs are fun and I'm learning a lot about how the voice works. Things my choir director told us now make sense."

— Emily Bradshaw, freshman music student

Preface

The Singing Book brings a new sense of adventure and fun to class voice, the private studio, and choirs. This book is designed to help the beginning singer develop fundamental habits of singing that are both healthful and easy and to provide useful guidelines and a repertoire collection for those who already have some background in singing. Using the principles outlined, singers will be able to perform in any style they wish, not just classical. The concepts in *The Singing Book* lay the foundations for a new generation of healthy and confident singers and at the same time furnish them with a book that is useful throughout their singing life.

The book is based on a multi-dimensional approach that includes a balanced use of mental, physical, and imaginative methods for performance. Mental approaches include techniques for visualization, focusing for success, and basic knowledge of how the voice works. The physical components have the two-fold goal of focusing both the body and the mind through exercises that create balanced right-left brain functioning and that work with effective concepts of postural and physical awareness. Finally, positive self-development, creativity, and imagination are encouraged throughout the process. Students are urged to experiment with vocal improvisations, to visualize scenes, to develop characters based on the song texts, and even to sing the book aloud as they read.

Key to this multi-dimensional approach is the concept of *co-responsibility,* which is emphasized and implemented through numerous sections labeled *Finding out for yourself* . . . . When students are given permission to experiment with both efficient and inefficient ways of singing in order to see and hear for themselves the habits that produce the best results, learning time is halved. The Finding out exercises can be performed in groups or alone with a video camera. The use of a video camera for teaching and feedback is a powerful learning tool. However, it is not always practical in a class situation. The exercises in *Finding out* sections are designed to give the singer an idea of what a video session might produce.

The book is divided into three sections. Part One teaches students to sing comfortably and easily; Part Two contains over sixty songs with comprehensive, interesting annotations and appropriate translations; and Part Three gives a detailed description of how the vocal mechanism works.

The book is organized in a way that gives the singer a chance to explore his or her own voice first and then begin singing without too many intellectual restrictions. By reading and working through the exercises in Part One, students will learn to focus their bodies and minds. Part One also includes easy physical warm-ups, suggestions for imaginative ways of learning songs, and easy vocal improvisations using everyday conversation. Finally, the first part of this book teaches students to handle performance jitters and to focus on confident performances.

Part Two of *The Singing Book* contains an anthology of over sixty songs, demonstrating a wide range of moods, rhythms, and tempos that are suitable for both men and women and that range from easy to challenging. A variety of world folk music, spirituals, patriotic songs, and rounds encourage healthy vocal technique, and the improvisation exercises encourage creativity and individuality and satisfy current NASM guidelines regarding vocal competency. Unison group songs and rounds offer beginning singers an opportunity to sing together before stepping out of their comfort zones and singing alone or in a duet. Representative art songs in a variety of languages from the Renaissance, Baroque, Romantic, and Modern eras are included in the anthology as well as songs from musical theater, television, film, and jazz standards. Annotations provide students with interesting background materials and performance suggestions for each of the songs.

When more in-depth knowledge is needed, teachers and students can turn to Part Three, which contains detailed text and illustrations relating to the logic and construction of the vocal mechanism. Part Three also provides information on vocal problems and instructions on how to keep a healthy voice. We have been deliberate in separating Parts One and Three in order to encourage students to begin to sing first without too much analytical-critical thinking getting in the way.

Supplementing the text is a 2-CD set that gives students three listening options for learning and practicing the songs. The songs are recorded in "split-track," with the melody and guide rhythm on one track and piano accompaniment on the other track. Using a computer or any stereo equipped with balance controls, students can adjust the speaker balance to hear either the melody/rhythm or piano accompaniment alone, or to hear both tracks played together. (Stereos without balance controls will play both tracks simultaneously.) Using the recordings will enable students to learn the music and become comfortable with the accompaniments before performing the songs in class.

Another excellent resource is *The Singing Book* Student Website (wwnorton.com/web/singing). Here, students and teachers can transpose and print sheet music in alternate keys for all of the folk songs, hymns, spirituals, and several art songs from the anthology. The Website also offers all of the public-domain songs from the first edition of *The Singing Book* in this format.

Class voice and studio repertoire sessions are excellent introductions to the art of singing in ways which will prove to be fun, imaginative, exciting, and satisfying to students and teachers alike. Often, group voice classes become required courses that students consider boring and instructors consider a chore. In many instances, the course is handled in the same way that many classical private studios are—as a kind of private lesson in a group format without regard to the various styles of singing and the varied interests and abilities of those required to take class voice. This book represents the antithesis of that philosophy.

We invite you to enjoy the journey of learning to sing and perform.

Meribeth Dayme and Cynthia Vaughn

Acknowledgments

No book of this scope can be written without incorporating information and feedback from every teacher, student, and mentor we have ever had. So to everyone one of you, thank you. We know that there is nothing new under the sun, that most information is just a new arrangement of existing knowledge. This book is no different.

To everyone who reviewed the manuscript of the first edition, we appreciate your comments and input. Special thanks go to Rita Farrell and Jane Vukovic, who gave us editorial suggestions and helpful encouragement. We would also like to thank all of the teachers, graduate teaching assistants, and voice class students who gave us invaluable feedback from their experience and teaching of the first edition.

Thanks also to the "Diction Divas" Candace Magner and Yvonne deChance, and to Jeson Yan, Alex Pudov, and Noemi Lugo for Chinese, Russian, and Spanish translations and pronunciation. Craig Tompkins (Canada) and Sylvana Santinelli (Mexico) offered many suggestions for French Canadian and Mexican songs to be used here and in future editions.

We would also like to thank the editorial staff at W. W. Norton & Company for their expertise and help. It has been an honor to work with them on this project. Maribeth Payne was instrumental in getting this project off the ground and Courtney Fitch has been extremely helpful and skillful in getting this second edition into shape. The Norton production team has also given us invaluable help and support.

Cynthia and Meribeth thank each other as well. It has been quite a team effort to put this book together. There have been many hours spent chatting on the Internet, many transcontinental phone calls, and many e-mails with attachments sent into the wee hours of the morning. Cynthia even managed to get to London and France to spend time with Meribeth there. Personally, Cynthia would like to thank her daughter Katy Vaughn for her sharp eye and twenty-something perspective, and Meribeth could not have done this without her personal coach, Louise Mita.

Our thanks would not be complete without acknowledging the dedication and talent of Beryl Maile, our illustrator, and our highly talented arrangers, Scarlett Antaloczy (editions 1 and 2) and Frank Ponzio and Cynthia Fox (edition 1). Thanks also to Ms. Fox for recording keyboard accompaniments for *The Singing Book* CDs. They worked to tight deadlines with wonderfully positive attitudes.

Putting *The Singing Book* together took a huge team of dedicated and skilled people. The combined experience, education, and wisdom of everyone involved is greatly appreciated. Many thanks to everyone.

INTRODUCTION Getting Started

Let's get right to the heart of the matter: Singing is fun, joyful, imaginative, exciting, and satisfying. It includes a variety of styles such as classical, musical theater, pop, jazz, rap, soul, and much, much more. *The Singing Book* is not just a textbook; it is designed to help you enjoy using your voice easily, healthily, and happily for the rest of your life. It is intended for those of you who are just beginning to sing, as well as choral singers and instrumentalists who want to improve. Along the way, you will develop a clear understanding of how the voice works and what it means to perform with purpose and a message in a number of the vocal styles listed above.

Any sustained sound that you make with your voice can be considered singing whether in the shower, in your car with the windows up, or on the karaoke stage. (Even your un-hums and ums and ers have a certain singing quality to them.) In those situations there is no one to tell you how to do it, and your analytical-critical left brain that wants to stop the sound before you begin is strangely absent.

Singing easily and healthily involves a balance of creativity, spontaneity, and knowledge of basic, healthy principles. This balance is important because much of your learning has been dedicated to analytical-critical thinking and data-specific information. For singing, it is important to balance the intellect with feeling, emotion, and intuition. The left brain is usually in charge of intellectual thinking and the right brain in charge of intuition and spontaneity. For singing and performance, a good connection between the right and left brain is necessary. Therefore, here are three principles that are important to your approach to singing.

Humans Are Meant to Sing

We "sing" all the time without realizing it. Listen to ordinary conversation and you will hear many musical sounds scattered throughout. There are many sustained sounds in every language. These form the basis of a natural way to move into singing. The sound *hummm,* often a response to conversation, could be considered a short hum, the basis for the beginning of a warm-up for many singers.

Preconceptions and self-sabotage regarding *singing* often get in singers' ways and stop them from making any sustained sound without criticizing it. These potential self-curses include everything from ideas that only highly trained singers perform in public to self-judgments about the quality of the voice as heard from the inside rather than the sounds heard by the audience. *Somehow we have the idea that "singing" has to be perfect rather than fun and enjoyable.* Yet we go about our normal day having "sung" quite often.

Vocabulary and Learning

When in doubt, always think positively. There is increasing evidence that positive or negative thinking and the vocabulary you use set you up to succeed or fail. Words and phrases like *I am capable of doing this, I can do this, I will do my best* will create an atmosphere in which you can reach your potential.

Unhelpful words that are best eliminated from your spoken and mental vocabulary include *right* and *wrong, should* and *ought, control* and *hold,* and *I always have trouble with. . . .* This kind of self-sabotage inhibits spontaneity, creativity, and intuition, and sets up an internal radio of nonstop comment and negativity in our brains. These and many more thought forms tend to lower the immune system temporarily. So, for this class, discard them; in fact, establish rules and agreements for their use, and give compliments for using *enjoy* and *imagination*: the "e" and "i" words.

With fun in mind, here is a crazy way to begin using this text. *Rather than just sitting and reading these words, sing them!* Now go back to the beginning of the chapter and sing everything you have just read in any way you wish. There are no "wrong" notes because you are making up the tune. Do this in class by having a "sung" conversation with a partner. When you can't think of something to sing, hum until you are ready. You can now say you have learned the basics of improvisation. Your assignment for the duration of your vocal study is to sing, rather than read silently, all the text in this book.

Finding out for yourself . . .

When you read the assignment to sing this text, did you think any of the following: "I can't do this, it is too childish," "People will think I'm nuts," or "I should be doing proper singing—something more sophisticated and classical"? These are good examples of an approach that is analytical-critical, creativity inhibiting, self-destructive, and under the control of a dominant left brain. However, if you said, "This sounds crazy and fun" or "What an imaginative way to begin singing" or any number of other positive things, then your inner child and your right brain thought it must be worth doing.

You can find out how your body reacts to positive and negative thoughts by using the following test with a partner. Person A is to stand and think thoughts like "I shouldn't be singing this way," "I can't do this," and "this is silly." Person B tests Person A's stability using two fingers to gently push on A's sternum (chest bone). Normally you will find that A cannot maintain his or her balance while thinking the negative thoughts. Now perform the same test using the following thoughts: "This is fun," "I am excited about doing this," "I am strong and centered in myself." The body will remain strong and unable to be pushed off center. Now that you know what negative thoughts do to your body, you can begin to understand what they do to your singing as well.

Technique Serves the Message

A vocally healthy, good technique is considered basic to singing well, whatever the style. This idea cannot be stressed enough. Many students become so involved with the technical aspects, however, that they forget about the message in the words and music. Yet singers who are good on stage are completely involved in the music and the audience adores them. Those who are only technically proficient complain about the poor technique of popular singers but are themselves somewhat boring. The truth is that you can do both—be completely involved and have good technique—and both are essential. A good technique provides the ease and freedom for your imagination and creativity to capture your audience. When you concentrate too much on your voice and how you sound, the message that comes across to the audience is "I am being very diligent about my singing." The message of the song and the music is then lost and the audience becomes bored very quickly.

Now that you have begun to use your creativity and imagination, it is important to have a pleasant, healthy voice. There are some key principles involved. You will probably need to change some old habits. That will take thought. However, this is part of the balance mentioned earlier.

The sections that follow are deliberately simple with minimal information given to allow you to experience your voice for yourself. More specific details of how the voice works are located in Part Three. You may *sing* Part Three any time you choose. First get started with Part One and Part Two, the songs, and then find out how your voice works and how to keep it healthy in Part Three. Don't forget to have fun with improvisation.

PART ONE

The First Steps to Singing Easily

S*inging is a* combination of mind, body, imagination, and spirit all working together. That is the context in which this text is written. The complete singer exhibits physical ease, awareness, imagination, and enjoyment.

Finding out for yourself . . .

Begin this process by asking yourself this question: "In the best of all possible worlds, how would I like my voice described?" If someone heard you sing and were to describe your voice to others, what would you like said about it? Make a list of the characteristics that are important to you. (For example, this list might include adjectives such as *warm, clear, bright,* and so on.) By knowing how you wish to sound, you can begin to make it happen.

CHAPTER ONE *Healthy Singing*

Vocal ease and health go hand in hand. They are the basis for a long-lasting technique and a beautiful sound. Your technique is the support or the framework for everything you want to do with your voice. Three basic principles of technique are presented here: physical balance, breathing, and presence.

Physical Balance

The first principle of healthy singing is good physical balance. Instrumentalists will tell you that the most wonderful technique in the world will not help when their instruments are unbalanced or misshapen. This is doubly true of the human voice whose instrument is the body. It is the equivalent of having a house built on shaky foundations with crooked walls. Those who can sing well, easily, and healthily despite posturally unbalanced and misshapened bodies are exceptional. Unfortunately, the most copied characteristics of admired singers are the faults and exaggerations, because they are usually the most obvious to the student with limited knowledge. These faults include poking the head forward to "sing to the audience," holding the body in a stiff and artificial manner, and adopting the super casual look of a pop singer.

FIGURE 1.1
Good posture

As you are used to your current habits of standing and sitting, you may find that the suggestions that follow feel awkward at first. When you are aligned well (ears in line with shoulders and hips) for the first time, your body will tell you that your balance is now not correct (see following Box). Use a mirror or a video to tell you how it really looks. Persist, and you will find that your muscles will adjust very quickly to a new way of standing and sitting.

As you know, how we *think* we look and how we actually look can be very different. It is important that you test for yourself what is said in this text. Here are some observations for you to make in a group or for yourself with the help of a video recording.

Efficient physical balance ensures that the parts of your instrument are aligned and in position to work together to produce a free sound. This means that your lungs, your voice box (larynx), and your throat (vocal tract) are all in a line and in a position of maximum efficiency for singing (see Figure 1.1).

Finding out for yourself . . .

First, how are you standing presently? Get a partner to coach someone to duplicate your posture exactly. After that person is standing or sitting exactly like you, notice what your profile is like. Get that person to describe how it feels to adopt your stance while you move around him or her to see how you look. (It is very effective to look at a side view of yourself with a video camera.)

Choose a few lines from any song and, with a partner, experiment with what happens to your singing, your body, and your tone quality when you do the following:

1. Sing with your weight on your heels.
2. Sing with an overly arched back.
3. Sing with your weight on your toes.

Now "superglue" your feet to the floor and reach for the ceiling with the crown of your head (that area where your cowlick sits near the back), don't adjust your chin up or down, keep your knees gently loose, and balance your weight evenly between the balls of your feet and your heels. The balance is correct when you can rise up on your toes by pushing through the feet without adjusting any other part of the body. You may find you have to move your weight more forward than you thought. Remember that the feet are superglued so the full foot will remain on the floor with your weight more forward. (This is a beginning and it does not matter if you are not perfect at it yet.)

4. Compare this final version with those in 1, 2, and 3 above. As awkward as it may feel, sing your phrases in this position. You will find the voice now is a more efficient instrument to sing/play.

Breathing Easily

The second principle is that breathing for singing needs to be accomplished easily and deeply. Notice that the word deeply is used. No one said to take a big breath. Deep and big are not the same. Deep, in this case, refers to the lower half of your body (including the abdomen and the lower ribs in the back) where you feel expansion on inhalation. You can take in a lot or a small amount of air as long as you feel the response deeply in your body.

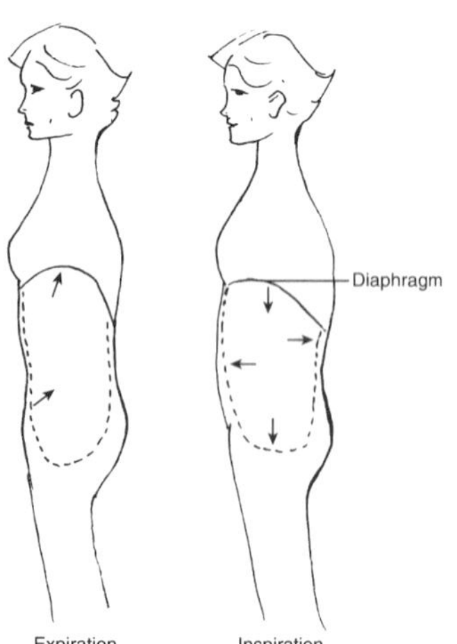

FIGURE 1.2
Deep breathing

Ideally, imagine you have a large tube from your mouth to your lower abdomen that forms a channel for your air. This tube does not change shape during the breathing process and nothing in the upper chest is disturbed. There is no gasping and no noise that comes from the mouth or throat and no extra movement of the shoulders or chest. Any visible action of breathing is seen in the lower ribs at the back and the lower abdomen (see Figure 1.2). Pay attention to your posture because when the back is overly arched (swaybacked), the lower ribs are not able to respond and it is difficult to get a deep breath. (A thorough discussion of breathing is in Chapter 8).

Never stop breathing. This may sound ridiculous to you. However, notice what you do the next time you "stop" to think. There is a good chance that you also stop the process of inhaling and exhaling. Mental and physical hesitation can cause us to stop breathing for the moment. It's all about flow, and in singing, especially airflow. When you gasp or grab a breath, the body wants to lock it in; there is a momentary pause, and the voice tends to seize up just when you want to sing. So, go with the flow.

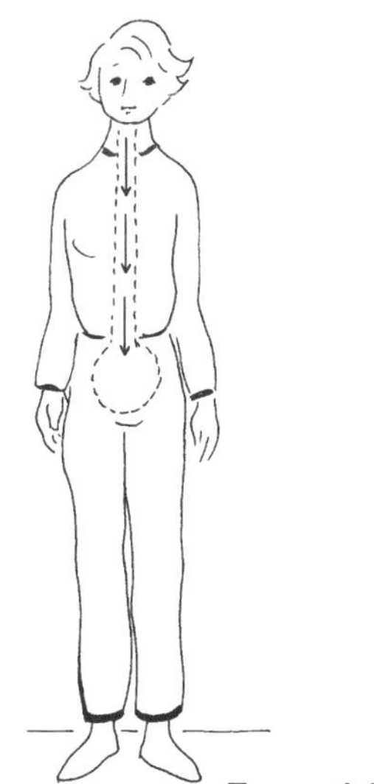

Figure 1.3
Imagery for deep breathing

Finding out for yourself . . .

This is an experiment in efficient and inefficient breathing and how it can affect your singing. Note: Let your partner do the listening. You cannot sing and listen at the same time. Your job is to do the "feeling." Sing a line or two of a song immediately after breathing in the manner below:

1. Take a huge breath letting your shoulders and chest rise.
2. Take a breath with a slouched posture.
3. Take a breath with an overly arched back.
4. Breathe with efficient physical alignment.
5. Breathe and feel as if you have an imaginary pipeline to the lower abdomen (see Figure 1.3).

Staying Present

The third principle is to stay present at all times. Being present implies that you are aware of what is happening around you while you are singing. This does not mean the same thing as being distracted. Presence is a state of being centered, of having a quiet alertness. In performance, this state acts as a powerful magnet to draw an audience to you. It enables you to be in touch with the music, yourself, and your audience. At the same time, it has a profound effect on your physical state and the freedom of your performance.

Presence is the first step to the development of a listening body and mind. You can tell the state of someone's presence by his or her alignment and the eyes. People who are present and aware seem to be able to see anything in the room without its being obvious. They use peripheral vision rather than a stare and they are *seeing* rather than *looking*. We need to do the same thing when we sing. Singing with the eyes looking up at the ceiling or down at the floor tends to focus the singer and the music inward rather than allowing it to fill the space around. This inhibits the freedom of the body and the participation of the audience.

Finding out for yourself . . .

(It is taken for granted that your posture is exemplary.) Have your partner note the differences (or use a video) when you sing a few lines of any song (the same lines each time) in the following ways:

1. With glaring eyes
2. With soft seeing eyes
3. Staring at the far wall or a person
4. With eyes looking heavenward (do not raise the head)
5. With eyes looking down (do not lower the head)
6. Using peripheral vision (seeing everything around you with calm eyes that are not roving)
7. Using peripheral vision and being the "dot" in the middle of a sphere that encompasses the whole audience (so that your awareness is 360 degrees)

No matter what you are singing or practicing, always stay fully present in the room. Do not take a mental vacation. Developing presence is an essential part of performance and doing so is important from the first moment you begin to sing—even during your vocal warm-ups. Warming up with your mind a thousand miles away will do nothing for your singing.

CHAPTER TWO *Preparing to Sing*

Preparing to sing is like preparing to participate in a sport. Every part of us needs to be available and ready to respond. The mind and body need equal attention from the very beginning. By beginning with focusing the mind, your body will be alerted to the need for action.

Focusing

Top athletes and competitors are taught to focus or visualize their goals before they ever set foot on the playing field. Research has shown that good visualization can be almost as effective as the actual physical practice. Certainly one key to being centered, remaining in the present and in charge of your practice and performance, is the ability to visualize what you want to happen. This can include anything from physical elements of your technique to positive attitudes about performance (including exams).

Here is an easy, short way to focus. Do this at the beginning of every practice session—and for that matter before you study any subject. You can do this even while waiting for a bus.

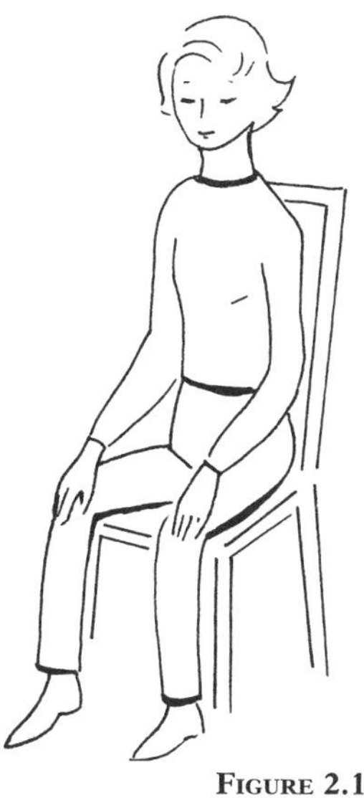

FIGURE 2.1
Being still

Finding out for yourself . . .

Note: For those of you who are used to moving and fidgeting, you may find it difficult to sit still for a minute. Start with thirty seconds instead (see Figure 2.1).

With your eyes open . . .

1. Sit (or stand) with two feet flat on the floor. Imagine that you have superglue attached to the bottoms of your feet. Everything is still. Nothing is twitching or moving.
2. Gently place your hands on something flat or your thighs. Imagine that you have superglue attached to the palms of your hands. Again, nothing is moving (except your breath).
3. Sit in this complete stillness for one minute. You may find that you begin to feel a different kind of energy and that

your thoughts begin to slow down. Enjoy this strange feeling. It will calm you and enable you to clear your mind of all the inner conversational debris that gets in your way.

4. Observe your breathing. Ideally, you will feel as if you are breathing in air from the bottom of the chair. Deep breathing has nothing to do with a big breath or the volume of air you take in. It has to do with a feeling of depth in the body. You can imagine that you are breathing in from the top of your spine to the very bottom of it. To breathe out you reverse the procedure. Deep breathing at its best is barely noticeable.
5. Some Qigong and yogic breathing techniques can be useful as well. They are extremely helpful in getting you to feel depth of breathing in the body. Here is one: As you breathe in, imagine the breath creating a circle behind you beginning at your coccyx (tailbone) and ending over the top of your head. (The circle starts at the coccyx behind and finishes at the lowest part of the pelvis in front.) Continue the circle in the front of your body by beginning your expiration over the top of your head and finishing your breath at the lower pelvis close to where you began. You will feel as if your air has begun deep in your body and you will feel the end of the expiration in the muscles of the lower abdomen.
6. Now visualize yourself creating an atmosphere in which you remain focused and able to do your best.

Focusing is the first step to readying your mind and body for the tasks ahead. The second step is to get the body moving in ways that will benefit your voice.

Movement

Here are some gentle physical warm-ups. They take less than two minutes to perform and are to be done at an easy slow pace and in a centered manner. These exercises consist of stretches and coordinated movements to free the body and get both sides of your brain working together. In all cases pay attention to your postural alignment.

RIB STRETCHES

The idea here is to give the ribs and waist a good stretch. The exercise is to be done slowly for the best effect. During these movements make sure the head is over the shoulders and not poked forward (see Figure 2.2).

a. Interlock your fingers and turn the palms outward.
b. Push your palms outward toward the ceiling until your arms are fully stretched.
c. Bend your elbows and bring the palms (still facing outward) toward the top of your head. Push the palms out and up to the right. Bring them back again and push them out to the left.

d. Repeat the exercise. This time as you do it, bend the knees as you bring the palms toward your body and straighten the knees when the palms and arms are fully stretched. You will find that when your arms are fully extended to the left or right the ribs get a nice stretch.

Figure 2.2
Rib stretches

CROSS CRAWL*

This exercise is similar to marching in place. You alternately move one arm to touch the opposite leg (knee) as you march. It is like walking and swinging your arms as you go. You would normally do it using alternating arm and leg (right leg up and left arm forward, then left leg up and right arm forward). As you touch the opposite knee, maintain your good spinal alignment (see Figure 2.3). You may do this exercise while singing if you wish. However, ten times for each side would be enough.

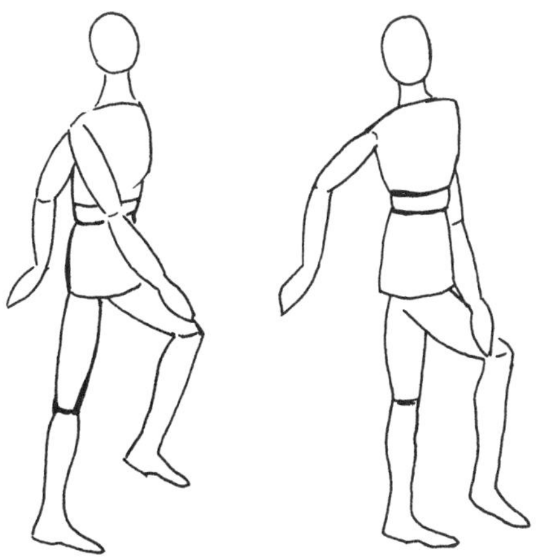

Figure 2.3
Cross crawl

*The Cross crawl, Lazy 8's, and Energy yawn are Brain Gym exercises based on studies by Paul E. Denison and Gail E. Denison.

LAZY 8'S*

This helps you focus and relax the eyes, neck, and shoulders.

Note: Keep the spine aligned and do not lean forward from the waist while you do this exercise.

Begin with either arm outstretched forward. Draw in the air an eight on its side (∞), beginning in the middle and moving up to either the right or left to make the pattern (Figure 2.4). It is important that your first movement be up!

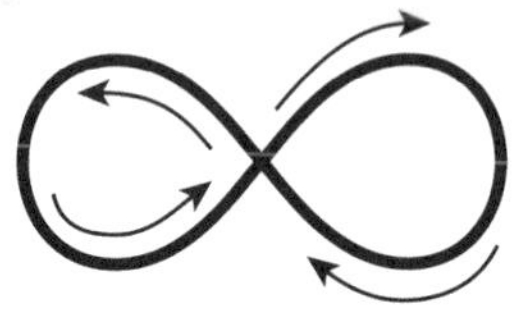

FIGURE 2.4
Lazy 8's

As you draw the eight slowly, smoothly, and evenly, carefully follow your fingertips with your eyes. Alternate left and right arms.

This exercise can also be done with both arms outstretched, palms together. And for more variety you can do this slowly with your nose, making the largest possible movement.

Repeat any of the above patterns ten times (see Figure 2.4).

ENERGY YAWN*

Somehow this exercise always helps people sing better. You can repeat it any time your jaw feels tight. If jaw tension is one of your problem areas, do this exercise several times during a practice session or several times during the day. Be sure to keep your head over your shoulders. There is a tendency to poke the head forward when performing this exercise.

FIGURE 2.5
Energy yawn

Open your mouth as if you are yawning. While maintaining the yawning position, strongly massage the area near the cheek bone above your back teeth (see Figure 2.5). Do this three times.

Warming Up Your Voice

Now that you have warmed up your body and gotten both sides of your brain working, it is time to give the muscles of your voice some special attention. The vocal warm-ups suggested here do not have to be done as scales. By playing and experimenting with sound, you can discover interesting ways of covering a wide range of pitches while relaxing the jaw, lips, and tongue.

Note: During all of the exercises below be sure to check your posture, levels of awareness, and presence. Here are some options for you:

1. Lip trills or "motor boats" going from the middle of your voice and as high as you can go, and then from the middle of your voice and as low as you can go.
2. Sirens up and down—not missing any pitches. This means lots of sliding up and down on an "ng" sound. You may also use a comfortable vowel sound for this.
3. Tongue trills or "raspberries" up and down in the same manner as numbers 1 and 2. (This is the same as a continual rolled "rr.")
4. Use any of the above methods to learn and sing the melodies of your songs.

*The Cross crawl, Lazy 8's, and Energy yawn are Brain Gym exercises based on studies by Paul E. Denison and Gail E. Denison.

5. Using vowels and other vocal sounds, improvise by starting with a rhythm or melody. Just let it develop in any way it wishes to go. Sometimes you can go on and on—especially in the shower. There is no rule that says you must sing anything recognizable for a warm-up.

Note: When you are using scales as warm-up material, vary the rhythm and beat so that you are not practicing the same way every time. That way lies boredom because when you are on automatic pilot, you lose presence and awareness of what you are doing.

Reminder: Singing this text is also a type of warm-up.

For those of you who want more ideas for warm-ups, see Appendix D at the back of the book.

Chapter Three Selecting Music to Sing

If you are new to voice classes, printed music can look like strange hieroglyphics and you may not feel ready to choose your own songs. (See Appendix E for the fundamentals of reading music.) At this stage of your vocal education, your teacher can choose the music best suited to you until you are able to read music and can choose for yourself. Help is also available on the CDs that come with this text. They contain the melodies, rhythms, and accompaniments of all the songs in this text, some of which may already be familiar to you.

There are some things you need to know about songs that will help you choose your music wisely. To do this, you will need to suspend your own perceptions of the limits of your voice at this point in time—and for the rest of your life. Remember, you are in this class to improve your voice and expand its capabilities. While studying singing, you have the potential to extend your vocal range, quality, and expression. Therefore, choosing a particular song may help you to sing smoothly or legato, extend your current pitch range, or bring out your personality and expression. What follows are some of the considerations you and/or your teacher may use when choosing a song.

Range and Tessitura

The range of the song includes the highest and lowest notes to be sung. However, it is the *tessitura*, or where the average or median of the pitches lies, that can often determine the difficulty of a song. For example suppose the highest note is an F5 and the lowest G3 (see Figure 3.1). There may be only one of those F's or one of those G's and the rest of the song may include mostly medium-range pitches. That song would be much easier than one that has many notes at the top or the bottom of the range throughout.

Range

Tessitura*

Figure 3.1
Range and tessitura

*Refer to Appendix E for location of notes on the keyboard.

Melody Some melodies are smooth and meant to be sung in a very connected manner (*legato*), such as ballads or love songs. Others are full of detached and sharp, accented notes (*staccato*). Teachers often assign specific styles to help beginning singers develop a versatile technique. Good singers can sing various melodic styles with ease.

Text The words and how fast or slow they have to be pronounced are another important consideration. Slow songs place emphasis on singing the vowels well while fast songs with lots of words get the tongue and lips moving. Rap is certainly a way of teaching singers how to articulate well and say words very quickly. Fast patter songs are also fun and helpful diction songs.

Fluency in several languages opens up the possibilities for much more music. Singing in a foreign language can often eradicate some poor speech habits in English. It is fun to learn songs in languages other than English, and several are included with this text.

Rhythm Rhythms can be simple or complex. Hymns have simple rhythms and much of the popular music of today has complex rhythms (compare "Amazing Grace," p. 108, to "True Colors," p. 190). Mastering basic rhythms is the first priority. Your teacher will know when you are ready to tackle a song with tricky rhythms.

Do You Like It? Finally, it is important for you to enjoy the music you are singing. After you have learned and lived with a song for several weeks, you may decide you do not like it. Perceived difficulty or seeing a note that looks or sounds too high is not a good reason for disliking a piece of music. However, if the song continues to irritate you, find one you do like. The world is full of good music.

Finding out for yourself . . .

The CD accompanying this book offers a fine way to hear the music. First listen to the melody and then the accompaniment. This will give you an excellent opportunity to decide how much you like the song.

CHAPTER FOUR *Learning Music Efficiently*

After you have selected the songs you wish to sing, your imagination is going to play a key role in learning your music and performing. Approach each song as if you are the director of a play. You choose the characters and know each one intimately (eye color, hair, height, weight, type of clothes, etc.); you design the set and costumes and be responsible for choosing every color and piece of material that appears on the stage. When you take this approach, your imagination will supply all the vocal color you need naturally and fill in the picture for the audience. Do this before you ever begin to learn the music. Take the text to each song you are singing and write a thorough description of each character. There is a worksheet, Appendix B, that will help you do this. It will give you the appropriate questions for setting the scene for each song you sing.

First, the Words

Your text is your message, and it is important. First, learn the words in their own natural rhythm and dramatize them as prose or poetry until they make complete sense to someone else. Do not be tempted to learn the tune yet. As an optional exercise, make a copy of your text and use colored pens to illustrate the various vocal colors you would like to include in your interpretation. For example, one phrase might be colored blue and the next a cream yellow. This stimulation of your imagination will help you when you begin to sing the song.

Second, the Rhythm

Everything has its own rhythm. All you have to do is tap into it. If instead you try to "make" the rhythm, that will only cause your body to tense and you will get slower and slower. What is meant by *make*? Well, think about this. You do not make your heart beat; it just beats. Your breathing has its own pattern, and each organ in your body has its own vibration as well. You can consider rhythm as the underlying heartbeat of the music. You do not make it happen; it is just there. First, there is the natural rhythm of the text alone, and second, there is the basic rhythm set by the composer. Each language has its own rhythm, as well. Stop and listen to someone speak French, German, English, or Chinese. When people learn a foreign language, it is not the pronunciation that usually trips them up; it is the rhythm of the language.

Physical rhythm, or the pulse, is the foundation of music. Using your whole body to feel the rhythm is very useful at this point. You can gain a lot by dancing your song to learn it.

Finding out for yourself . . .

RHYTHMIC EXERCISES

1. First, tap into the pulse of a song by walking or marching and clapping loudly the basic beat of the song. Do not bother with the exact rhythm yet; just get the feel of the music. You can do this with the rhythm and melody tracks on the CD.
2. Next, begin to singsong or chant the actual rhythm of the song on one pitch using any syllable such as lah [la] or doo [du] to this basic beat. Then singsong the words of the song, on one pitch, to the rhythm while walking and clapping. Do not allow your left brain to trap you into lacking courage or to stop where you perceive a mistake; just keep walking and clapping. Be aware that when you feel insecure, your body will want to hesitate. By walking and clapping you will be able to overcome this tendency. This is why it is not helpful to tap a toe or finger (they are too small and can be bullied easily by your analytical brain). The moment you become unsure, the tapping will stop. Please do not stop until the end of the song! Don't worry about being perfect.
3. A way of checking that you know the rhythm is to singsong it in a staccato manner using any syllable such as hah [ha] or lah [la] or tee [ti] or hee [hi]. This means that each note is short and sharp and totally disconnected from the note before. Rhythmic mistakes show up quickly when you do this because you are filling in with silence rather than sound.
4. Here is one you can do after you have learned the melody. Sing to your own pulse. Find the pulse in your wrist or on your neck. While keeping your finger lightly on your pulse sing a familiar song. Make sure you stay in touch with your own inner beat while singing. If you find you cannot feel your pulse, you have probably allowed physical tension to interfere.

Third, the Melody

With the words and rhythm firmly in place, you can learn the melody with confidence. The melody is available for you on the CD. First, feel the melody and the phrasing by moving your arms and hands to the shape of it. Next, while continuing to follow the phrasing with your arms, use a vocally easy syllable such as pah [pa], lah [la], dee [di], or loo [lu] to sing the melody. This makes singing the melody easier, and it also acts as a vocal warm-up. When you are confident of the notes or pitches, add the words.

Finally, Putting It All Together

All the pieces are now in place and you are finally ready to put everything together. If you have worked to assimilate this time-consuming process, you will find that your musicianship is more accurate. That is because you have built in imagination and expression and are not stumbling or stopping and starting because of inaccurate words or rhythms. This process is one that builds confidence at each step.

CHAPTER FIVE *Practice Habits*

Consistency is the key word here. A little every day is the best approach to singing. Vocal muscles need intelligent and varied repetition for you to create healthy singing habits. It would be ideal for you to spend thirty to forty-five minutes practicing per day. However, ten minutes is better than nothing. At the beginning, it does more harm than good for you to sing more than forty-five minutes. Therefore, singing is not something you can cram the day before a class.

You do not have to be in a studio to practice. You can do loads of work away from a piano or CD player. Visualization can be done anywhere. The words can be learned and recited in your room, on street corners, even in front of theater students who may later expect you to reciprocate.

Once you have learned the words and rhythm, you can think or inwardly say or sing your words in rhythm as you walk across campus or down the street. Interestingly, you have to stay on beat because your walk is steady.

Practicing in a Small Room

Almost every singer who practices in small rooms sings too softly. The reason for this is that the ear will constantly adjust the sound to the room it is in. Think of it this way—if you are singing *piano,* or softly, in a small room, and you were to sing at that same dynamic level on a stage, you would not be heard. Your practice room "soft" would become triply soft in a large space. Because your habitual dynamic levels would be soft, you would find that singing in a much larger situation would cause you to strain and push your voice in larger spaces. Translated, this means that a good target to reach for when practicing in small spaces is a medium volume.

Checklist for Practice Session

1. Spend thirty seconds to one minute focusing.
2. Check your posture.
3. Make sure you are seeing peripherally and are fully aware and present during the entire session.

4. Do two minutes of physical warm-up using the stretching and exercises for connecting your right and left brain (Brain Gym).
5. Do five minutes of vocal warm-up, including an easy song to sing as an exercise.
6. Vary the remaining time between learning new music and rehearsing songs you know. It is important vocally and mentally to practice songs that are in the learning stage, the developing stage, and the performance-ready stage.
7. Your imagination is also needed in a practice session to make the words of a song take shape. Here is a way to encourage it. As you sing your song, use your hands to fully illustrate the text. In other words, be a ham and enjoy it. The rule is very strict: Your hands must draw a picture. For example, when you are singing about a "long road," you must allow your hand to indicate a very long road; when singing about a person, indicate where that person is and what he or she looks like. Pretend your audience is wearing earplugs and needs to see the song mimed. Be thorough in your visual presentation. You will be surprised at how quickly the song will come to life.
8. Never leave the studio without singing one song with full involvement with the message, as if you are performing before an audience of thousands. This means that you are not allowed to stop yourself in the middle if it isn't going the way you want. You must continue. Besides, if you are paying that much attention to the technique, you have forgotten the message.

Chapter Six *Performing*

Nothing is more satisfying than the supportive energy of a live audience willing you to be wonderful. This is why many singers do their best with an audience. Note that your perception of your performance and the audience's perception of your performance may be entirely different.

You have a memory of having sung a song many times. Each one of these times is firmly entrenched in your mind. What's more, you have compared (either consciously or subconsciously) all of these times and put each one on a scale of best and worst (see Figure 6.1).

Figure 6.1
Your memory bank of singing the song

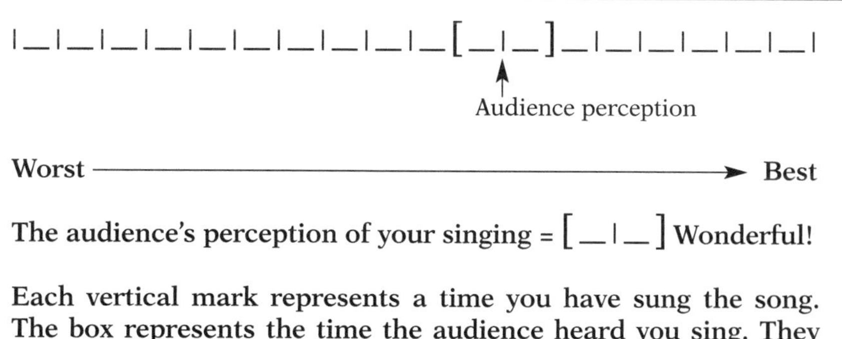

Audience perception
Worst
Best
The audience's perception of your singing = [— | —] Wonderful!
Each vertical mark represents a time you have sung the song. The box represents the time the audience heard you sing. They think it is wonderful. However, you are remembering all the times you have sung it and it does not satisfy your "best." Give up this kind of self-sabotage. Who needs a saboteur like that?

You have the dubious privilege of knowing where each performance fits on this scale. Your audience does not. They have heard it once or twice at most. They are judging you on a limited knowledge and may perceive it to have been sung wonderfully. Meanwhile, on your scale you may have sung it somewhere near mediocre. You must honor their perception of your singing. The best reply to *"You were wonderful"* is *"Thank you."* Whatever your thoughts are about your performance, *keep them to yourself.* For you to turn around and say, *"Oh, no, I can do it so much better,"* or *"That was terrible!"* is the equivalent of saying *"You do not know what you are talking about."* The fact is, they know their own taste and appreciation. Respect that! You may well be able to sing it better, but a musically unsophisticated audience may not know that. Your self-criticism does not increase the listener's pleasure or understanding.

We often give the audience credit for knowing everything that is going on inside us as we sing. So many times when singers see a video of themselves, they say "I was going through hell, and yet I look so calm and in control." But there may be a difference between how you think you sound and look, and how you actually sound and look. Remember this!

Finding out for yourself . . .

Positive thoughts from the audience help the singer enormously. When singing for your classmates or peers, experiment with the following:

- **Have someone sing a song for the class. While he or she is singing, have the class mentally send positive thoughts of support and care for the person performing. *Will* that person to sing well. *Note:* Do not tell the singer what you are doing.**
- **Now do the opposite. While that person is singing, ask the class to send critical negative thoughts.**
- **Ask the singer about the differences in performing in each situation.**
- **Always send positive caring thoughts to the person singing. No mental criticism allowed. It is not helpful to you or the performer.**

Nerves

Of course you want to be confident when you perform. Confidence comes with the process of disciplined practice and attention to learning combined with positive thinking. Believe it or not, one way of becoming confident is to pretend you are. "Fake it until you make it" is not a bad adage when it comes to performing in public. The audience does not usually see your perceived wobbly legs and knotted stomach. It is worth repeating here: "How you perceive yourself and how others see you are very different."

When people are nervous, it means that they are thinking about themselves more than the message or the music. This is usually the time the words are forgotten. At no time do you want to call attention to yourself by thinking thoughts such as "Is this OK?" or "Oops, I sang a wrong rhythm." Focus on the message of the music and communicating with your audience. By working through the worksheet in Appendix B, you will have a strong basis for remembering the words and delivering a meaningful message.

By using the focusing technique you learned earlier, you can see yourself on stage or in performance being comfortable, remembering the words, and being fully involved with the message.

Presence This topic has been discussed earlier. However, it can never be stressed enough. Your presence is a combination of your spirit, physical balance, seeing as you sing, your desire to be there, the music, and the message of the music. Remember you are sharing that with the audience at all times. You and your sound are the drop that creates ripples going out in all directions so that you fill the entire space.

The Message Before you sing, ask yourself: "What is the one thing I would like my audience to take away from this performance?" It could be many things. It is up to you to choose one as the "bottom line." (An example: *I would like to create an atmosphere in which the members of my audience go away feeling better for having come to hear me.*) Having an underlying goal for your whole performance will help you be comfortable with your audience and will help you believe you have something to offer them.

Never forget that each song has its own message. Your careful preparation of the text, your full involvement in its message, and your presence all contribute to a compelling performance.

PART TWO

Improvisations and Songs

Improvisation

Traditional Songs, World Songs, and Rounds

Popular Songs

Art Songs and Arias

Men and women have used music and song to express and lift their spirits, energies, and emotions for as long as we know. Songs have been used to develop religious fervor, to create energy for work, to urge men to war, to serenade loved ones, and to lull babies to sleep. Whenever we express our thoughts and words through music, the effect is many times more powerful. Singing "I love you" on a high note can certainly magnify the intensity and meaning of the words beyond any stated declaration of them.

The oral tradition of handing down songs has existed for thousands of years and continues today. Children are taught the songs their parents and grandparents were taught. We sing many of these "traditional" songs today. Part Two devotes a whole section to this type of song. In fact, Part Two contains the widest possible variety of songs, which in turn provides a basis for expressing yourself in music. The improvisations give you the freedom to experiment with your voice and to be creative with the music. Annotations are included to help you understand the context of each song and to aid your interpretations. The accompanying CDs make it easy to learn your music, while the Student Web site allows you to listen to many of the songs in various keys and to print a copy of that song as performance-ready sheet music.

Many of the songs in this book are timeless and have a history of inspiring people to sing. There are tunes you "can't get out of your head," which is why many of them have been sung for decades. You can sing these songs anywhere, even to your computer. Years ago, before electronic diversions of computers, video games, iPods, TVs, and radios, people gathered around the piano to sing for their entertainment. Today this happens formally in choirs and informally in karaoke bars, at football games, or at Christmas, when groups gather to sing carols.

The late, great American folk singer Burl Ives remarked "Now songs are, roughly, of two kinds: The songs sung at us . . . and the songs sung by us." This book is all about "the songs sung by us." The songs that follow will help your vocal development, but they were chosen for their beauty, fun, tradition, and inspiration. You are encouraged to use these songs to explore and improve your unique vocal instrument and to discover a wealth of traditional, classical, and popular solo vocal repertoire.

Improvisation

Improvisation is a creative process. It is spontaneous and there are no set rules or text. You have already begun to improvise music by singing this book and having sung conversations with partners. Jazz and pop styles are full of improvisation. So is the Baroque music of Bach and Handel—it is just incorporated into the music much of the time. In fact, there is a tradition of classical singers improvising in the seventeenth and eighteenth centuries and today in contemporary music.

The key to improvisation is giving yourself permission to vocalize without *any* self-criticism. Yes, you will sing clinkers—just call them "atonal" music.

Here are some ways to begin:

1. Begin with a group rhythm improvisation. Use tongue clicks, claps, the chair, or anything that can contribute to the sound for this. One person can begin with a single sound, and others can join in gradually until you build up a nice rhythm section. You can also do this alone with your own recordings.
2. Next, use the above exercise to get started and then gradually add vocal sounds, vowels, isolated words, and phrases until you build up vocal energy. Play with different rhythms and jazz sounds as well.
3. Listen to the CD improvisation accompaniments and hum along with any pitches you like. Let your ear, not your intellect, guide you.
4. If you are a little timid, just add a note and hold it until you sense it is time to change it.
5. Where there are long notes on the recording sing notes to fill in the gaps with syllables like tah [ta], lah [la], tee [ti], or doo [du].
6. Change your hums to vowel sounds or to something like Dooby-doo.

7. Be really daring and choose a familiar nursery rhyme tune to sing on top of the CD accompaniment.
8. Improvise with your favorite recording.
9. For the truly brave—record yourself singing along with your CD and then play it back.

Just as instrumentalists have "jam" sessions, so can singers. You have some class exercises that begin to address this. For inspiration, you might listen to Bobby McFerrin or legendary jazz great Ella Fitzgerald's vocal improvisations on numerous recordings. There is a memorable moment in Ella's famous live recording of "Mack the Knife" when she forgets the words and totally improvises, never missing a beat!

Now it is up to you to go bravely into the unknown and make "child's play" with music. When you learned to walk, everyone was proud of your first step. Be the same with yourself in regard to improvisation.

Dance Your Dream Come True

Rhythmic Song

Music by
Scarlett Antaloczy

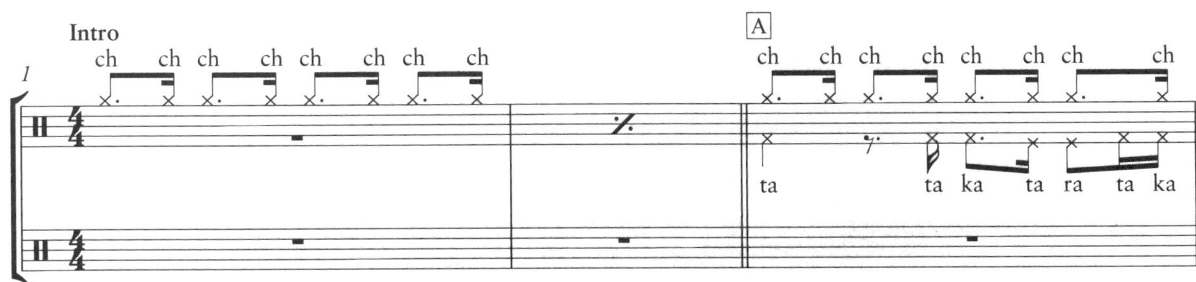

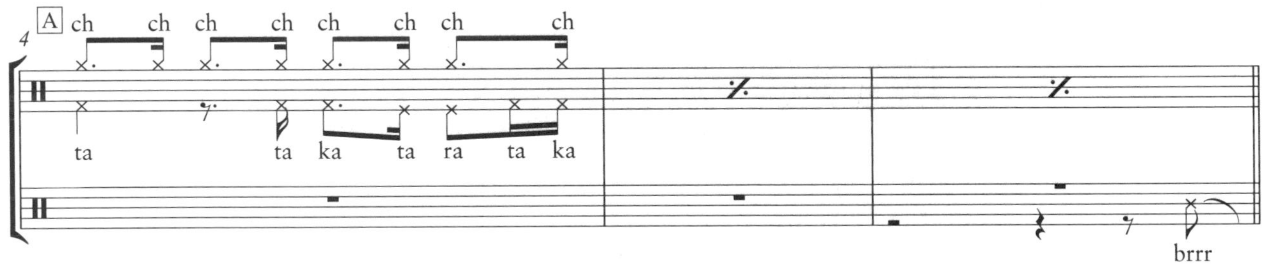

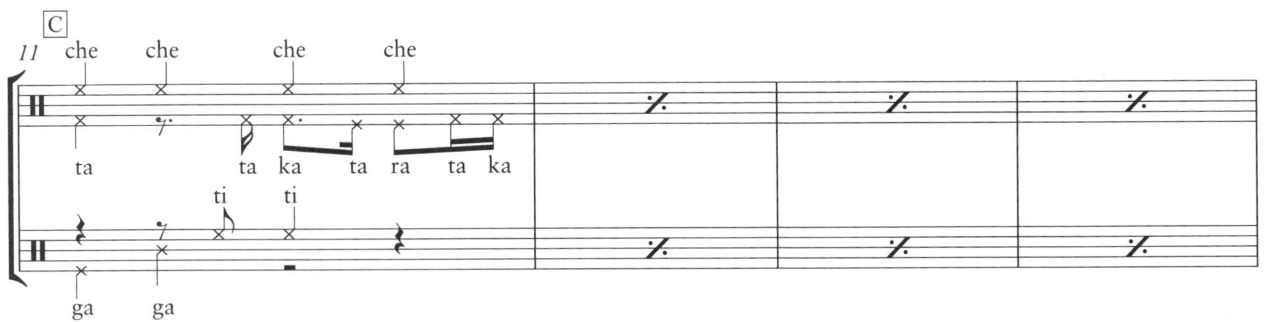

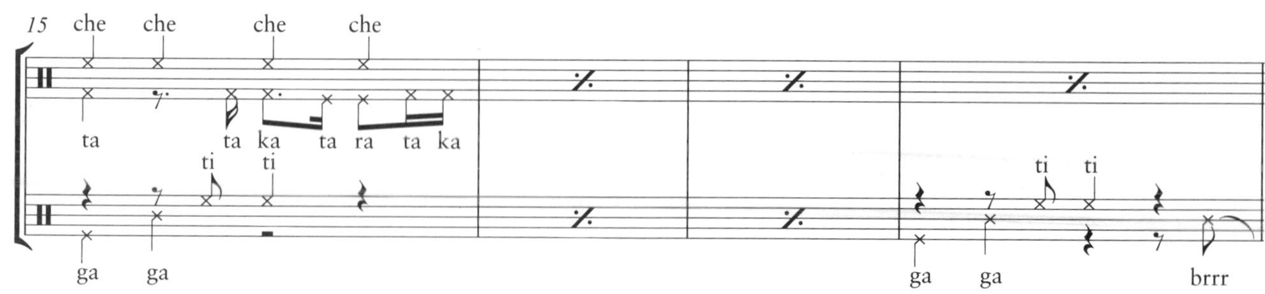
15
che che che che
ta ta ka ta ra ta ka
ti ti
ti ti
ga ga
ga ga brrr

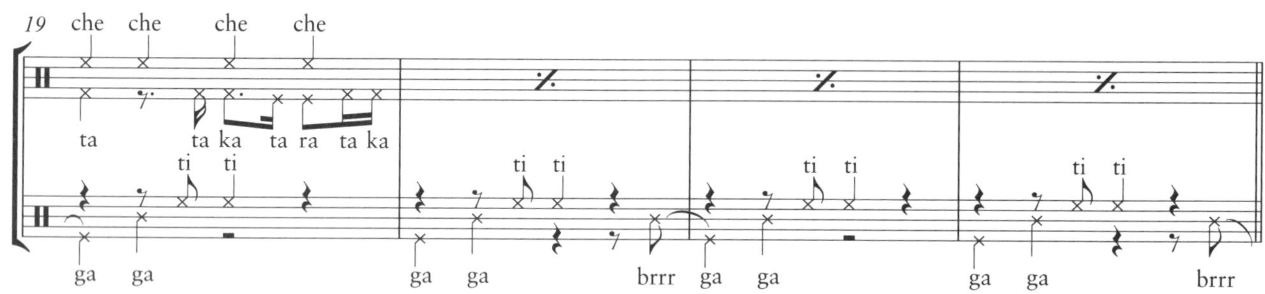
19
che che che che
ta ta ka ta ra ta ka
ti ti
ti ti
ti ti
ti ti
ga ga
ga ga brrr
ga ga
ga ga brrr

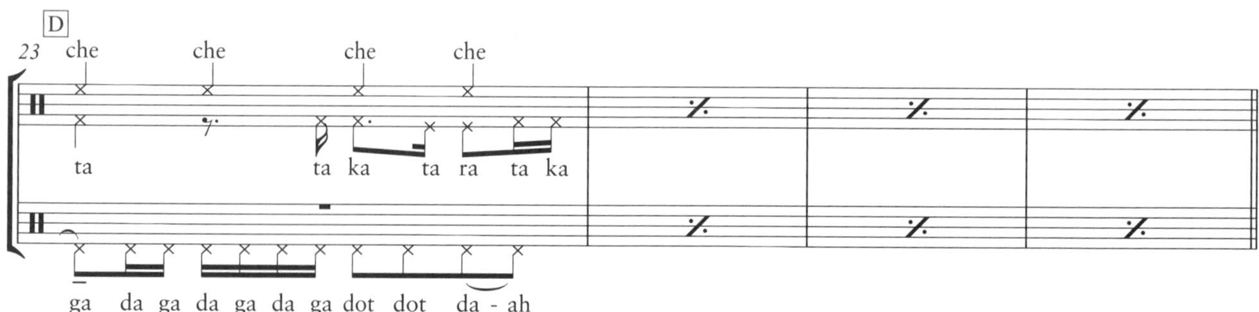
D
23
che che che che
ta ta ka ta ra ta ka
ga da ga da ga da ga dot dot da - ah

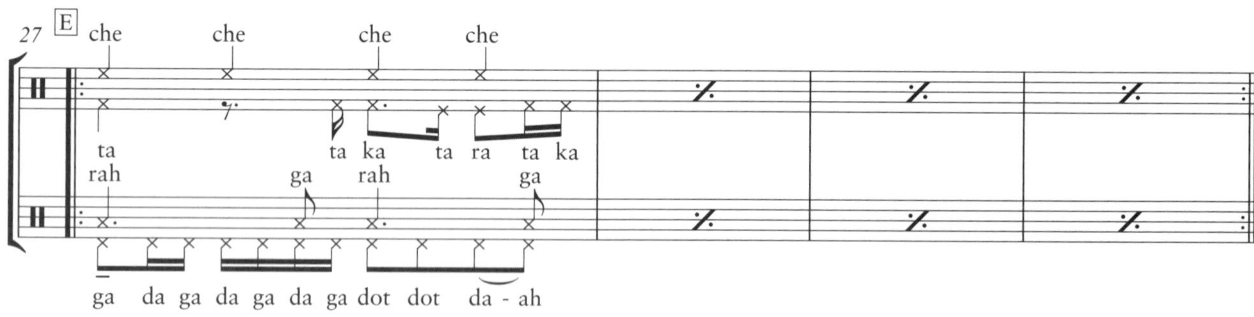
27
E
che che che che
ta ta ka ta ra ta ka
rah ga rah ga
ga da ga da ga da ga dot dot da - ah

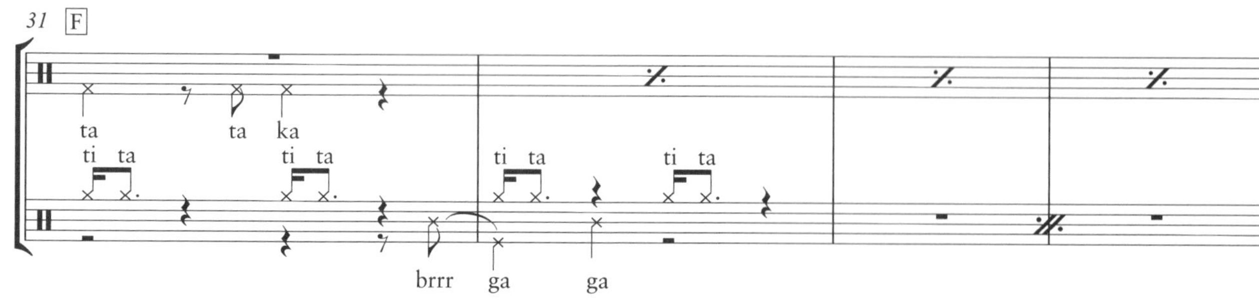
31
F
ta ta ka
ti ta ti ta
ti ta ti ta
brrr ga ga

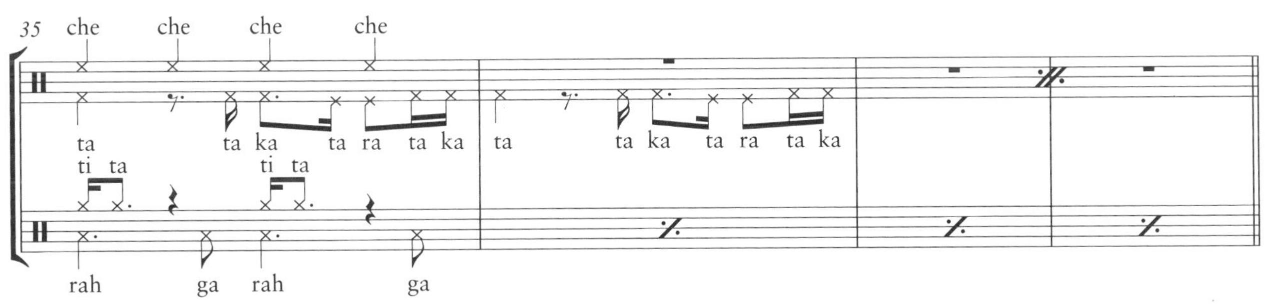
35
che che che che
ta ta ka ta ra ta ka ta ta ka ta ra ta ka
ti ta ti ta
rah ga rah ga

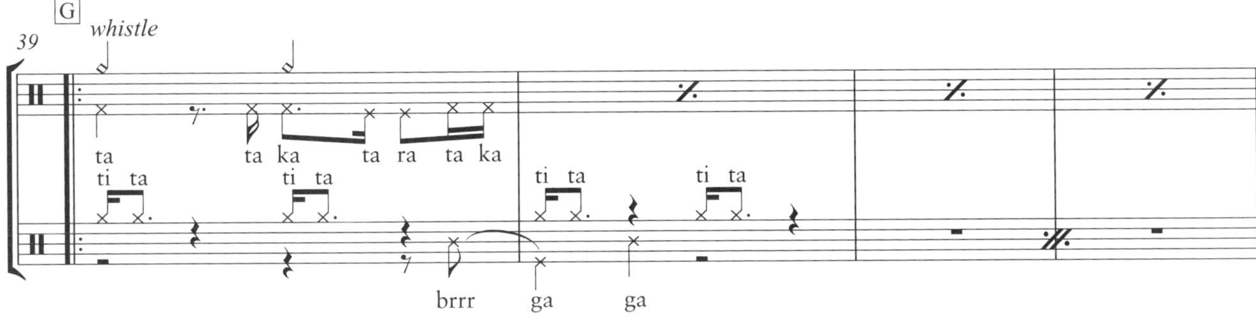
G
39
whistle
ta ta ka ta ra ta ka
ti ta ti ta ti ta ti ta
brrr ga ga

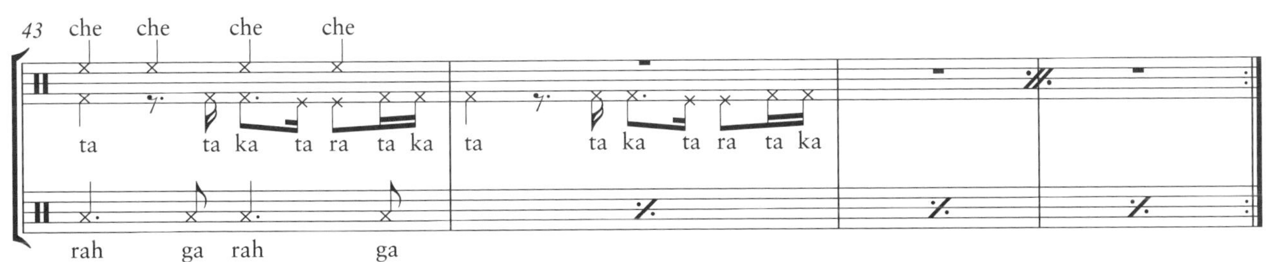
43
che che che che
ta ta ka ta ra ta ka ta ta ka ta ra ta ka
rah ga rah ga

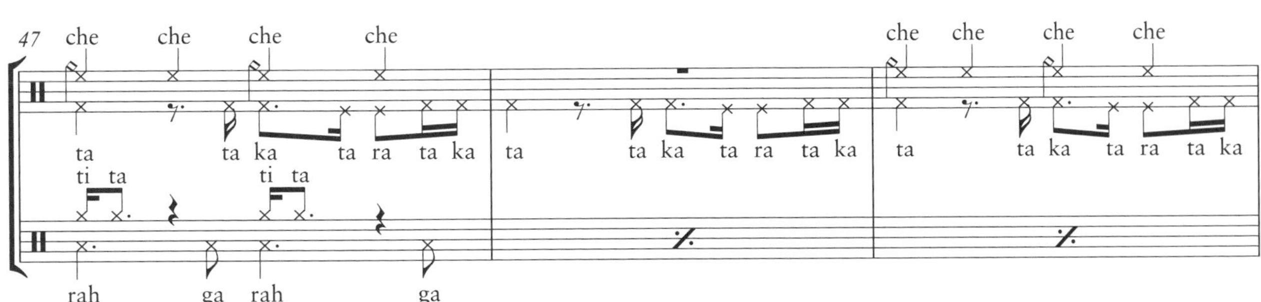
47
che che che che che che che che
ta ta ka ta ra ta ka ta ta ka ta ra ta ka ta ta ka ta ra ta ka
ti ta ti ta
rah ga rah ga

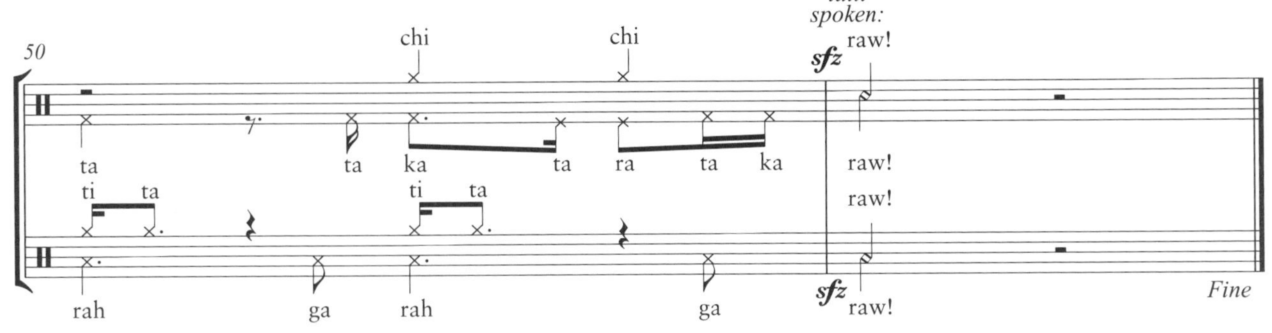
50
chi chi
tutti spoken:
sfz raw!
ta ta ka ta ra ta ka raw!
ti ta ti ta raw!
rah ga rah ga
sfz raw!
Fine

Circle of Friends

Improvisational vocalise

Music by
Scarlett Antaloczy

14
A
Improv 4 times
F
Dm7
Gm7
Gm9 7 Gm7
C7sus4
ah
ah
ah
(guide vocal 2nd and 3rd time improv)
(piano comp.)
18
B
Improv 4 times
F
Dm7
Gm7
Gm9 7
C7sus4
da
da
(guide vocal)
22
A
F
Dm7
Gm7
1.
C7
2.
C7
da
da
da
ah
ah
27
B
F
Dm7
Gm7
C7sus4
G♭maj7
Fmaj9
ad lib.
da
doo
da
ah

Ballad (Major Key)

Music by
Scarlett Antaloczy

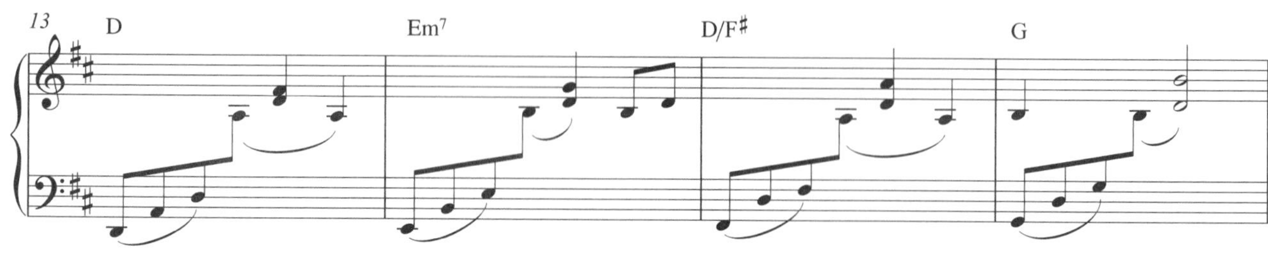

17
Bm
F♯m7
Em7
A7sus4
A7

21
Bm
G
Bm
G♯ø7
C♯7
F♯m

26
G
F♯m
A7sus4
A7
D
rit.

30
Em7
D/F♯
G
Bm

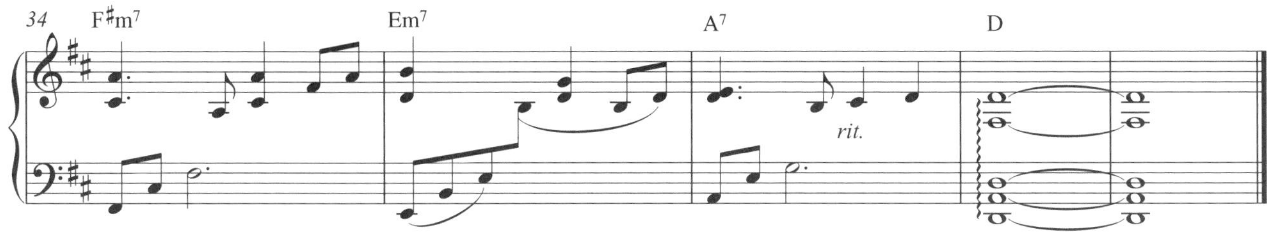
34
F♯m7
Em7
A7
D
rit.

Swingin' in Minor Blues

Music by
Scarlett Antaloczy

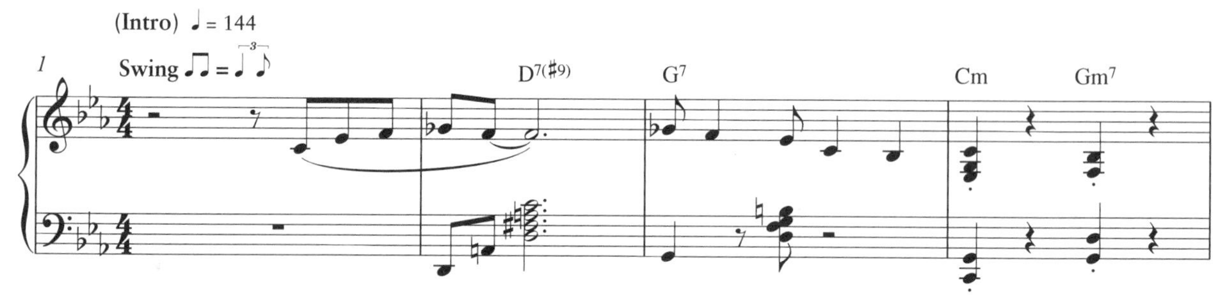

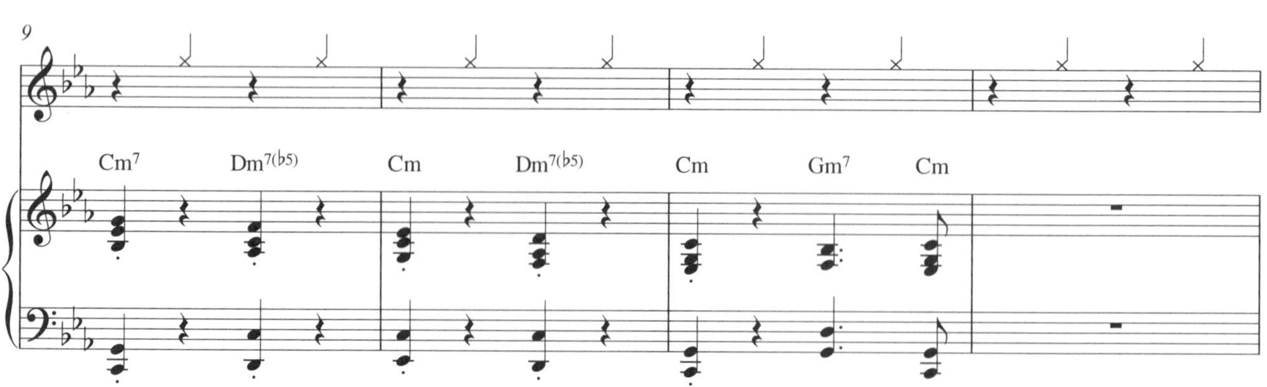

13
Fm7
Gm7
Fm7/A♭
Gm
Fm
Cm
Fm
17
Cm7
Dm7(♭5)/C
Cm
Dm7(♭5)
Cm
Gm7
Cm
21
D7(♯9)
G7
Cm
Gm7
Cm
25
(walking bass line)
Cm7
Dm7(♭5)
Cm7
Dm7(♭5)
Cm
Gm7
Cm

29
Cm7
Dm7(♭5)
Cm7
Dm7(♭5)
Cm7
Gm7
Cm
33
Fm7
Gm7
Fm7/A♭
Gm7
Fm
Cm/E♭
Fm
37
C pedal
Cm7
Dm7(♭5)/C
Cm
Dm7(♭5)
Cm
Gm7
Cm
41
(yeah!)
D7(♯9)
G7
Cm
Gm7
Cm

Traditional Songs, World Songs, and Rounds

Unison Songs and Rounds

Unison means "one sound." Such single line melodies were the earliest type of song. It must have been interesting to be there when the first person came in late in a song and it actually sounded all right. That is how one might imagine rounds began. It is fun to imagine that you can come in at almost any time and still make nice music with other people. This is why rounds are so much fun and satisfying for group singing. Also people are comfortable because if they did not learn the song on the first go, they have plenty of repeats to catch up.

World Songs

World songs, or folk songs, are myths and legends handed down in song. They were sung from generation to generation in every culture and form an important part of the oral tradition. Some tunes cross cultural boundaries and are found in a number of countries at once. The melodies were rarely written down and were sung either *a capella* (without accompaniment) or accompanied by folk instruments like guitars or dulcimers. Fortunately for us, in the eighteenth to twentieth centuries, men like James Childs, Cecil Sharp, Béla Bartók, and John Jacob Niles traveled to rural areas to collect and preserve the traditional songs. These first "songcatchers," as they were sometimes called, listened carefully to the songs and wrote down the various versions of the words and music. Later they used recording equipment to collect the actual raw singing of songs that were fast disappearing. Composers like Joseph Haydn, Benjamin Britten, and Aaron Copland wrote their own arrangements of folk songs for solo voice with piano accompaniment; other composers used folk tunes in classical instrumental music.

Spirituals

Spirituals are distinctly American songs. These unaccompanied religious folk songs with African rhythmic and modal influences sprang up from the mid 1700s to about 1900, first as work songs for slaves and later as escape and revival songs. In the countryside, slaves gathered, sometimes in secret, to sing for hours at "camp meetings." Before slavery was abolished in 1865, slaves were drawn to songs about the Israelites' trials under the bondage of Egypt. There was a double meaning for Christian slaves. While they longed for heaven, here on earth they were desperate to "cross the River Jordan" and to enter the "the promised land" of "Canaan"—meaning anywhere North of the Ohio River.

Spirituals about trains and chariots were metaphors for the Underground Railroad, a network of abolitionists who helped slaves escape to the North. In the cities, as the religious Revival movement grew, blacks and whites gathered in stadiums and large tents for revival meetings.

For a while after the Civil War, few people wanted to sing the old spirituals that reminded them of the horrors of slavery. Before the end of the century, however, trained musicians began to arrange them in a European classical way for choruses and solo artists. European audiences were enchanted by American spirituals. Even now, touring American choruses and opera singers regularly include spirituals in their European concerts. From the cotton fields to symphony halls, the songs endure.

Hymns

Many traditional church hymns of the Christian-based religions also have a long history of inspiring hope and stirring passion in believers. From the very earliest biblical times the words "hymn" and "psalm" were used interchangeably to mean a religious song.

The first Catholic hymns were sung in Latin, and by the eleventh century there were nearly 300 Latin hymns in the liturgy. During the Reformation in Germany, Protestant hymns were written in the vernacular (or common) language. Martin Luther, and later J. S. Bach, wrote many hymns and "chorales" that are still an important part of the Lutheran and other Protestant churches.

Meanwhile, in England, John and Charles Wesley took hymns in a new direction in the early Methodist church. They felt that the old-fashioned psalm tunes were too rigid to express personal emotion, so the Wesleys followed a more secular musical style. The well-known hymn "Love Divine, All Loves Excelling" is actually an adaptation of a purely secular poem, Dryden's "Fairest Isle, all isles excelling." A turning point came in 1819 when the English legal court released state churches from "authorized" old-version hymns and decreed that churches could freely write their own versions of hymns and psalms.

By 1861, churches of many denominations in England and America were openly writing their own hymnals—whatever suited their theology and parishioners. The task of writing these new hymns usually fell to clergy of the individual churches, who were kept busy writing not only the Sunday sermon but also the weekly prayer meeting hymn. It is no wonder that the first published edition of *Olney Hymns* in 1779 (see "Amazing Grace") contained nearly 300 songs by the Reverend John Newton.

Patriotic Songs

Patriotic songs were usually written after some big event—to display the pride of winning a battle, for instance, or seeing something so beautiful that the love for one's country just welled up into a song. For months after the September 11, 2001, terrorist attacks in New York, Washington, D.C., and Pennsylvania, you could frequently hear patriotic songs in concerts and on radio and TV. Singing and hearing "God Bless America" and "The Star-Spangled Banner" was a way of encouraging and uniting people after a national tragedy.

There's Music in the Air (p. 51)

Sentimental songs were extremely popular in the Victorian era when poetry on the topics of love, joy, angels, and death reflected the ideals of the time. The memorable tunes and repeated phrases of these songs appealed to all social classes and were played in fashionable homes, in music halls, and by hurdy-gurdy musicians on the streets. The words to "There's Music in the Air" were written by hymnist Fanny J. Crosby and the music by George Friederick Wurzel, whose pen name was "George F. Root."

My Country 'Tis of Thee (p. 52)

The Reverend Samuel French Smith wrote the words of this well-known patriotic song, while the tune was "borrowed" from an old English manuscript called *Thesaur's Musicus of 1744*. (Throughout the history of music you will find many borrowed tunes.) "My Country 'Tis of Thee" is a favorite choir audition song because the melody begins and ends on the same note. Choir directors want to see if the singer can maintain the key from the beginning to the end.

Suggested recordings of "My Country 'Tis of Thee" (iTunes):

GENRE: *Folk* □ ***Patriotic Songs of America,*** 2005, Madacy

GENRE: *Rock* □ ***Crosby and Nash,*** 2004, Sanctuary

⏩If you like this patriotic song, take a look at the song "This Is My Country"

MUSIC ALONE SHALL LIVE (P. 53)
OH, HOW LOVELY IS THE EVENING (P. 54)

Rounds and folk dances such as Germany's "Die Musici" and "O wie wohl is mir am Abend" were extremely popular in England during the seventeenth and eighteenth centuries. A round, or "circular canon," consists of two or more musical phrases of equal length. Two, three, four or more singers enter the song at various times to create their own harmonies. Singers circle back to the beginning and repeat the song as many times as they wish. Early rounds were not written down but were spread by composers and troubadours traveling from town to town, and even from country to country. While the melodies of many rounds remained relatively intact over the centuries, the words changed freely. You can discover the same tune set to English, Latin, or foreign texts, ranging from sacred to secular to downright indecent topics. Singing and drinking (not necessarily in that order) were the tradition of "Catch Clubs" in Victorian England, which featured humorous, bawdy rounds known as "catches." The rounds sung, however, on "ladie's night" were on more delicate subjects such as blind mice, rowing boats, music, and lovely evenings.

BABYLON (P. 55)

This round, by American composer William Billings, is a setting of Psalm 137, a lament for the Jewish people who were exiled from their homeland. Billings, a Boston tanner's apprentice by trade, became well known for his sacred music after the publication of his *New England Psalm Singer* in 1770. Two hundred years later, Babylon became a metaphor for Vietnam, when singer/songwriter Don McLean featured Billings' round on his classic American rock album *American Pie.*

Suggested recording of "Babylon" (iTunes):

GENRE: *Rock* □ Don McLean: ***American Pie,*** 1971, BGO

⏩If you like this song, take a look at Don McLean's "Till Tomorrow"

DONA NOBIS PACEM (P. 56)

Ancient Latin rounds were influenced by sacred liturgy and chants. Tunes were borrowed freely from Catholic canonic chants that were often sung outside the church by ordinary people. Some Latin rounds used liturgical lyrics, such as "dona nobis pacem" or "alleluia." Others, such as "Ego sum pauper" (online bonus song), used secular words about everyday situations like poverty, marriage, and unrequited love. There are reports of Latin rounds as early as 1065, but the first printed collections of Middle English and Latin rounds and songs were published by Thomas Ravenscroft around 1600. The oldest Ravenscroft round is "Sumer is icumin" ("Summer is a-coming"). The best-known Ravenscroft round is "Dona Nobis Pacem," which is attributed to the sixteenth-century composer Palestrina.

Suggested recordings of "Dona nobis pacem" (iTunes):

GENRE: *Pop* □ Beth Nielsen Chapman: ***Hymns,*** 2004, Emergent

GENRE: *Children's Music* □ Susie Tallman: ***Lullaby Themes for Sleepy Dreams,*** 1998, Rock Me Baby

⏩If you like this song, take a look at the song "Panis angelicus"

AH, POOR BIRD (P. 57)
SHALOM, CHAVERIM (P. 57)
AH, POOR BIRD/SHALOM (P. 58)

These modern rounds most likely evolved from the same tune. Though "Shalom, chaverim" is an Israeli folk song and "Ah! Poor Bird" is an American round, both songs have similar melodies and harmonic structures. After you learn each song separately, try combining them as a duet, using the English version of the Hebrew song. The songs fit together like a musical puzzle, and even the words make sense: "Farewell my friends . . . take thy flight . . . We'll meet again."

Suggested recordings of "Shalom, chaverim" (iTunes):

GENRE: *Folk* □ Judy Caplan Ginsburgh: ***Shalom Yeladim/Hello Children,*** 1993, Judy Caplan Ginsburgh

GENRE: *Folk* □ The Weavers: ***The Weavers at Carnegie Hall,*** 1957, rel. 1990, Vanguard

⏩If you like this world song, take a look at the Indonesian song "Suliram"

THREE ALLELUIA ROUNDS (P. 59)

If you are tempted to dismiss rounds as simple children's songs, then consider that many of the leading classical composers wrote rounds and canons. (Canons are similar to rounds, except both voices end at the same time instead of repeating continuously.) Purcell, Haydn, Mozart, Beethoven, Mendelssohn, Schubert, and Brahms all wrote rounds. Here, the first "Alleluia" example is a simple two-part round by Mozart. The second Mozart "Alleluia" round is much more challenging and uses melodic material that Mozart later recycled for his solo motet *Exsultate, Jubilate* for soprano and chamber orchestra. Mozart may also have "borrowed" some tunes from fellow composer William Boyce, who is said to have remarked, "Mozart takes ordinary things and turns them into pearls." The final "Alleluia" round by William Boyce is no mere child's play, however, and it will challenge the most accomplished singers. Though rounds and canons lost their popularity during the nineteenth century, modern composers such as David Diamond, Vincent Persichetti, and Randall Thompson have all composed rounds.

SHENANDOAH (P. 60)

Many traditional songs made their way to America from England, Scotland, and Ireland, but "Shenandoah" is a truly American folk song. It most likely began as a land ballad about a trader who fell in love with a Native American tribal chief's daughter named Shenandoah. As early as 1820, Missouri river boatmen carried the song to the deep-sea sailors, where it was particularly popular as a capstan chantey. As they sang, sailors pushed the massive capstan bars around to lift the ship's anchor. The song is still popular today and strikes a chord with anyone who is homesick for a distant place or far away lover.

Suggested recordings of "Shenandoah"(iTunes):

GENRE: *Classical* □ Paul Robeson: ***Paul Robeson Sings "Ol' Man River" and Other Favorites—Recorded 1928–39,*** rel. 1990, Angel

GENRE: *World* □ Sissel: ***Sissel,*** 2002, Decca U.S.

⏩If you like this song, take a look at the folk song "Morning Has Broken"

THE HOUSE OF THE RISING SUN (P. 63)

Green Day and U2 rocked Monday Night Football on September 25, 2006, with a modified verse of an American folk classic: "There is a house in New Orleans, they call the Superdome." Millions downloaded the live version of the song, and as a result the studio single of "House of the Rising Sun/The Saints Are Coming" was nominated for a Grammy award for Best Rock Performance by a Duo or Group. Long before the devastation of Hurricane Katrina, this southern folk ballad told a cautionary tale about a real or fictional New Orleans brothel (or possibly a prison). The best known recordings are by male vocalists—notably Eric Burdon of The Animals and rock legend Bob Dylan—but the original folksong, as compiled and recorded by folklorist and songcatcher Alan Lomax (on 1941's *Our Singing Country*), was from a decidedly female perspective: "It's been the ruin of many a poor girl." Folk singer Joan Baez's version may be closest in spirit to the original tune. This song has been recorded by such diverse artists as Dolly Parton, Bachman-Turner Overdrive, The Rolling Stones, Johnny Cash, and B. B. King.

Compare these recordings of "House of the Rising Sun" (iTunes):

GENRE: *Folk* □ Kristia Di Gregorio: ***Any Given Night,*** 2005, Crimson and Gold

GENRE: *Rock* □ Shawn Mullins: ***9th Ward Pickin' Parlor,*** 2006, Vanguard

GENRE: *Jazz* □ Nina Simone: ***The Lady Has the Blues,*** 2003, Tomato

⏩If you like this song, take a look at "Sea Fever" as sung by William Topley on the album ***Sea Fever***

SCARBOROUGH FAIR (P. 66)

The earliest printed version of this popular English riddle song, "The Elphin King," dates back to 1670 and is derived from an ancient Viking epic. Riddle songs involved seeming contradictions, such as "I gave my love a cherry without a stone." At first glance, the story seems to be about the impossible demands of a jilted lover ("Tell her to make me a cambric shirt . . . with no seam or needlework"). But folklorists claim the song is a conversation between a maiden and a demon, the Elphin King. In plant mythology certain herbs were said to have supernatural powers. Parsley warded off the "evil eye" while sage assured wedded bliss, long life, and health. In 1579's *The Garden of Health,* William Lengham recommended bathing in rosemary "to make thee lusty, lively, joyfull, likeing and youngly" and a woman wearing thyme in her bosom was said to be irresistible. Modern audiences are most familiar with Simon and Garfunkel's hit recording of "Scarborough Fair" in 1968, which climbed pop charts with magical charm.

Suggested recordings of "Scarborough Fair" (iTunes):

Genre: *World* □ Celtic Woman: ***A New Journey,*** 2007, Manhattan

Genre: *Folk* □ Simon and Garfunkel: ***Parsley, Sage, Rosemary and Thyme*** (remastered), 2001, Sony

▸▸If you like this song, take a look at the English folk song "Barbara Allen"

Danny Boy (p. 70)

The melody of the song we know as "Danny Boy" was first published in 1855 in *Ancient Tunes of Ireland* as "Londonderry Air." However, it is unlikely that the poet and credited songwriter of "Danny Boy" ever set foot in Ireland. In 1910, Fred E. Weatherly, an English lawyer and prolific songwriter, wrote words and music to a song he called "Danny Boy." It was not a commercial success until his sister Margaret sent Weatherly the "Londonderry Air" tune that she heard played by an Irish immigrant fiddler in a Colorado gold rush camp. The tune was a perfect match to Weatherly's original lyrics and became a hit soon after Boosey published the song in 1913. Even today, grown men weep when "Danny Boy" is sweetly sung by an Irish tenor. It is also appropriate for a woman to sing "Danny Boy." Weatherly was a smart businessman who usually kept the gender neutral in his popular songs so that he could sell more copies to amateur singers.

Suggested recordings of "Danny Boy" (iTunes):

Genre: *Folk* □ The Irish Tenors: ***Heritage,*** 2004, Razor & Tie

Genre: *Classical* □ Mario Lanza: ***Be My Love,*** 1972, rel. 1991, RCA Victor

▸▸If you like this song, take a look at the folk song "The Last Rose of Summer"

The Water Is Wide (p. 72)

Cecil Sharp (1859–1924) was the most famous of "songcatchers." Without his efforts, much British and American folk music from the sixteenth to nineteenth centuries, such as "The Water Is Wide," would have been lost. In 1902 he visited English countryside villages to collect and record authentic specimens of English folk music. When the oral tradition of folk songs began to die out in Britain, Sharp found it to be flourishing in America. During World War I, Sharp and his secretary traveled to America's Appalachian mountain region to collect songs, including "The Water Is Wide," or "O Waly, Waly," as it was known in seventeenth-century Britain. ("Waly, Waly" is a form of the Anglo-Saxon "wa la wa" meaning "Woe, alas, woe.") This nearly lost song inspired generations of recording artists including folk legends Bob Dylan, Pete Seeger, and Joan Baez, and modern artists like Sarah McLaughlin, Charlotte Church, Jewel, James Taylor, Barbra Streisand, and Wendy Matthews. The tune is timeless and the text is universal. As Pete Seeger wrote, "We have to cross the oceans of misunderstanding between the peoples of this world."

Suggested recordings of "The Water Is Wide" (iTunes):

Genre: *Folk* □ Connie Dover: ***The Border of Heaven,*** 2000, Taylor Park

Genre: *Rock* □ James Taylor: *New Moon Shine,* 1991, Sony

▸▸If you like this song, take a look at the folk song "Red River Valley"

Salley Gardens (p. 76)

The melody is the traditional Irish tune "The Maids of Mourne Shore." However, this is not a folk song in the true sense because the text was not written by an unknown, long-forgotten poet but was penned by Ireland's greatest poet, William Butler Yeats (1865–1939). Yeats was an Irish nationalist who rebelled against English rule and culture. He was a founder of the National Literacy Society in Dublin, and in 1923 he was the first Irishman to win the Nobel Prize in literature. His poetry remains very popular today, especially in Ireland where musicians like Van Morrison and the Cranberries recently recorded *Now and in Time to Be,* a CD of settings of Yeats's poetry.

Yeats's writings were influenced by ancient Celtic myths, mysticism, and unrequited love, and his poetry has been called musical and magical. When a beautiful woman, Maud Gonne, spurned Yeats's obsessive attention, the poet created some of the world's best love poetry, including "Down by the Salley Gardens." Interestingly, the girl in the poem isn't named "Sally." In this song "Salley" means a willow garden or a bog field that is useless for growing or grazing—just the ideal place for clandestine lovers to meet! A "weir" is a fence or dam set in a stream to catch fish.

Suggested recordings of "Salley Gardens" (iTunes):

GENRE: Folk □ Mae Robertson and Don Jackson: ***The Sun Upon the Lake Is Low,*** 1997, Lyric Partners

GENRE: Classical □ Graham Johnson, ***Britten: Folk Song Arrangements,*** 2005, Naxos

▸▸If you like this song, take a look at the folk song "Black Is the Color of My True Love's Hair"

SUO-GÂN (P. 79)

This beautiful Gaelic air is featured prominently in Steven Spielberg's 1987 film *Empire of the Sun,* starring 13-year-old Welsh native Christian Bale. The future star of *Newsies* and *Batman Begins* lip-synched "Suo-gân," which literally means "lullaby." A few years later, Welsh singer Charlotte Church included "Suo-gân" on her debut album and in concert performances. "Suo-gân" (pronounced [si-o-gan]) is one of the most popular traditional songs in Wales, a country that is famous for its singing societies. The Gaelic language, with its liberal use of consonants, is quite a challenge to non-natives; however, E. T. Davies writes, *"Y mae'r Alawon hyn erbyn heddiw more boblogaidd fel y cydnabyddir hwy yn Alawon Cenedlaethol Cymru, nid yn unig yug Nghymru, ond hefyd mewn gwledydd dros ei gororau."* "These tunes are now so well-known that they have become the common heritage not only of the Principality but also of countries far beyond its borders."

Suggested recordings of "Suo-gân" (iTunes):

GENRE: *Soundtrack* □ John McCarthy, dir., and James Rainbird: ***Empire of the Sun,*** 1987, Warner

GENRE: *Classical* □ Charlotte Church: ***Voice of an Angel,*** 1999, Sony

▸▸If you like this song, take a look at the Welsh song "Ar Hyd Y Nos" ("All Through the Night")

RED IS THE ROSE (P. 82)

Many songs have been written about red roses, including the recent hit by country singer Alan Jackson, "Like Red on a Rose." Famed Scottish poet Robert Burns penned "My love is like a red, red rose that's newly sprung in June," and the best known rose poem is probably the childhood rhyme, "Roses are red, violets are blue." The Irish folk song "Red is the Rose" uses the same traditional melody as the Scottish song "Loch Lomond." The Irish version has a lilting dance rhythm on the words "lily of the valley," a flower that symbolized sweetness and a return to happiness in Victorian times. The language of flowers, Floriology, associates certain flowers and colors with specific emotions or sentiments (see *Flor, blanca flor* on p. 85). The red rose represents deepest love and may also be associated with great respect and courage. This kind of love is said to transcend even death; mythology claims that a red rose cannot grow on a grave.

Suggested recordings of "Red Is the Rose" (iTunes):

GENRE: *Folk* □ Jill Anderson: ***Cool of the Day,*** 2001, Red Chair

GENRE: *Folk* □ The Irish Tenors: ***Heritage,*** 2004, Razor & Tie

▸▸If you like this song, take a look at the folk song "Londonderry Air"

FLOR, BLANCA FLOR (FLOWER, WHITE FLOWER) (P. 85)

The traditional ranchera song "Flor, blanca flor" is the type of Mexican folk song most associated with *mariachi* bands. *Ranchera* (literally, ranch songs) originated before the Mexican revolution in the mid 1800s and were typically traditional songs of love, nature, or patriotism. These songs usually have an instrumental introduction and conclusion, with a verse and refrain in the middle as standardized by Silvestre Vargas and Rubén Fuentes in the early twentieth century. The "blanca flor," or white flower, in Mexican culture symbolizes innocence and eternal love. It is a fitting tribute that the beloved Mexican-American *tejano* singer Selena, tragically killed at age 23 in 1995, was known as "La Flor" (The Flower) and "La Rosa Blanca" (The White Rose).

Suggested recording of ranchera songs (calabashmusic.com)

Genre: *Mexico* □ ***Traditional Songs of Mexico,*** 2006, Calabashmusic

⏩If you like this song, take a look at "Cielito Lindo"

Niño precioso (p. 89)

This lullaby comes from Nicaragua and is also sung as a Christmas carol. Lullabies, with their gentle swinging rhythms, accompanied by the comforting sounds of a mother's voice, have lulled babies to sleep throughout the world. Compare "Niño precioso" to the Welsh lullaby "Suo-gân" (p. 79). "Niño precioso" has a limited vocal range and the rocking 3/4 rhythm typical of lullabies. The sudden change of tempo and rhythm at the chorus mimics the child stirring from sleep, perhaps due to the chilly air ("Que hoy hace frio"). Luckily, the rocking rhythm returns at the end of the song so that baby and mother (or father) can get some rest. Shhhhhh . . . sing the ending softly.

Suggested recording of Latin American lullabies (iTunes):

Genre: *Children* □ Maria del Rey: ***Lullabies of Latin America,*** 2004, Music for Little People

⏩If you like this song, take a look at "Duérmete mi niño"

Santa Lucia (p. 93)

There has been some confusion about whether "Santa Lucia" is a place or a person. The original Italian sailing song was inspired by the beautiful Bay of Naples outside the city of Santa Lucia near Mt. Vesuvius. In Scandinavia, Sankta Lucia (Saint Lucia) is a holiday tradition in which a young girl wearing a wreath of candles guides children bearing cakes and gifts. The Sankta Lucia Festival version of the song uses the same Italian melody with completely different Swedish words. The Italian version of "Santa Lucia," like other popular Neapolitan songs such as "O Sol Mio" and "Sorrento," has been recorded by opera singers Luciano Pavarotti and Placido Domingo and by popular singers Perry Como and Tony Bennett. Neapolitan songs are now being rediscovered by the new generation of classically trained pop singers: Josh Groban, Andrea Bocelli, and Charlotte Church.

Suggested recordings of "Santa Lucia" (iTunes):

Genre: *Classical* □ Enrico Caruso: ***Caruso: Italian Songs*** (remastered), rel. 2002, RCA

Genre: *Folk* □ Luciano Pavarotti: ***20th Century Masters: The Best of Luciano Pavarotti: The Millennium Collection,*** 2004, Decca

⏩If you like this song, take a look at the folk song "Torna a Surriento"

L'hirondelle messagère (p. 97)

"Have you flown to far countries? Have you seen my love?" the young maiden asks the swallow in this traditional French Canadian folk song. She dispatches the "swallow messenger" to fly to her loved one with assurance that she will faithfully await his return from sea. The swallow as a messenger of good news or ill omens is a common symbol in the folklore of many countries, including Denmark, Africa, England, France, and Canada. "Ah! toi, belle hirondelle," as this song is also known, was a hit record for the 1970s Canadian folk-rock group Garalou and is featured on their 1997 *Réunion* album and in a recent YouTube video.

Suggested recording (smithsonianglobalsound.org):

Genre: *World* □ Emile George, ***Voix du Sol Français, Vol 2: La Francophone: France and Its Diaspora,*** 1976, Folkways

⏩If you like this song, take a look at the French Canadian song "À la claire fontaine"

Dubinushka (Hammer Song) (p. 100)

"Dubinushka" was originally a barge hauler's work song set to a poem by B. Bogdanof in 1865. After the "Bloody Sunday" massacre in Russia the song became a powerful revolutionary song to protest the oppression of the people. The verses that were added later urge the laborers to wake up and use their work hammers to smash the oppressors who crush their strength and spill their blood.

Bloody Sunday took place on January 9, 1905. Troops fired on peaceful demonstrators who were seeking help from the Czar and were walking to the Winter Palace in St. Petersburg. Nearly 1,000 people were killed, and among those outraged at the senseless shootings were many prominent Russian musicians, including Rachmaninoff, Rimsky-Korsakov, and the famous operatic bass, Fyodor Chaliapin. Protests and workers' strikes sprang up everywhere and included underpaid chorus singers and orchestra members. Chaliapin shocked the audience and angered the government by singing "Dubinushka" during an opera performance at the Bolshoi Theater, and Nicholas the Second demanded his immediate dismissal. However, the theater owners feared such action would spark a full-blown revolution. Protected by his immense popularity, Chaliapin continued to lead the singing of "Dubinushka" for crowds of as many as 5,000 Russian workers.

Suggested recording of "Dubinushka" (iTunes):

GENRE: *Classical* □ Feodor Chaliapin: ***The Chaliapin Edition, Volume 2: 1908–1911,*** rel. 2001, Arbiter

⏩If you like this song, take a look at "Volga Boat Song"

DANCE OF YOUTH (QING CHUN WU QU) (P. 102)

This popular Chinese folksong is known by many titles, including "Little Bird." It comes from the Xin Jiang province of northwest China, near the Russian border, and has been passed from generation to generation of Chinese and Chinese American singers. "Dance of Youth" is among the folksongs that were collected by one of the best-known Chinese songcatchers, Wang Lou Bin (1913–1996). Some scholars believe that Wang Lou Bin may have gathered the melody and added his own poem. During Chinese festivals, young people dance ("wu") together and sing this song. It is often accompanied by gymnasts. The moral of the song is "This is our youth, so enjoy the moment and be merry! Enjoy life."

Suggested traditional recording of "Qing Chun Wu Qu" (iTunes):

GENRE: *World* □ ***Liu Tang Ge De Sheng Jin Dian Ge Qu Ban, Vol. 4,*** 2006, Pacific Audio

⏩If you like this song, take a look at "Gan Lan Shu" (Olive Tree)

EV'RY TIME I FEEL THE SPIRIT (P. 106)

This fiery revivalist song from 1874 was sung by both blacks and whites after the abolition of slavery. No composer is credited, and the song was possibly written by a former slave. During slavery, most slaves were allowed to sing but were strictly forbidden to play instruments or dance in public. In the 1890s, however, the African traditions returned with much shouting, stomping, dancing, and clapping. There was a lot of repetition of text, and a song could go on and on—as long as the spirit moved. The songs often depicted colorful stories of the Old Testament, such as God speaking to Moses through a burning bush: "Out of His mouth came fire and smoke."

Suggested recording of "Ev'ry Time I Feel the Spirit" (iTunes):

GENRE: *Classical* □ Paul Robeson: ***The Power and the Glory,*** 1991, Sony

⏩If you like this song, take a look at "Swing Low, Sweet Chariot"

AMAZING GRACE (P. 108)

By now, many Americans know the story of how the slave trader John Newton came to write this hugely popular hymn. It is probably true that the tune to "Amazing Grace" was originally a slave song that Newton had heard. It is also true that on May 10, 1748, in a deadly storm, Newton's fervent prayers for mercy were answered. His ship did not sink and Newton vowed to God that he would be a changed man.

It is not as commonly known that after Newton's conversion he continued to sail slave ships until illness forced a career change. It was only then that Newton devoted himself to religious studies in Greek and Hebrew, and eventually became a beloved minister in the Church of England at Olney. Newton's job demanded that he write a new song for each weekly prayer meeting. It was here, along with the famous English poet William Cowper, that Newton wrote several editions of *Olney Hymns,* which included the song that came to be known as "Amazing Grace." The song has an incredible universal appeal and has been recorded by rock groups, country singers, pop singers, classical singers, choirs, and orchestras;

it has also been used as background music for Olympic gymnasts and television commercials.

Suggested recordings of "Amazing Grace" (iTunes):

GENRE: *Gospel* □ Mahalia Jackson: ***In My Home Over There,*** 1998, MCA

GENRE: *Pop* □ Hayley Westenra: ***Pure,*** 2003, Decca

⏩If you like this song, take a look at "Be Thou My Vision"

WAYFARING STRANGER (P. 111)

Fans were stunned to see White Stripes guitarist Jack White playing the role of a civil war troubadour in the 2003 Oscar-winning film "Cold Mountain." White sings "Wayfaring Stranger" and other traditional Appalachian songs in the film and soundtrack. "Wayfaring Stranger" was passed down from generation to generation until it was written down by songcatchers such as John Jacob Niles. The words are pure Kentucky; however, like many southern folk tunes, the tune probably came from our ancestors in the British Isles. During the 1930s, the acclaimed folk singer Burl Ives traveled the U.S., introducing many southern folk songs to the northern and western regions. Ives became known as the Wayfaring Stranger and adopted the title for his popular 1940s radio show and 1948 autobiography.

The song's reference to crossing over the River Jordan had a double meaning during the Civil War. When the slaves sang about boarding trains bound for Glory, or crossing rivers, they were secretly but openly singing about the underground railroad or crossing the Ohio River to find freedom in the North. No doubt the song also provided assurance that this world's woes are fleeting.

Suggested recordings of "Wayfaring Stranger" (iTunes):

GENRE: *Blues* □ Eva Cassidy: ***Songbird,*** 1998, Blix Street

GENRE: *Folk* □ Kristin Chenoweth: ***As I Am,*** 2005, Sony

GENRE: *Country* □ Loretta Lynn: ***Van Lear Rose,*** 2004, Interscope

⏩If you like this song, take a look at the spiritual "Flee as a Bird"

I'VE GOT PEACE LIKE A RIVER (P. 113)

Spirituals such as "I've Got Peace Like a River," "This Little Light of Mine," and "We Shall Overcome" took on new life in the 1960s. The river signified freedom for slaves (see "Wayfaring Stranger," p. 111) and was a symbol for peace and political freedom in the Civil Rights Movement crusades and marches. Peace was a constant theme in the life and singing of Coretta Scott King, widow of the slain civil rights leader Dr. Martin Luther King, Jr., as she continued her husband's work by performing "freedom concerts" across the country. In her eulogy, theologian Dr. Sam Roberts gave thanks for Scott King's voice of beauty, saying, "Art is ultimately used to redeem the ugliness of bigotry around us. Freed from the strictures of mortal cares and infirmities of body, her soul now exults in the words of an old spiritual, 'I've got peace like a river, I've got peace like a river, I've got peace like a river, in-a my soul.'"

Suggested recording of American spirituals (iTunes):

Genre: *Classical* □ Marian Anderson: ***Spirituals,*** 1952, rel. 1999, RCA

⏩If you like this song, take a look at the spiritual "Wade in the Water"

HOW CAN I KEEP FROM SINGING? (P. 116)

This hymn, from the Revival period in America, was written by the Reverend R. Lowry in about 1865. (It is not an old Quaker or Shaker hymn, as some sources suggest.) This beautiful hymn isn't well known in churches, yet it frequently rises to the surface in times of national crisis as a song of the indomitable American spirit.

Doris Plenn added a verse during the McCarthy era: "In prison cell and dungeon vile our thoughts to them are winging, when friends by shame are undefiled, how can I keep from singing?" The song appeared during the Vietnam era and, more recently, after the terrorist attacks on September 11, 2001. Numerous print and TV journalists wrote and recited the words, "Through all the tumult and the strife I hear the music ringing. It sounds an echo in my soul, how can I keep from singing?"

Suggested recordings of "How Can I Keep From Singing?" (iTunes):

GENRE: *Folk* □ Judy Collins: ***Portrait of an American Girl,*** 2005, Wildflower

GENRE: Jazz □ René Marie: ***How Can I Keep From Singing?,*** 2000, MAXJAZZ

▸▸If you like this song, take a look at "Let It Be"

AMERICA THE BEAUTIFUL (P. 119)

When Katherine Lee Bates wrote these lyrics after visiting Colorado's Pikes Peak, she created a song that evokes the emotion produced by the beauty that is prevalent across the United States. The Reverend Samuel Ward set the poem to music. Though Bates and Ward never met, their song became immensely popular. "America the Beautiful" remains a favorite patriotic song and has often been suggested as a new national anthem. Elvis Presley, Ray Charles, and many other artists have recorded the song, and opera singer Denyce Graves sang a particularly stirring and heartfelt rendition at the National Prayer Service after September 11, 2001.

THE STAR-SPANGLED BANNER (P. 121)

On the morning of September 13, 1814, Francis Scott Key was inspired to write the words that would become known as "The Star-Spangled Banner." Key had witnessed a tattered American flag still flying over Fort McHenry after the colonists defended Baltimore from bombardment by British war ships. Nearly two hundred years later, an eerily similar image inspired an entire nation as rescue workers in New York City raised a tattered American flag on a pile of rubble that had once been the World Trade Center. Since this song's official adoption as national anthem in 1931, critics have suggested alternate anthems, "America the Beautiful" being the strongest contender (See "America the Beautiful," p. 119). However, despite criticism that "The Star-Spangled Banner" is too difficult to sing, or that it was set irreverently to a British drinking song ("To Anacreon in Heaven"), or that it is too militaristic, the song remains the national anthem of the United States of America. So, here is your opportunity to learn the words and the vocal technique to brave that octave-and-a-half range. The next time you hear the familiar opening strains of "O say can you see . . ." at a sporting event, you'll be confident enough to sing along.

O CANADA! (P. 123)

"O Canada!" did not become the official Canadian national anthem until 1980, though the original French version was written in 1880 by Calixa Lavallée and Sir Adolphe-Basile Routhier. This French version remains unchanged, unlike the English version that underwent several changes, including a national contest. In the end, a version of Robert Stanley Weir's 1908 lyrics was adapted in 1968. "The True North strong and free," meaning loyal or faithful, is a quote from Alfred, Lord Tennyson.

Reflecting Canada's dual languages, "O Canada!" is often sung in French and English at sporting events in Canada the U.S. The opening lines are usually sung in French, then switch to English after "Des plus brillants exploits." Others prefer to sing the first two and last three lines in French to avoid sexist language or religious connotations. A third option is to avoid the English text altogether. We have included French and English lyrics and leave the choice to the singer.

There's Music in the Air

Words by Fanny Crosby
(1820–1915)

America
Music by George F. Root
(1820–1895)

For background and performance notes, see page 42.

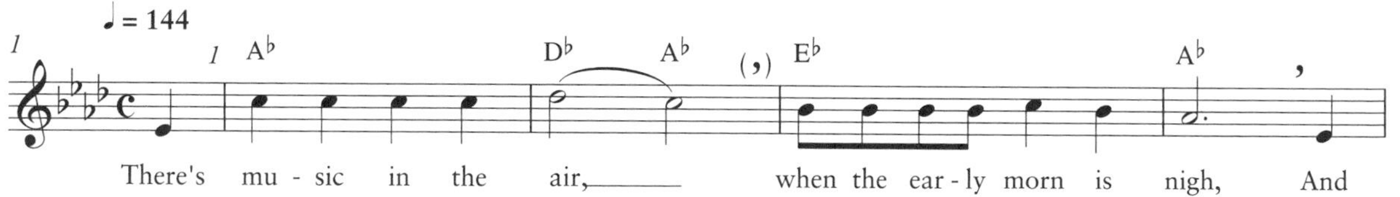
♩ = 144
A♭ D♭ A♭ (,) E♭ A♭ ,
There's mu - sic in the air, when the ear - ly morn is nigh, And

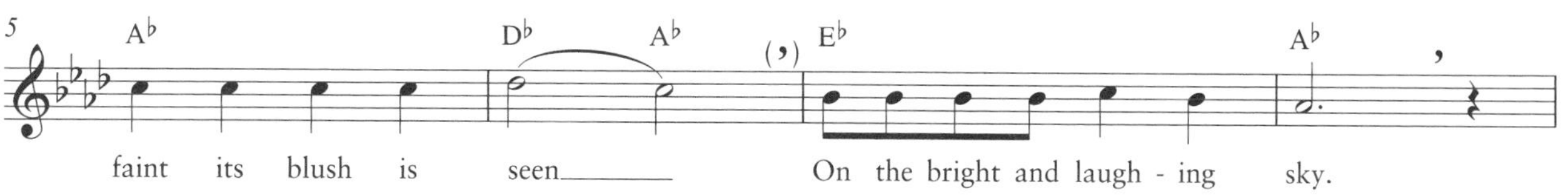
A♭ D♭ A♭ (,) E♭ A♭ ,
faint its blush is seen On the bright and laugh - ing sky.

D♭ A♭ (,) E♭ A♭ ,
Many a harp's ec - stat - ic sound Thrills us with its joy pro - found

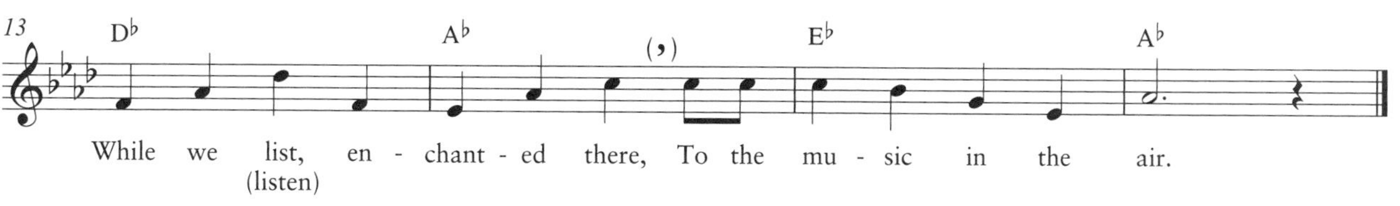
D♭ A♭ (,) E♭ A♭
While we list, en - chant - ed there, To the mu - sic in the air.
(listen)

My Country 'Tis of Thee

Words by Samuel F. Smith
(1808–1895)

America
Music by Henry Carey
(1687–1743)

For background and performance notes, see page 42.

♩ = 84
1
G
D
G
G
My coun - try 'tis of thee, Sweet land of lib - er - ty, Of thee I sing.

7
G
D7
Land where my fa - thers died, Land of the Pil - grims' pride,

11
G
C
G
C
G
D7
G
From ev - 'ry mount - tain side, Let free - dom ring!

Music Alone Shall Live
(Round)

Germany

For background and performance notes, see page 43.

♩=100
1
F
C
F
2
F
C
All things shall per - ish from un - der the sky. Mu - sic a - lone shall live,

7
F
3
F
C
F
mu - sic a - lone shall live, mu - sic a - lone shall live, ne - ver to die.

Oh, How Lovely Is the Evening

(Round)

Germany

For background and performance notes, see page 43.

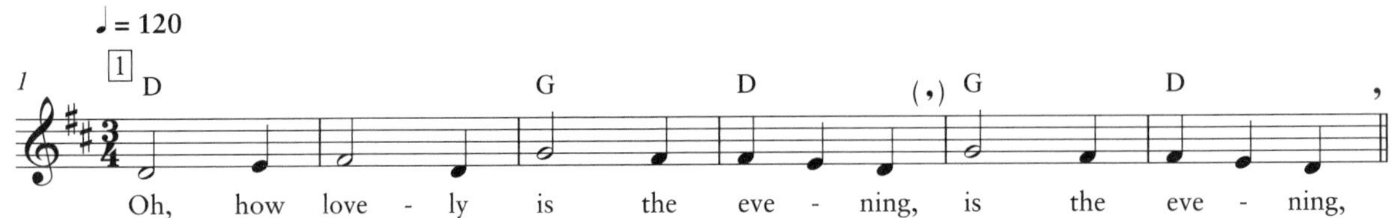

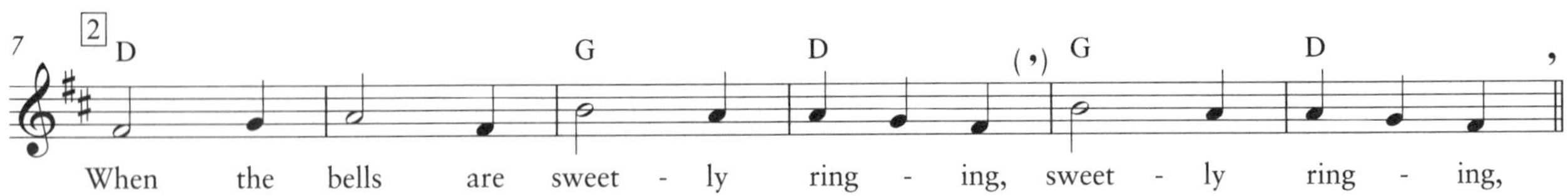

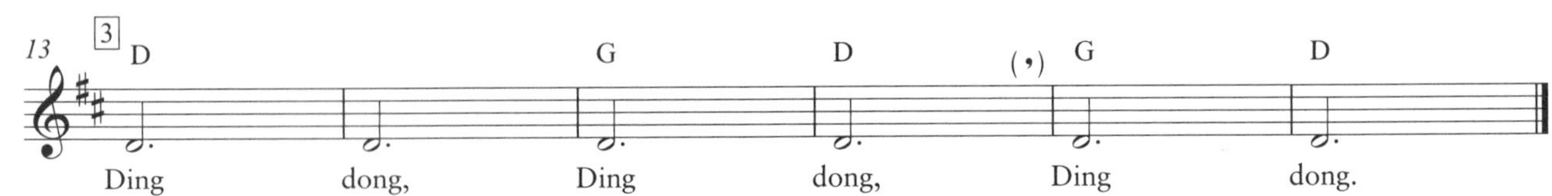

Babylon
(Round)

Words from Psalm 137

America
Music by William Billings
(1746–1800)

For background and performance notes, see page 43.

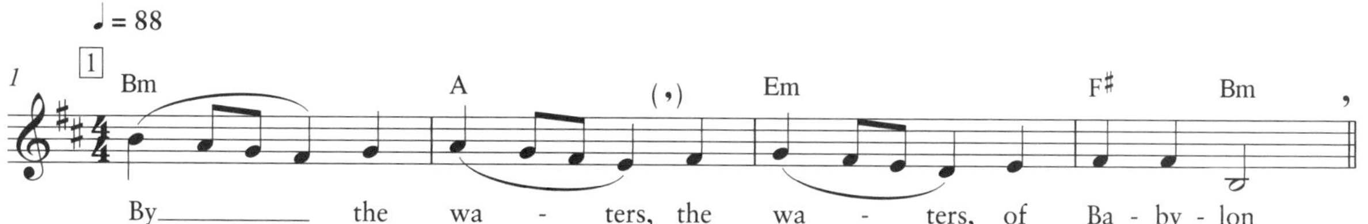
♩ = 88
1
Bm A (,) Em F♯ Bm
By the wa - ters, the wa - ters, of Ba - by - lon

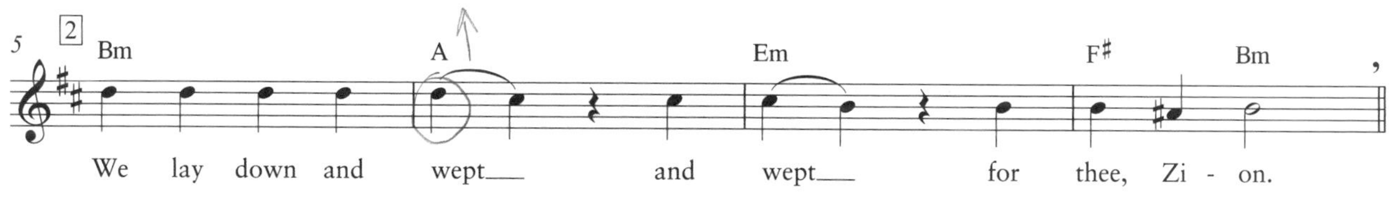
2
Bm A Em F♯ Bm
We lay down and wept and wept for thee, Zi - on.

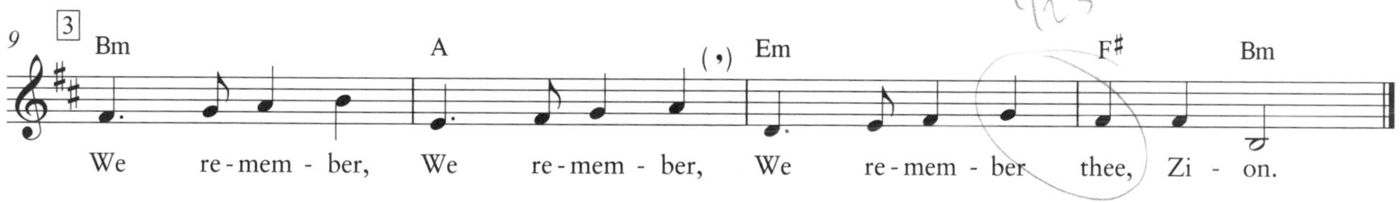
3
Bm A (,) Em F♯ Bm
We re-mem - ber, We re-mem - ber, We re-mem - ber thee, Zi - on.

PART TWO
Traditional Songs

Dona nobis pacem
(Round)

Latin

For background and performance notes, see page 43.

Dona nobis pacem.
[dɔna nɔbis patʃɛm]

Grant us peace.

Ah, Poor Bird

(Round)

America

For background and performance notes, see page 43.

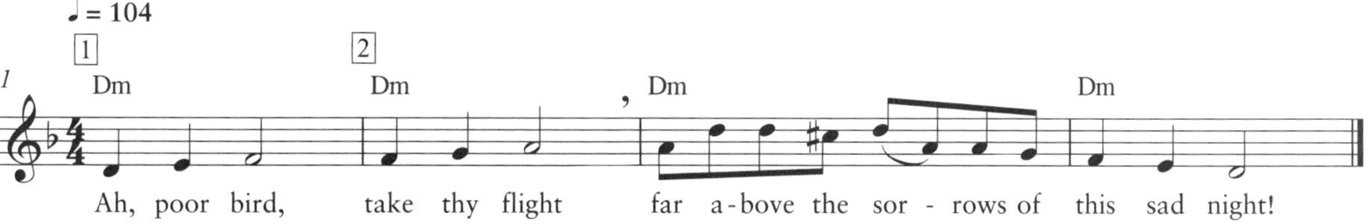

Shalom, chaverim

(Round)

Israel

For background and performance notes, see page 43.

Shalom,* chaverim, shalom, chaverim [ʃalɔm, xavɛrim, ʃalɔm, xavɛrim]	**Farewell, friends, farewell, friends,**
shalom, shalom. [ʃalɔm, ʃalɔm]	**farewell, farewell.**
Le hit raot, le hit raot, [lə xit ɾaot, lə xit ɾaot]	**Until we meet again, until we meet again,**
shalom, shalom. [ʃalɔm, ʃalɔm]	**farewell, farewell.**

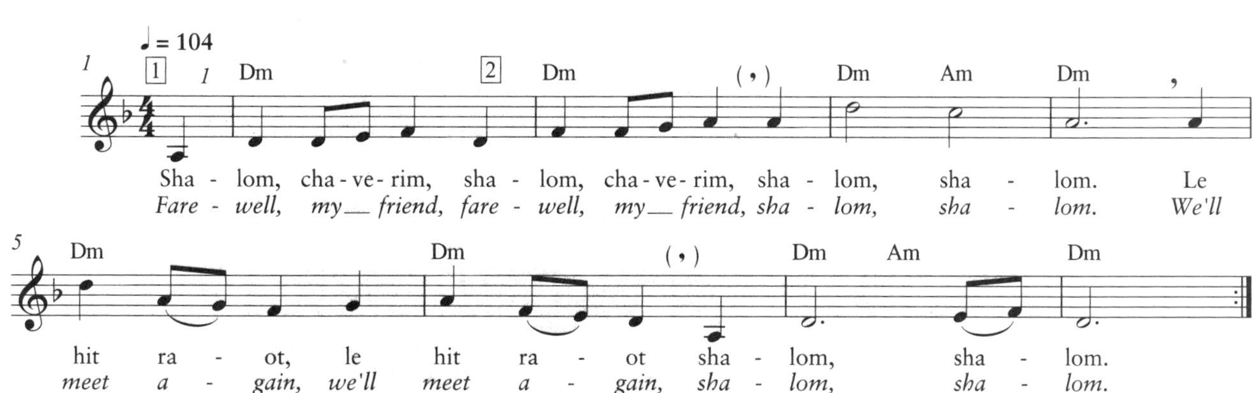

Alternate text: Glad tidings we bring / of peace on earth / good will toward men. / Of peace on earth, / of peace on earth / good will toward men.

**Shalom* can mean hello or good-bye. (Hebrew translation and pronunciation by Cynthia Lee Fox.)

PART TWO

Traditional Songs

Ah, Poor Bird/Shalom

(Duet)

Israel, America

For background and performance notes, see page 43.

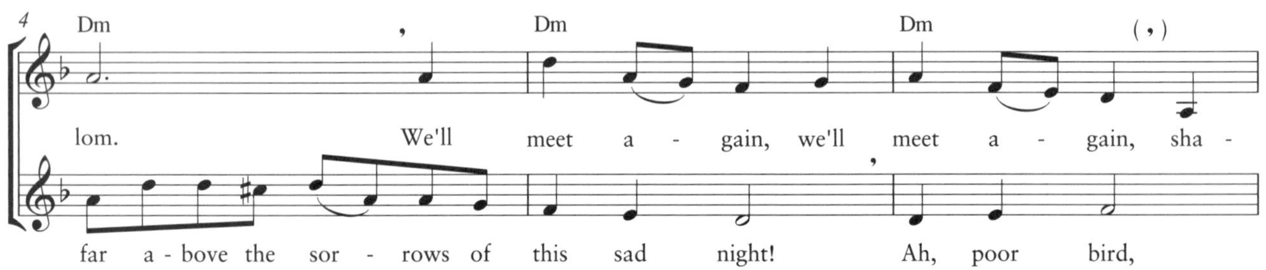

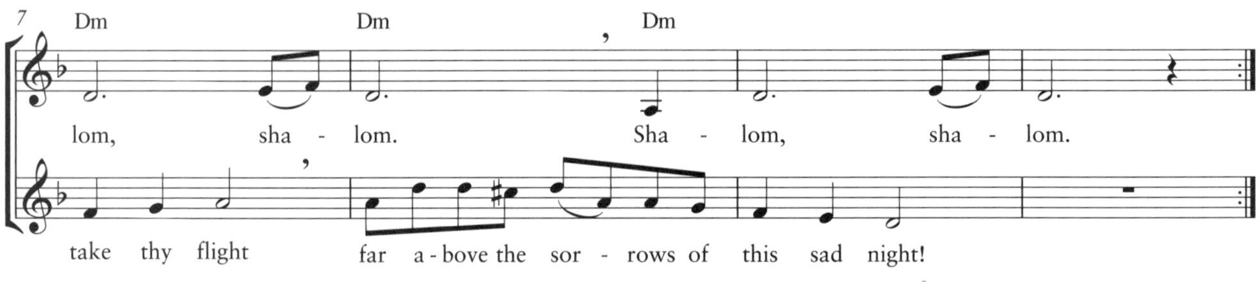

Three Alleluia Rounds

Music by W. A. Mozart
(1756–1791)

For background and performance notes, see page 44.

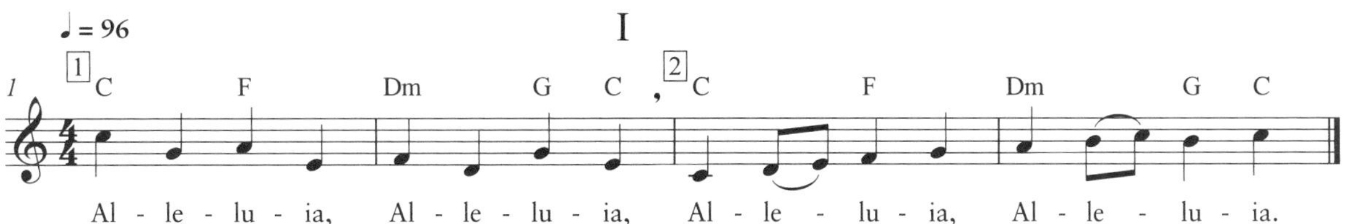

Music by W. A. Mozart

Music by William Boyce
(1711–1799)

Shenandoah

America
Arranged by Frank Ponzio

For background and performance notes, see page 44.

16
D G D/F♯ G
Shen-an - doah I'm bound to leave you. A - way you roll-ing
19
D G Em Em/D D A
riv - er. O Shen-an - doah I'll not de - ceive you. A -
22
D A D/F♯ G A7 Bm A
way I'm bound a - way, 'Cross the wide Mis-sour - i.
26
D D
For sev-en years I've been a

29
G
G
D
rov - er A - way you roll - ing riv - er. But

32
G
D
A7
D
D/F#
I'll re - turn to be your lov - er A - way I'm bound a -

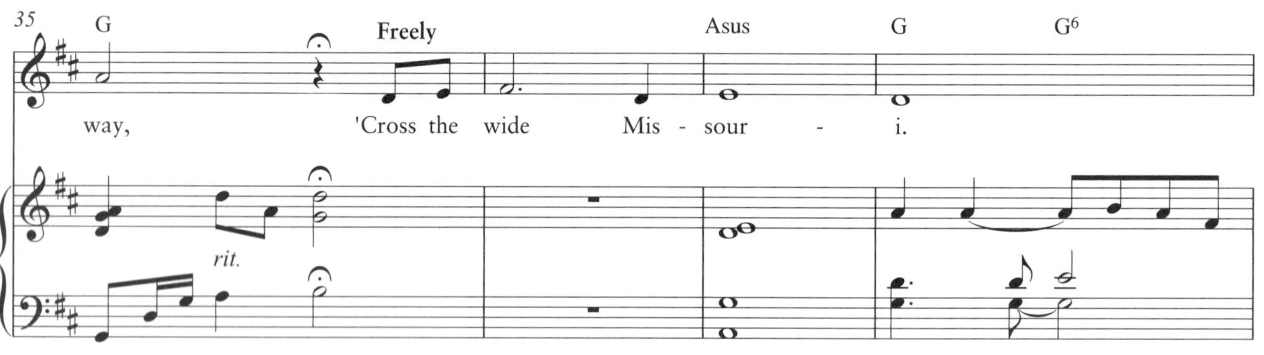
35
G
Freely
Asus
G
G6
way, 'Cross the wide Mis - sour - i.
rit.

39
G
D/F#
G
A7
D

The House of the Rising Sun

America
Arranged by Scarlett Antaloczy

For background and performance notes, see page 44.

*girl

11
Dm A7 1. Dm A7 2. Dm A7
me, oh, Lord, I'm one.
ram - bler lead me a - 2. If - stray.
14
Em B7 Em G A C
3. O mo - ther tell your chil - dren not to
go - in back to New Or - leans my
p
17
Em G B7sus4 Em G
do what I have done, but shun that house in
race is al - most run, I'm go - ing back to
20
A C Em B7 1. Em B7
New Or - leans they call the Ris - ing Sun.
spend my life be - neath the Ris - ing 4. I'm

PART TWO
Traditional Songs

Scarborough Fair

England
Arranged by Scarlett Antaloczy

For background and performance notes, see page 44.

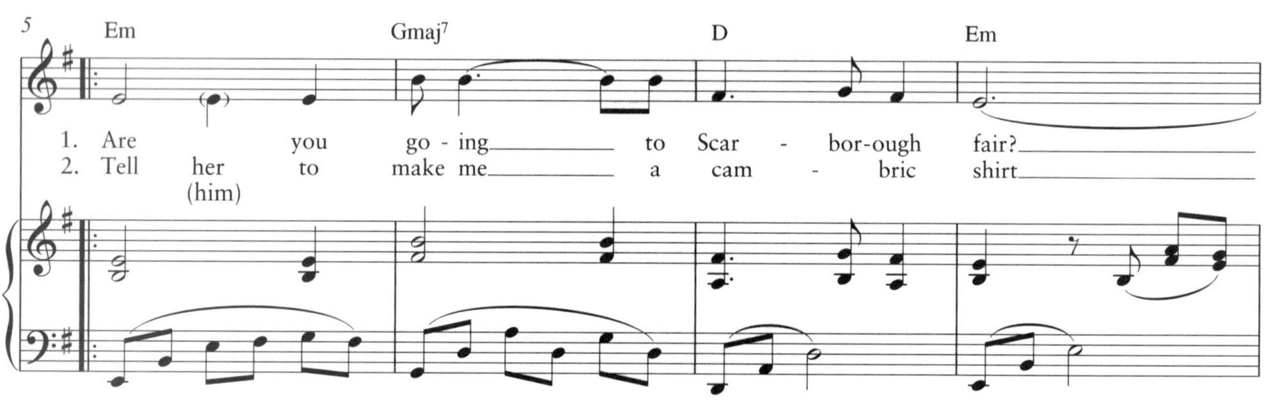

13
Em
D/Em
Em
D/Em
thyme.
Re -
With -
17
Em
Gmaj9
Em/G
D/A
G/B
D
mem - ber me to one who lives there.
out a seam or fine need - le work.
21
Em
Dmaj9
rit.
Cmaj7(♯11)
D6
She once was a true love of
(He)
1.
25
Em
D/Em
Em
D/Em
mine.
p

2.
Em
D/Em
Em
Em
C/E
mine.
mf
E7sus4
E7sus4/G
E7sus4/D
Em
Tell her to wash it in yon - der dry well.
(him)
D/Em
G
Em
Bm
Em
D/G
G
A7sus4
Pars - ley, sage, rose - ma - ry, and
D/Em
D/Em
Cmaj7
D
Cmaj7
thyme.
Where

45
B7sus4
Cmaj7
A/C♯
G
D9
wa - ter ne'er sprang nor drop of rain fell.
3
49
D
mf
Em
Dmaj9
Cmaj7(♯11) D6
For she once was a true love of
(he)
mf
53
Em
D/E
Em
Gmaj7
D6
Cmaj7(♯11) D6
mine.
She once was a true love of
(He)
mp
rit.
58
Em7/A
Em
D/Em
Em
mine.
rit.
p
pp

Danny Boy

Words by Fred E. Weatherly
(1848–1929)

Traditional Irish Tune
"Londonderry Air"
Arranged by Frank Ponzio

For background and performance notes, see page 45.

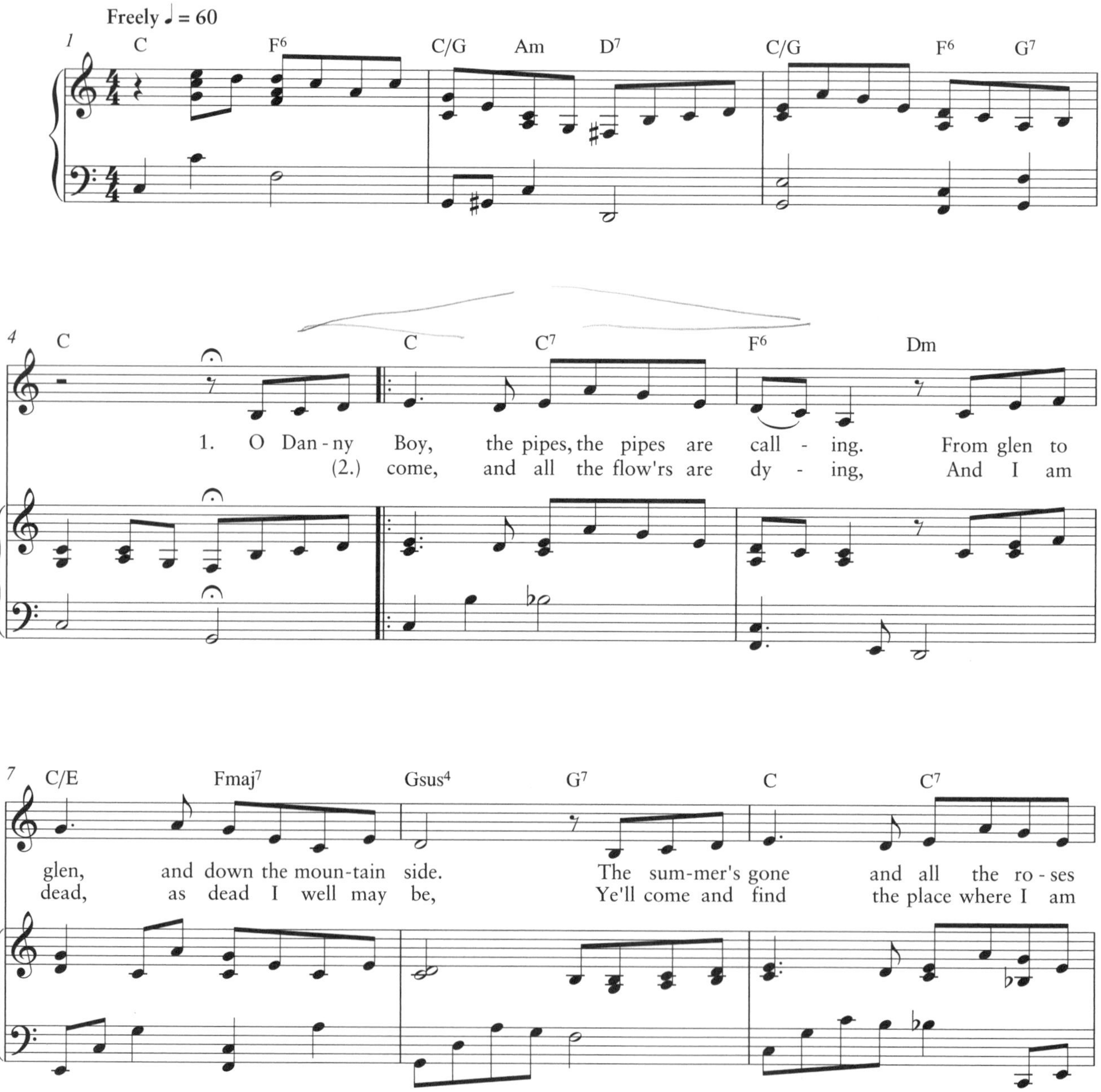

Freely ♩ = 60
1 C F6 C/G Am D7 C/G F6 G7
4 C C C7 F6 Dm
1. O Dan - ny Boy, the pipes, the pipes are call - ing. From glen to
(2.) come, and all the flow'rs are dy - ing, And I am
7 C/E Fmaj7 Gsus4 G7 C C7
glen, and down the moun - tain side. The sum - mer's gone and all the ro - ses
dead, as dead I well may be, Ye'll come and find the place where I am

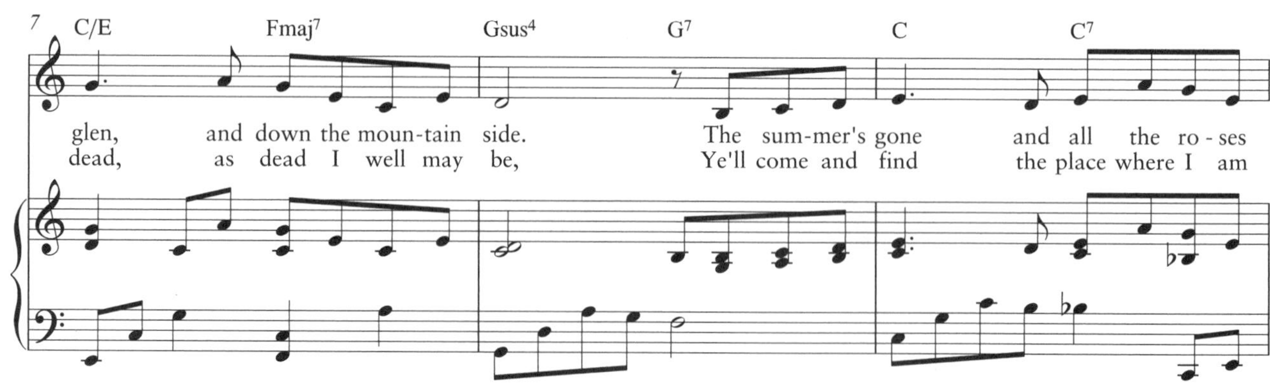

10 F6 F♯dim C/G Gsus4 G7 F C

fall - ing, It's you, it's you must go and I must bide. But come ye
ly - ing, And kneel and say an "*A - ve*" there for me; And I shall

13 Am G/F C/E C C/B Am G/F

back When sum-mer's in the mead - ow, Or when the val - ley's hushed and white with
hear, tho' soft you tread a - bove_ me, And all my grave will warm - er, sweet - er

16 Gsus4 G7 C F6 C/G Am

snow. 'Tis I'll be there in sun-shine or in shad - ow, O, Dan - ny
be, For you will bend, and tell me that you love_ me, And I shall

slight rit. *a tempo* *rit.*

19 C/G F6 G7 1. C 2. C

Boy, O Dan - ny Boy, I love you so. But if ye me.
sleep in peace un - til you come to

The Water Is Wide

Traditional English Tune
"Waly, Waly"
Arranged by Scarlett Antaloczy

For background and performance notes, see page 45.

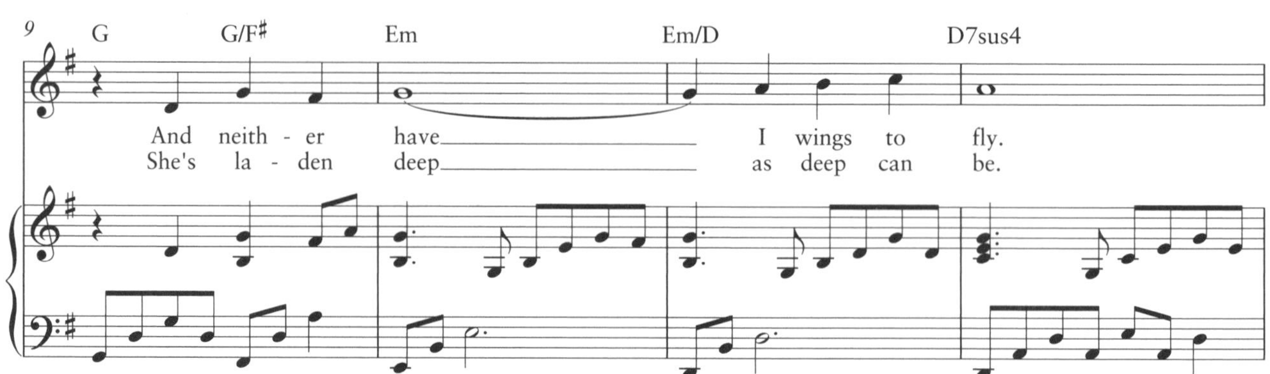

13
D D/C Bm7 Cmaj9(add13)
Build me a boat that can car - ry two,
But not so deep as the love I'm in,
17
G/D D7sus4 G
And both shall row my love and I.
I know not if I sink or swim.
21
D7sus4 G C/G D/G G G/F♯
rit.
I leaned my back a - gainst an old oak. I thought it
rit.
26
Em D D D/C
was a trust - y tree. But first it

30
Bm7
Cmaj9(add13)
G/D
bend - - ed and then it broke, Thus did my love
35
D7sus4
Interlude
G/B Am/C G/D F/E♭ F G/B♭ Am/C G/D Bm
prove false to me.
p
40
G/B Am/C G/D F/E♭ F G/B Am/C G/D E9/B
Broader
O love is
♩ = 80
44
A D/A A A A/G♯
hand - - - some and love is fine. Pure as a

48
F♯m9
E
E E/D A/C♯ E7/B
jew - el when first it is new. But love grows
52
C♯ø7
F♯7
Bm9
G7
ff
old And wax - eth cold
56
C♯m
rit.
Dmaj7/E D Em/D A/C♯
rit.
Bm/D A/E
and fades a - way Like the morn - ing dew.
60
G/F G A/C♯ Bm/D A/E C♯m A
mf
mp rit.
ppp

Salley Gardens

Words by W. B. Yeats
(1865–1939)

Traditional Irish Tune
"Maid of the Mourne Shore"
Arranged by Frank Ponzio

For background and performance notes, see page 45.

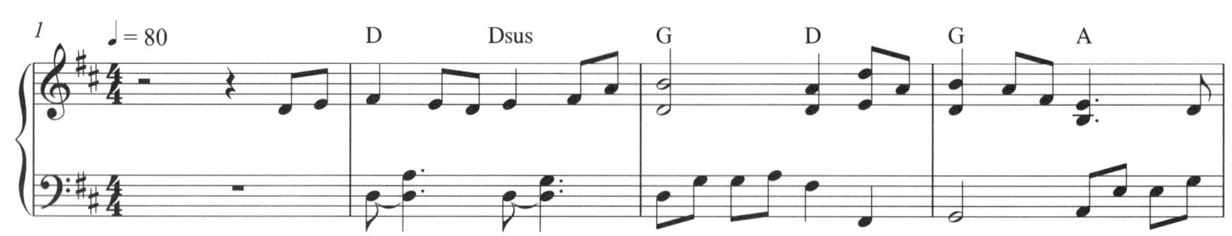
1
♩= 80
D
Dsus
G
D
G
A

5
D
D
A
G
D/F♯
(,)
G
A7
Down by the Sal - ley Gar - dens my love and I did
(his) (he)

9
D
D
A/C♯
G
D
(,)
G
A
meet. She passed the Sal - ley Gar - dens with lit - tle snow white

13
D Bm G F♯m
feet. She bid me take life ea - - sy, as the
(him)
16
G A D D Dsus
leaves grow on the tree, But I be - ing young and
(he)
19
G D/F♯ G A7 D Em D
fool - ish with her did not a - gree. In a
23
D A7 G D/F♯ G
field by the riv - - er my love and I did
(his) (he)

26
Dsus D D A G D/F♯ G A7
(,)
stand and_ on my_ lean - ing_ shoul - der she_ placed her_ snow white
(his)_
30
D Bm G F♯m D
(,)
hand. She bid me_ take life eas - - y as the
(him)_
33
G A Dsus D D G6
grass grows on_ the_ weirs, But_ I was_ young and_
(he)
36
G F♯m D/F♯ Em7 Asus D
(,)
rit.
fool - ish and_ now am_ full of tears.
(is)_
rit.

Suo-gân
Lullaby

(Welsh Gaelic)

Huna blentyn ar fy mynwes [hina blɛntɪn arr va manwɛs]	**Sleep my baby on my bosom.**
Clyd a chynnes ydyw hon; [klid a xanɛs adiju hɔn]	**Warm and cozy may you rest,**
Breichiau mam* sy'n dynn amdanat, [brraikiai mam sɪn dɪn amdanat]	**Mother's arms are around you tightly,**
Cariad mam sy dan fy mron; [kariad mam si dan va mrɔn]	**Mother's love in my breast.**
Ni cha' dim amharu'th gyntun, [ni xaif dim amharɪθ gantin]	**Not a thing shall mar your resting,**
Ni wna undyn â thi gam; [ni una indɪn a θi gam]	**Nor a person do you harm.**
Huna'n dawel, annwyl blentyn, [hinan dawɛl anwɪl blɛntɪn]	**Be at rest my darling baby.**
Huna'n fwyn ar fron dy fam. [hinan vuin arr vrɔn da vam]	**Sleep my baby on your mother's breast.**

**mam* is Welsh for "mother."

Suo-gân

(Lullaby)

Gaelic words by Robert Bryan
English version by Huw Lewis

Wales
Arranged by Scarlett Antaloczy

For background and performance notes, see page 46.

1
Lilting ♩ = 72

5
A
F
C7
F
Through the win-dow by your can - dle Shines a moon-beam
Hun - a blen-tyn ar fy myn - wes Clyd a chyn - nes

8
Gm/C
Dm/F
F
C7
soft and clear: Sleep my ba - by, fear no dan-ger,
yd - yw hon; Brei - chiau mam sy'n dynn am - da - nat,

11
F
Gm/C
C^{13}_{7}
Dm/F
B
Dm
Am
none can harm you, mo - ther's* near; In the tree - tops
Car - iad mam sy'n dan fy mron. Ni cha' dim am -
14
B♭
F
Dm
Am
Gm⁷
C⁷sus⁴
rit.
winds are sigh - ing, Birds are fly - ing to their nest.
har - u'th gyn - tun, Ni wna un - dyn â thi gam,
17
E♭/F
B♭
D♭maj⁷
E♭⁷
Dm/C
Am/C
Warm and co - sy, no more cry - ing, Sleep my ba - by,
Hun - a'n da - wel ann - wyl blen - tyn, Hun - a'n fwyn ar
a tempo
20
1.
2.
Gm/C
C^{13}_{7}
Dm/F
Gm⁷
C⁷
F
be at rest. be at rest.
fron dy fam. fron dy fam.

*father's

PART TWO

Traditional Songs

Red Is the Rose

Traditional Irish Tune
"Loch Lomond"
Arranged by Scarlett Antaloczy

For background and performance notes, see page 46.

*lad

13
G9
F♯m
G
G♯11
You choose the rose love and I will make the vow, and I'll
moon shone its rays on her* locks of gold - en hair, She†
17
D/F♯
F7♯11
A7
D
A7
be your true love for - ev - - er.
swore she'd‡ be my love for - ev - - er.
Chorus
21
D
Bm
Em
G
Red is the rose that by yon - der gar - den grows,
25
D
Bm
G
A
G9
Fair is the li - ly of the val - - ley, Clear is the

*his
†He
‡he'd

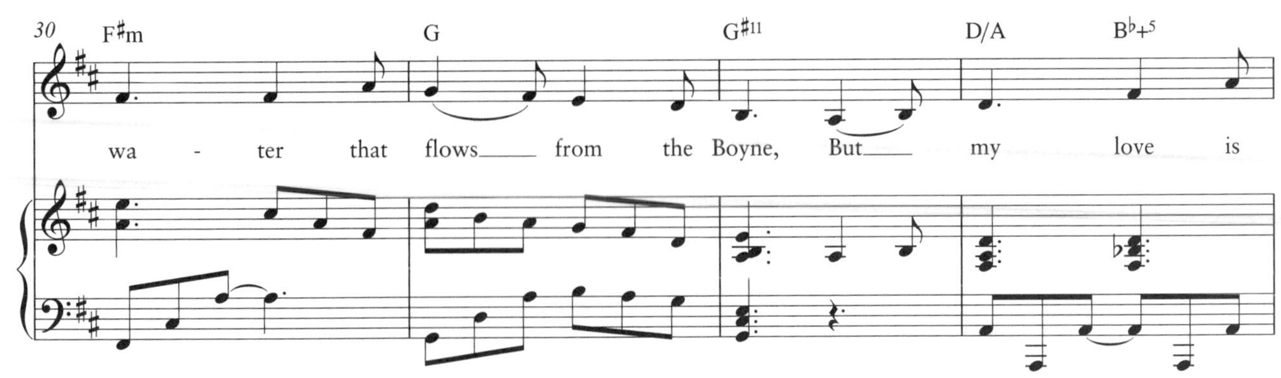
30
F♯m
G
G♯11
D/A
B♭+5
wa - ter that flows___ from the Boyne, But___ my love is

34
A/B
A7
1.
D
2.
D
fair - er than an - - y. 2. 'Twas - y.

Flor, blanca flor
Flower, White Flower

(Latin American Spanish)

Flor, blanca flor, flor de las flores, [flɔɾ, blaŋka flɔɾ, flɔɾ dɛ las flɔɾɛs]	Flower, white flower, flower of flowers,
chaparrita de mi vida regálame tus amores. [tʃaparrita dɛ mi vida rregalame tus amɔɾɛs]	Chaparrita* of my life give to me your love.
En el mar tengo‿una palma [ɛn ɛl maɾ tɛŋgɔuna palma]	Near the sea I have a palm
con las ramas hasta‿el cielo [kon las rramas astaɛl tʃjelo]	with branches to the sky.
donde se refugia mi‿alma [dɔndɛ sɛ rrɛfudʒa mialma]	My soul takes refuge
cuando no‿encuentra consuelo. [kuando no ɛnkuɛntra konsuelo]	when it does not find comfort.
Flor, blanca flor, flor de las flores, [flɔɾ, blaŋka flɔɾ, flɔɾ dɛ las flɔɾɛs]	Flower, white flower, flower of flowers,
chaparrita de mi vida regálame tu‿alegría. [tʃaparrita dɛ mi vida rregalame tualɛgɾia]	Chaparrita of my life give me your happiness.

**chaparitta* (or the masculine form *chaparitto*) is an endearment similar to "little sweetheart."

Flor, blanca flor

(Flower, White Flower)

(Duet)

English version
by Cynthia Vaughn

Mexico
Arranged by Scarlett Antaloczy

For background and performance notes, see page 46.

17
F
B♭
se re-fu - gia mi al - ma__ cuan-do no en - cuen-tra con-sue - lo.__
soul can find its re - fuge__ There is no oth - er com - fort.__
21
F
B♭
Flor, blan - ca flor, flor de las flor-es, cha-par-
Flow - er so white, flow - er of flow ers, cha-par-
25
F
B♭
Chorus
ri - ta de mi vi - da,__ re-gá - la - me tu a - le - gri - a. En el
ri - ta of my life,__ oh you bring to me such plea - sure. Near the
29
F
B♭
mar ten-go u - na pal - ma__ con las ra - mas has - ta el cie - lo, don - de
sea I have a palm tree__ and its bran - ches reach the sky,__ where my

33
F
B♭
se re - fu - gia - mi al - ma cuan - do no en - cuen - tra con - sue - lo.
soul can find its re - fuge when there is no oth - er com - fort.
37
F
B♭
Flor, blan - ca flor, flor de las flor - es, cha - par -
Flow - er so white, flow - er of flow - ers, cha - par -
41
F
B♭
ri - ta de mi vi - da, re - gé - la - me tu a - le gri - a.
ri - ta of my life, oh you bring to me such plea - sure.
45
49

Niño precioso
Precious Child

(Latin American Spanish)

Niño precioso, mas que el armiño, [niɲo presjoso mas kel armiɲo]	**Child more precious then the finest cloth,**
risueño niño Dios del amor. [rrisweɲo niɲo djos del amoɾ]	**Smiling boy, God of love.**
Duerme tranquilo, duerme‿entretanto, [dwɛɾme traŋkilo dwɛɾmentɾetanto]	**Sleep calmly, sleep while**
Eleva un canto mi‿humilde voz. [eleva un kanto miumilde vos]	**My humble voice raises a song.**
Duerme, chiquitito que hoy hace frio. [dwɛɾme tʃikitito ke oi ase fɾio]	**Sleep little boy who is cold.**
Duerme, chiquitito yo velaré. [dwɛɾme tʃikitito jo velaɾe]	**Sleep, little boy, I will keep vigil.**

— *translation by Noemi Lugo*

PART TWO

Traditional Songs

Niño precioso
(Precious Child)

English version
by Cynthia Vaughn

Nicaragua
Arranged by Scarlett Antaloczy

For background and performance notes, see page 47.

Gently ♩ = 84
Dm
Dm/C
Gm
A7sus4
p

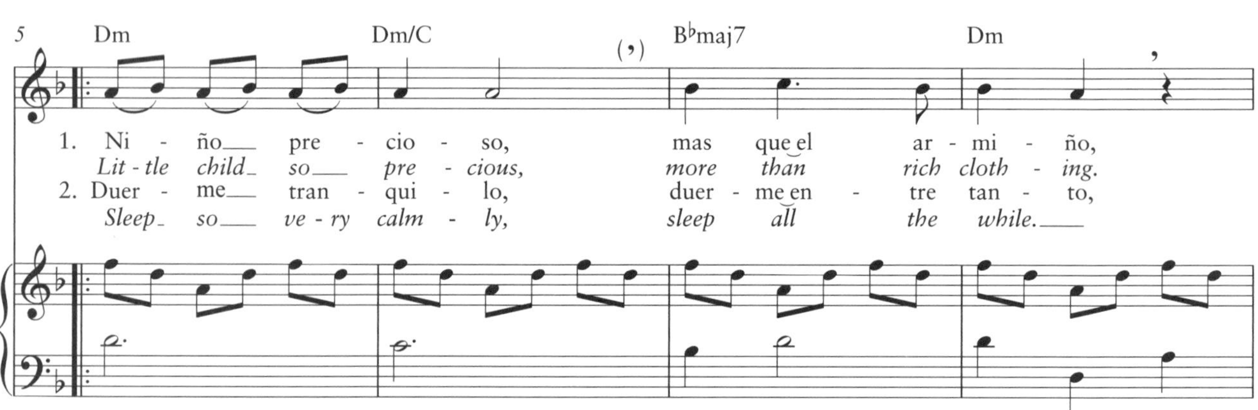
Dm
Dm/C
(,)
B♭maj7
Dm
1. Ni - ño pre - cio - so, mas que el ar - mi - ño,
Lit - tle child so pre - cious, more than rich cloth - ing.
2. Duer - me tran - qui - lo, duer - me en - tre tan - to,
Sleep so ve - ry calm - ly, sleep all the while.

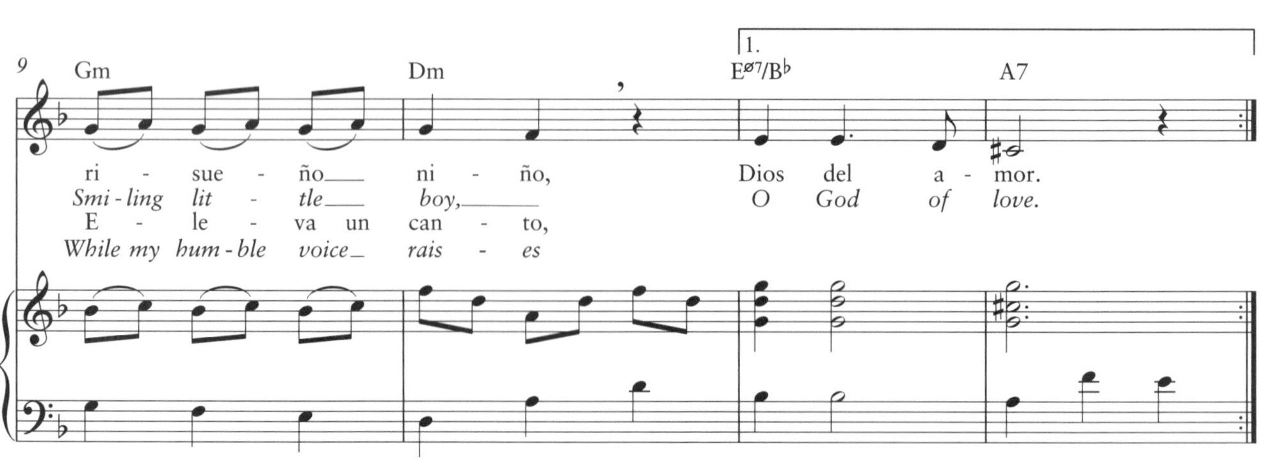
Gm
Dm
1.
E∅7/B♭
A7
ri - sue - ño ni - ño, Dios del a - mor.
Smi - ling lit - tle boy, O God of love.
E - le - va un can - to,
While my hum - ble voice rais - es

Refrain
♩ = 92
13 E⌀7/B♭ A7 Dm F/A Gm7 Dm Dm/C
mi-hu - mil - de voz. Duer - me, chi - qui -
a song of love. Sleep, O sleep, my
17 Gm7 C C/B♭
ti - to que hoy ha - ce
dear one, shiv - er - ing and
21 F E⌀7 A Dm Dm/C
fri - o. Duer - me chi - qui -
cold. Sleep, O sleep, my
25 Gm7 A Amaj7 A7
ti - to yo ve - la
dear one, I will watch

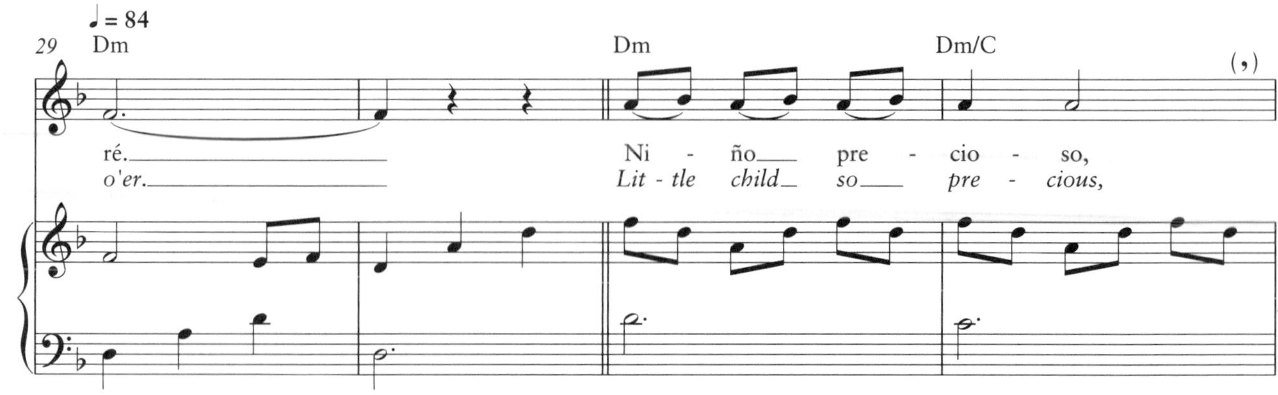
♩ = 84
29
Dm
Dm
Dm/C
(,)
ré.
o'er.
Ni - ño pre - cio - so,
Lit - tle child so pre - cious,

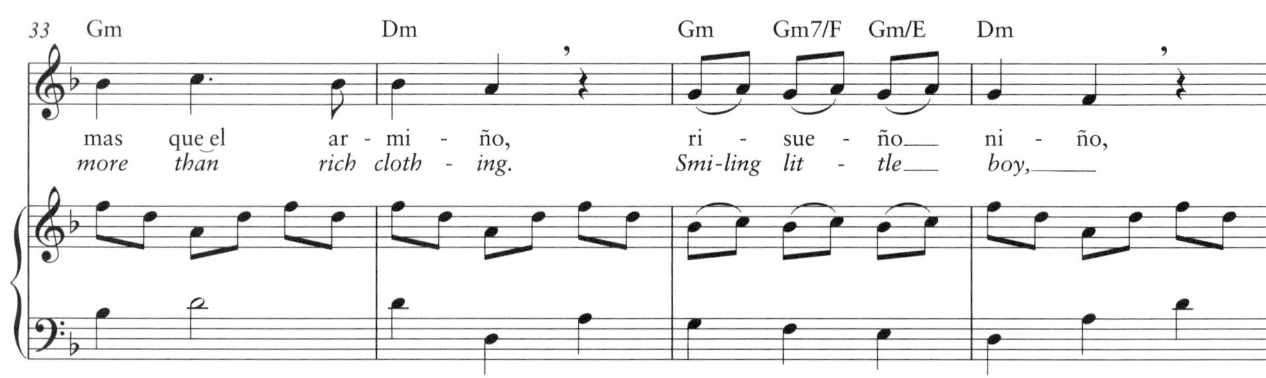
33
Gm
Dm
Gm
Gm7/F
Gm/E
Dm
mas que el ar - mi - ño,
more than rich cloth - ing.
ri - sue - ño ni - ño,
Smi-ling lit - tle boy,

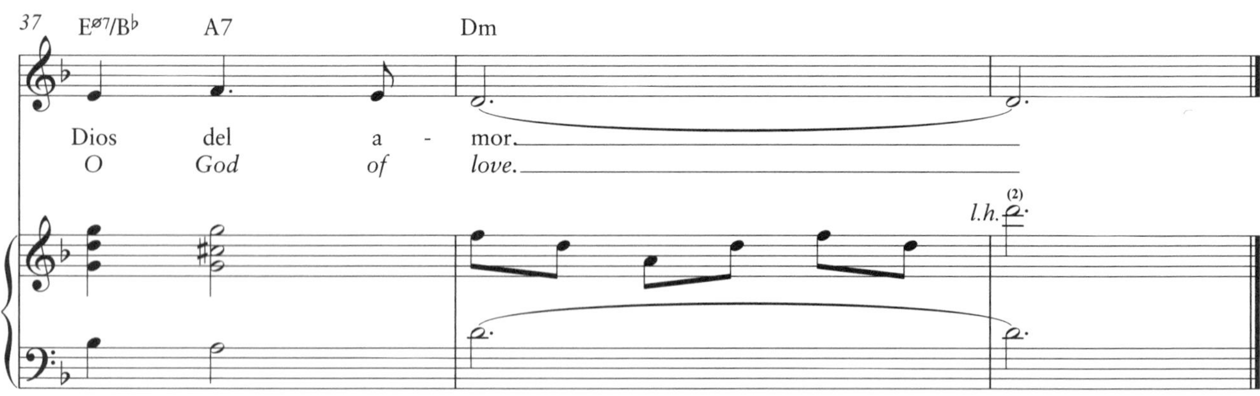
37
A7
Dm
Dios del a - mor.
O God of love.
l.h.
(2)

Santa Lucia

Saint Lucia

(Italian)

Sul mare luccica l'astro d'argento [sul mɑɾe luttʃika lɑstrro dɑrrdʒɛnto]	**On the sea sparkles the star of silver**
Placida‿è l'onda, prospero è il vento. [platʃidae londa prrɔspeɾoeil vɛnto]	**Placid are the waves, prosperous is the wind.**
Venite‿all'agile barchetta mia! Santa Lucia! [vɛnite ɑlladʒile bɑrrkettɑ miɑ sɑntɑ lutʃiɑ]	**Come to my agile little boat! Saint Lucia!**
Con questo zeffiro così soave. [kon kwesto dzeffiro kozi soɑve]	**With this zephyr* so sweet.**
Oh, com'è bello star sulla nave! [o kome bɛllo stɑrr sullɑ nɑve]	**Oh, how it is beautiful to be on the ship!**

Note: It is important to observe the double consonants in Italian (lu<u>cc</u>ica, barche<u>tt</u>a, ze<u>ff</u>iro, be<u>ll</u>o, su<u>ll</u>a . . . .). Give the double consonants a little extra time.

*A zephyr is a warm, gentle breeze.

PART TWO

Traditional Songs

Santa Lucia
(Saint Lucia)

Traditional English version

Italy
Words and Music by Teodoro Cottrau
(1827–1879)
Arranged by Scarlett Antaloczy

For background and performance notes, see page 47.

♩ = 100
1
C
Dm
G7
C
mf
rit.

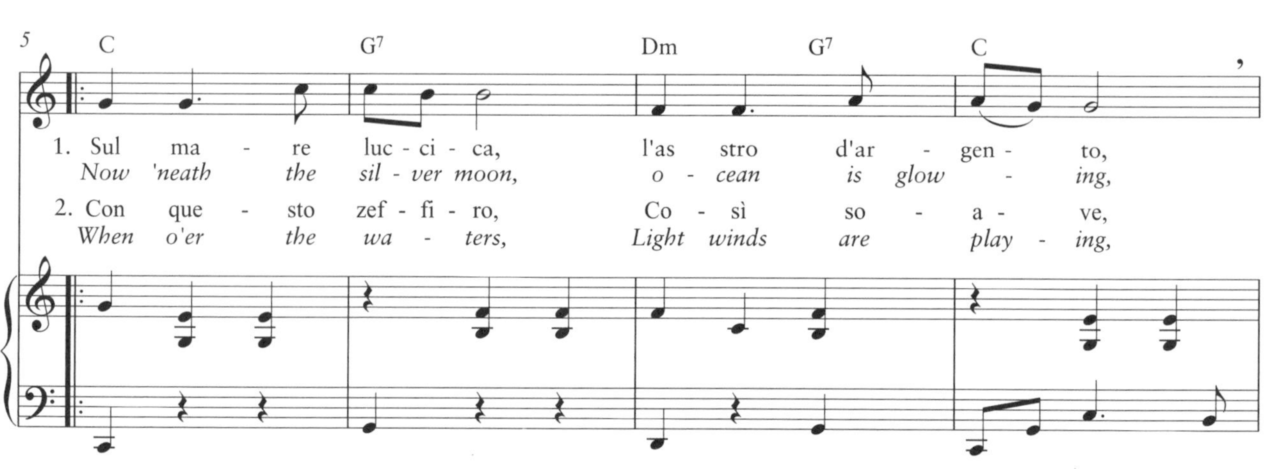

5
C
G7
Dm
G7
C
1. Sul ma - re luc - ci - ca, l'as stro d'ar - gen - to,
Now 'neath the sil - ver moon, o - cean is glow - ing,
2. Con que - sto zef - fi - ro, Co - sì so - a - ve,
When o'er the wa - ters, Light winds are play - ing,

9
A
A7
Dm
G7
C
pla - ci - da è l'on da, pros - pe - ro è il ven - to.
O'er the calm bil - lows, soft winds are blow - ing.
Oh! co - m'è bel - lo, Star sul - la na - ve!
Thy spell can soothe us, All cares al - lay - ing.

13
C G7 Dm G7 C
Sul ma - re luc - ci - ca, l'as - tro d'ar - gèn - to,
Here balm - y breez - es blow, Pure joys in - vite us,
Con que - sto zef - fi - ro, Co - sì so - a - ve,
To thee, sweet Nap - ol - i, What charms are gi - ven,

17
A A7 Dm G7 C
pla - ci - da è l'on da, pro - spe - ro è il ven - to.
And as we gent - ly row, All things de - light us.
Oh! co - m'è bel - lo, Star sul - la na - ve!
Where smiles cre - a - tion, Toil blest by Hea - ven!
5

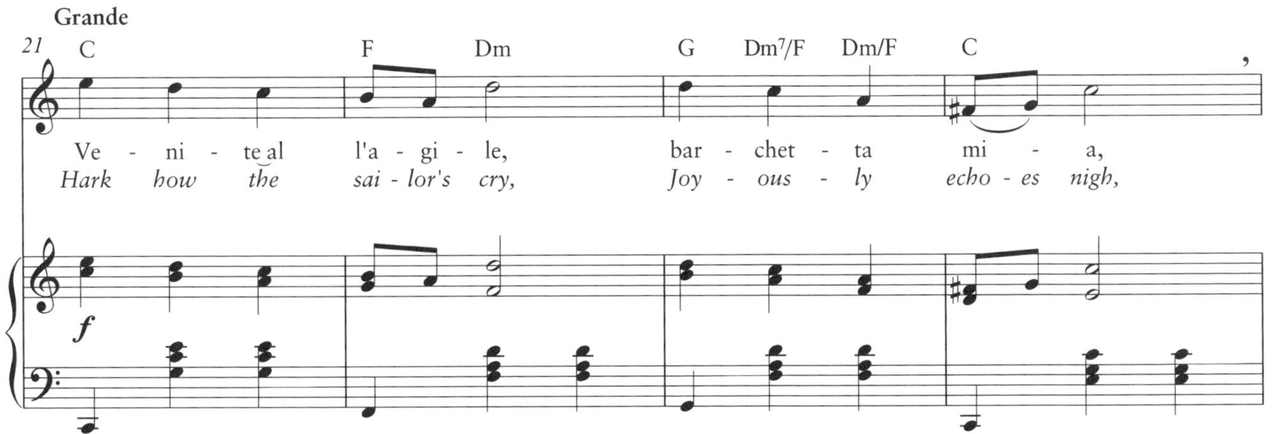
Grande
21
C F Dm G Dm7/F Dm/F C
Ve - ni - te al l'a - gi - le, bar - chet - ta mi - a,
Hark how the sai - lor's cry, Joy - ous - ly echo - es nigh,
f

25
C
Dm
F
G7
C
San - ta Lu - ci - a, San - ta Lu - ci - a.
3
3

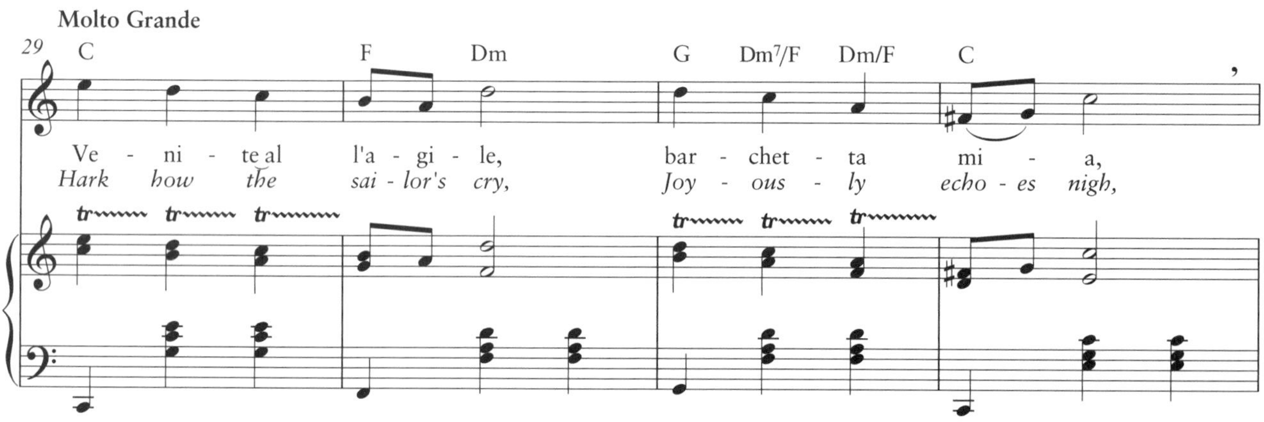
Molto Grande
29
C
F
Dm
G
Dm7/F
Dm/F
C
Ve - ni - te al l'a - gi - le, bar - chet - ta mi - a,
Hark how the sai - lor's cry, Joy - ous - ly echo - es nigh,
tr

33
C
Dm
F
G7
rit.
C
San - ta Lu - ci - a, San - ta Lu - ci - a.
3
rit.

L'hirondelle messagère

The Messenger

(French)

Ah! toi, belle‿hirondelle, qui vol'ici, [a twa bɛlirõdɛlə ki vɔlisi]	**Ah, you beautiful swallow who flies here,**
As tu vu dans ces‿iles mon‿Alexis [a ty vy da sɛzilə mõnalɛksi]	**Have you seen on the island my Alexis**
Qui est par ti dans les voyages‿en‿es longsjours? [ki e par ti dã lɛ vwajazəʒãne lõʒur]	**Who has voyaged many days?**
Il te donnera des nouvelles de son retour. [il tə dɔneɾa dɛ nuvɛlə də sõ rətuɾ]	**Did he give you news of his return?**

L'hirondelle messagère

(The Messenger)

English version
by Cynthia Vaughn

Canada
Arranged by Scarlett Antaloczy

For background and performance notes, see page 47.

13
D/C
Gm/D
D7
E♭maj7
A13♭9
F
B♭
C7
jours? Il te don - ne - ra des nou - vel - les de son re - tour.
choose? Will he re - turn swift-ly to me? Bring me good news.
17
1.
C7/D
C7
2.
C7/D
C7
Gm7/B♭
C7
E♭/G
Gm
Ah! Ah Ah
Oh
rit.

PART TWO

Traditional Songs

Dubinushka

(Hammer Song)

English version
by Cynthia Vaughn

Russia
Arranged by Scarlett Antaloczy

For background and performance notes, see page 47.

♩ = 120
Dm A Dm
Dm
I have heard man - y songs in the land that I love, They have
mf

Gm
Dm A Dm
Gm
told me of sad - ness and sor - row. Yet there's one song that I will

A Dm
A
Dm A Dm rall.
sing all my life, It's the song that brings hope for to - mor - row.

Ex, Dubinushka, uhnem!
[ɛx dubinuʃka uxnjɛm]

Oh, green stick, away (heave-ho)

Ex, zelyonaya sama pojdot, sama poydyot!
[ɛx zɛlɔnaja sama paidjɔt sama paidjɔt]

Oh, it will yield if you push (strike) hard, push (strike) hard!

Podyornem, Da uhnem!
[padjɔrrnɛm da uxnjɛm]

Push, yes away (heave-ho)

— *Russian translation and pronunciation by Alex Pudov*

**Dubinushka* is a large wooden club or sledgehammer.

Dance of Youth

(Qing Chun Wu Qu)

English version
by Jeson Yan

China
Arranged by Scarlett Antaloczy

For background and performance notes, see page 48.

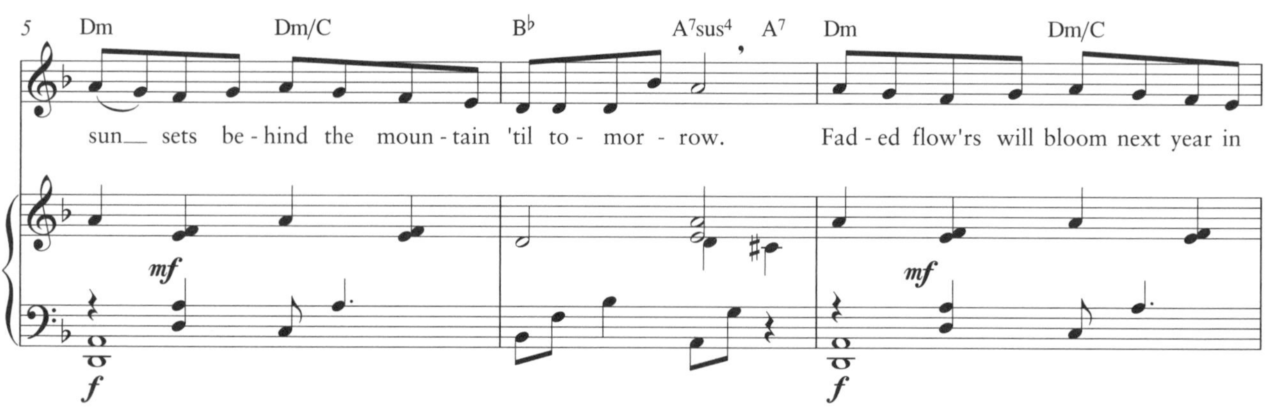

Dm Dm/C B♭ A7sus4 Dm Dm/C B♭ Asus4
youth will not re-turn like pret-ty bird flown a-way. Youth will not re-turn like pret-ty bird flown a-way.
mf
f
Dm Dm/C B♭ Asus4 Gm Asus4 Dm
mf Pret-ty lit-tle bird flew__ far a-way. My youth will not re-turn like pret-ty bird flown a-way.
p La la la la la la la la la la la la la la la la la la la la la la la.
1.
Dm Am/C B♭ Am Gm Asus4 Dm Gm7
2.
E7sus4 Bm7/D Cmaj7 Bm7 Am Bm C B7sus4
The
f

27
Em
Em/D
C
B7sus4
B7
Em
Em/D
sun_ sets be-hind the moun-tain 'til to- mor - row.
Fad - ed flow'rs will bloom next year in
mf
f
mf
f
30
C
B7sus4
Em
Bm
C
B7sus4
joy and sor - row.
Pret - ty lit - tle bird flew a - way with no trace. My
p
33
Em
Em/D
C
B7sus4
B
Em
Em/D
C
B7sus4
youth will not re-turn like pret-ty bird flown a-way.
Youth will not re-turn like pret-ty bird flown a-way.
mf
f
37
Em
Em/D
C
B7sus4
B7
Am
B7sus4
1.
Em
mf Pret-ty lit-tle bird flew_ far a-way. My youth will not re-turn like pret-ty bird flown a-way.
p La la la la la la la la la la la la la la la la la la la la la la la.

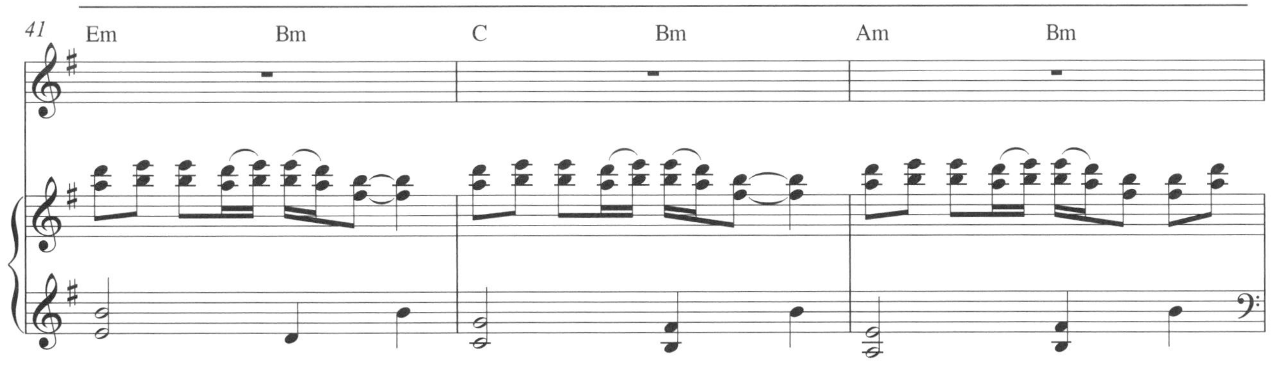

青春嘆

太陽下山明朝依舊爬上来，

花儿謝了明年還是一樣地開。

美麗小鳥飛去無影蹤，

我的青春和小鳥一樣不回来。

啦……，啦……，

我的青春和小鳥一樣不回来！

Ev'ry Time I Feel the Spirit

America, c. 1874
Arranged by Scarlett Antaloczy

For background and performance notes, see page 48.

17
D G D
D Em D
F♯m Em7 A7sus4
D G D
round me it looked so fine till I asked my Lord if all were mine. Ev' - ry
leads me I'll ne - ver fear for I am shel-tered by His care.
21
G D/F♯ D Em D D7
time I feel the spir - it mov - ing in my heart I will pray. Ev' - ry
25
1.
G D/F♯ D Em D G D
time I feel the spir - it mov - ing in my soul I will pray. Oh I have
2.
29
D Em A7sus4 G F D
rit.
(optional vocal ad lib.)
cresc.
in my soul I will pray.
tr
rit.

PART TWO

Traditional Songs

Amazing Grace

Words by
William Cowper
(1731–1800)

America
Music by John Newton
(1725–1807)
Arranged by Scarlett Antaloczy

For background and performance notes, see page 48.

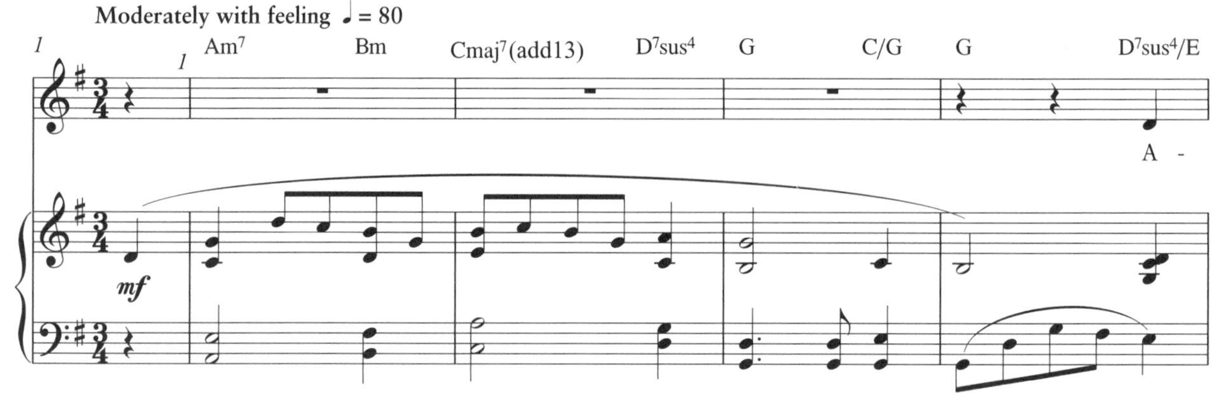

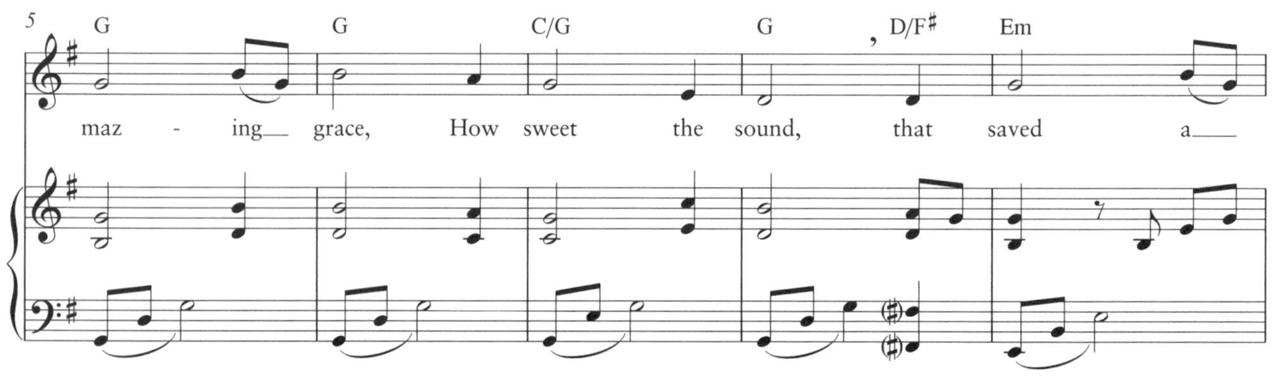

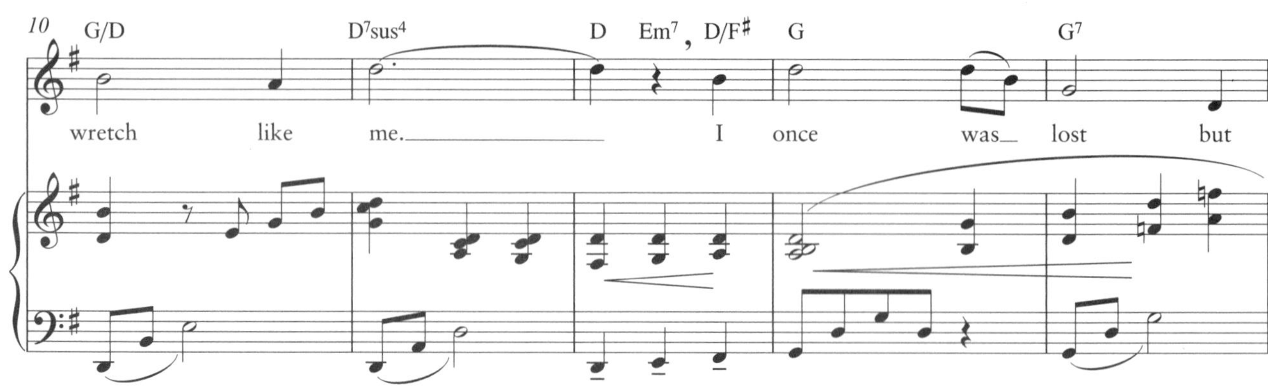

15
C G D/F♯ Am7 Bm Cmaj7(add13) D7sus4 G
now am found, Was blind but now I see.
20
D7sus4/E G G C/G D/G
'Twas grace that taught my heart to fear and
25
Em G/D D7sus4 D Em7 D/F♯ G G7
grace my fears re - lieved. How pre - cious did that
31
C G D/F♯ Am7 Bm Cmaj7(add13) D7sus4 G C/G
grace ap - pear the hour I first be - lieved.

36
G
D7sus4/E
G
G7/F
C/E
Cm/E♭
— Through ma - ny— dan - gers, toils, and snares I
41
G/D
C♯ø7
A7sus4
D
Em7
D/F♯
have al - read - y come.— 'Tis
45
Dm/G
F/G
G
G7
Dm/G
C
G
D/F♯
grace— hath— brought me safe— thus— far, And
49
Am7
Bm
Cmaj7 (add13)
D7sus4
G
rit.
C/G
G
grace will— lead me home.—
rit.

Wayfaring Stranger

America
Arranged by Scarlett Antaloczy

For background and performance notes, see page 49.

Optional text for a second verse:

I know dark clouds will gather round me,
I know my way is rough and steep,
But golden fields lie just before me
Where weary eyes no more will weep.

Chorus

I'm going there to meet my father,
I'm going there no more to roam,
I'm just a-going over Jordan,
I'm only going over home.

I've Got Peace Like a River

America
Arranged by Scarlett Antaloczy

For background and performance notes, see page 49.

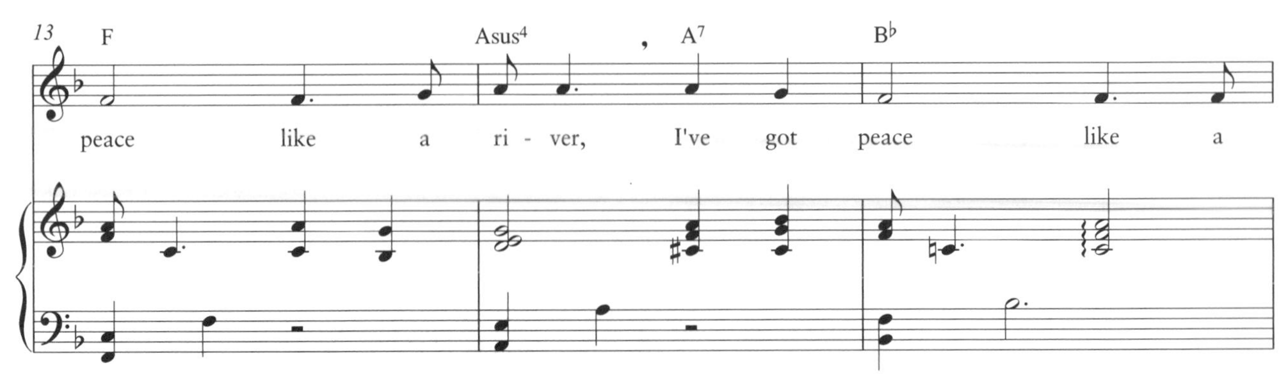
13
F
Asus4
A7
B♭
peace like a ri - ver, I've got peace like a

16
C7sus4
G9
C7
ri - ver, I've got peace like a ri - ver in my

19
F
Broadly
rit.
F7sus4
soul. mm I've got
rit.

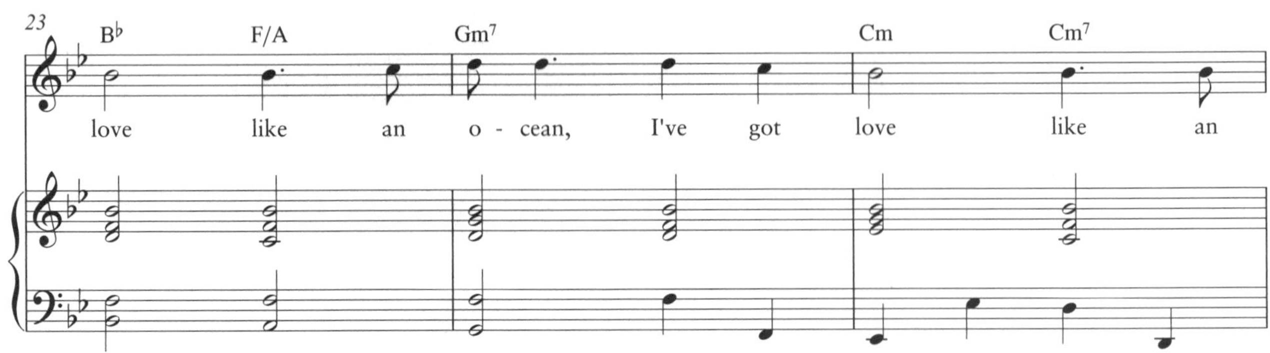
23
B♭
F/A
Gm7
Cm
Cm7
love like an o - cean, I've got love like an

26
Cm
D/F♯
Gm7
C7
o - cean, I've got love like an o - cean in my
29
E♭9
F7sus4
F7
C7
B♭
D7
soul. I've got love like an o - cean, I've got
33
E♭
C7
love like an o - cean, I've got love like an o - cean in my
37
B♭
rit.
E♭7
ad lib.
B♭7
soul. mm peace in my soul.
rit.
trem.

PART TWO

Traditional Songs

How Can I Keep from Singing?

America, c. 1865
Words and Music by Reverend R. Lowry
(1826–1899)
Arranged by Frank Ponzio

For background and performance notes, see page 49.

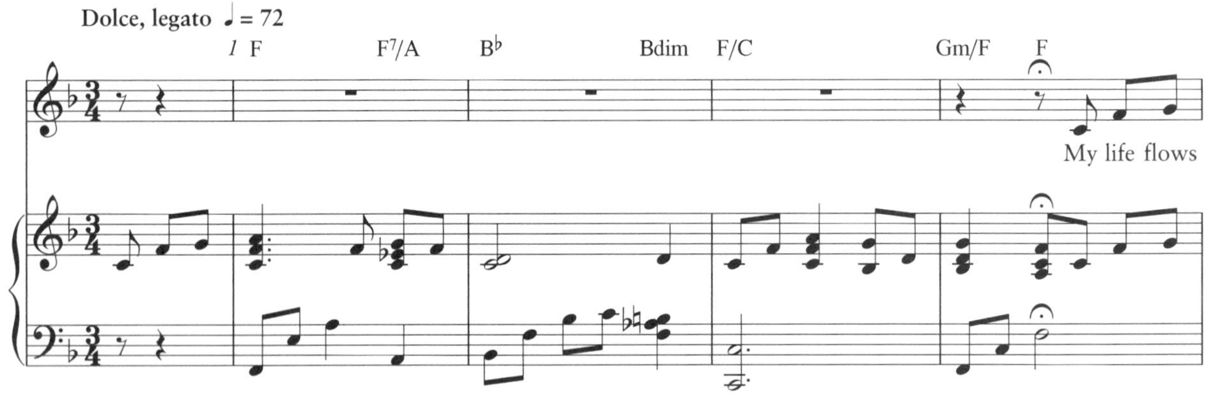

13 Am D7 Gm7 Csus C♯dim Dm G/B C7
all the tu - mult and the strife I hear the mu - sic ring - ing. It
17 F F7 B♭ Am Gm7 C7 Gm/F F
finds an ech - o in my soul; How can I keep from sing - ing?
21 Csus Broadly F F7/A B♭ Bdim F C/E Dm7
I lift my eyes, the cloud grows thin, I see the blue a -
25 Gm7 C7 F F7/A B♭ Bdim F/C
bove it. And day by day this path-way smooths since first I learned to

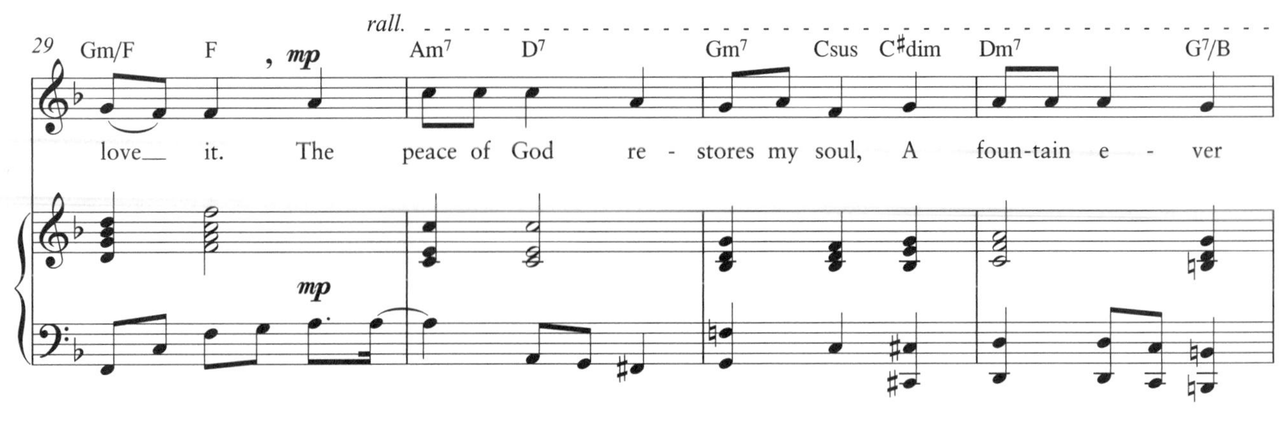
rall.
29 Gm/F F mp Am7 D7 Gm7 Csus C#dim Dm7 G7/B
love__ it. The peace of God re - stores my soul, A foun-tain e - ver
mp

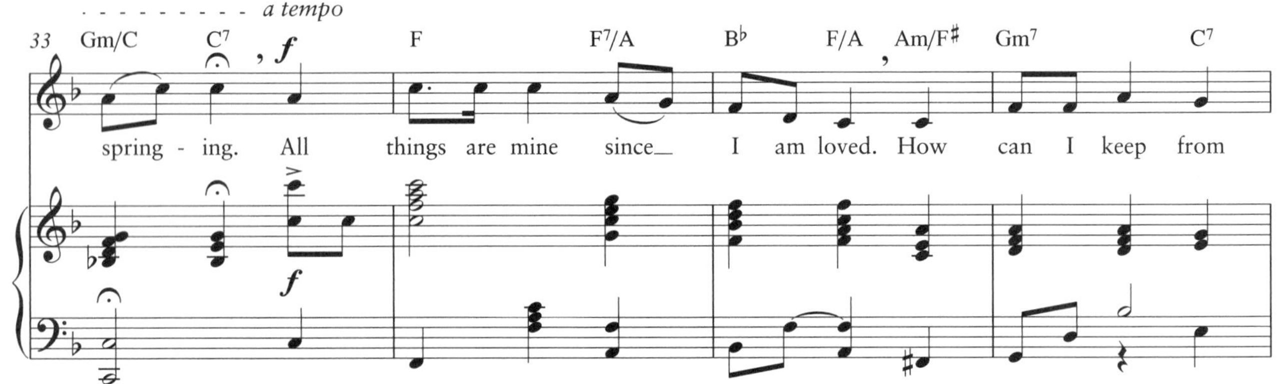
a tempo
33 Gm/C C7 f F F7/A B♭ F/A Am/F# Gm7 C7
spring - ing. All things are mine since__ I am loved. How can I keep from
f

rit.
37 Gm/F B♭ Am Gm7 C7 B♭/F F/C
sing - ing? How can I keep from sing - ing?
mf

America the Beautiful

Words by
Katherine Lee Bates
(1859–1929)

America
Music by Samuel A. Ward
(1847–1903)
Arranged by Scarlett Antaloczy

For background and performance notes, see page 50.

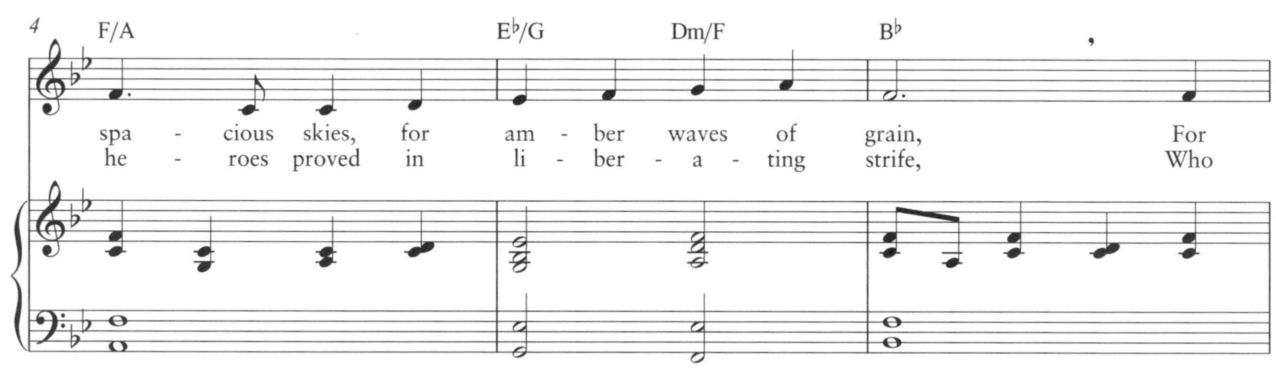

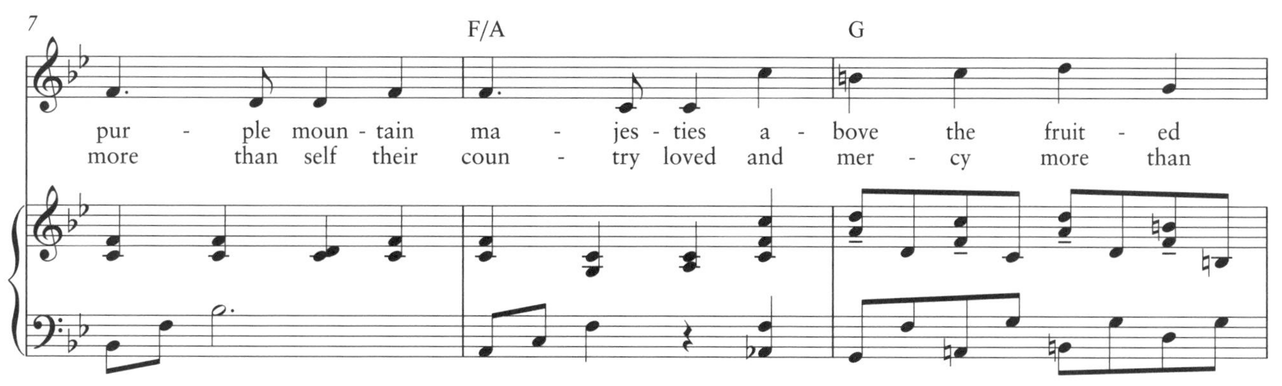

PART TWO
Traditional Songs

10
C7sus4 C F13/7 B♭ F/A E♭/G F (,) E♭/G F/A E♭ F/A
plain. A - mer - i - ca, A - mer - i - ca, God shed His grace on
life.

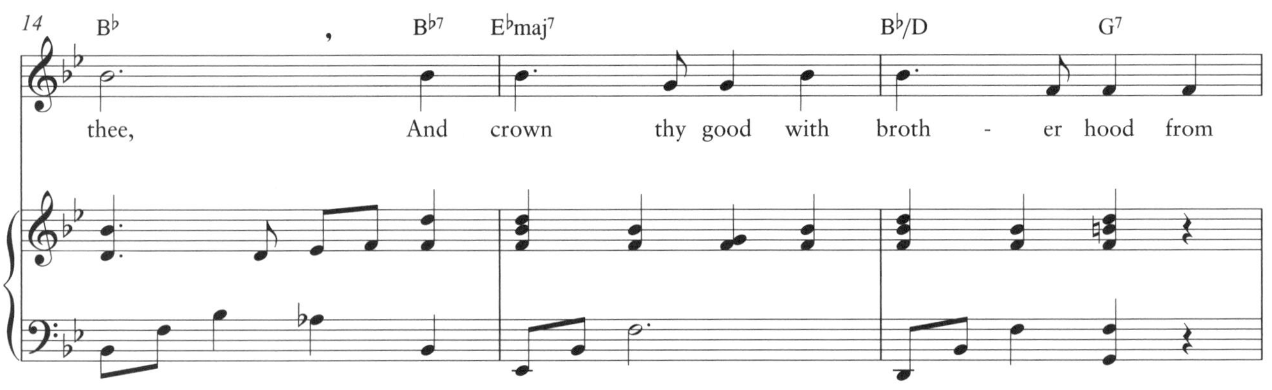
14
B♭ B♭7 E♭maj7 B♭/D G7
thee, And crown thy good with broth - er hood from

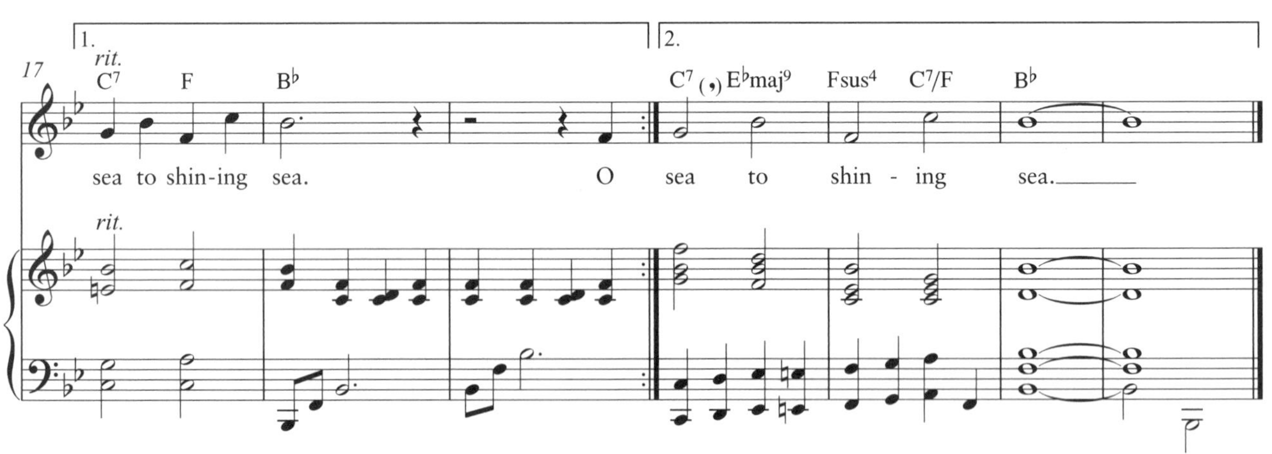
1.
2.
17
rit.
C7 F B♭ C7 (,) E♭maj9 Fsus4 C7/F B♭
sea to shin-ing sea. O sea to shin - ing sea.
rit.

The Star-Spangled Banner

National Anthem

Words by
Francis Scott Key
(1779–1843)

America
Music by
John Stafford Smith
(1750–1836)

For background and performance notes, see page 50.

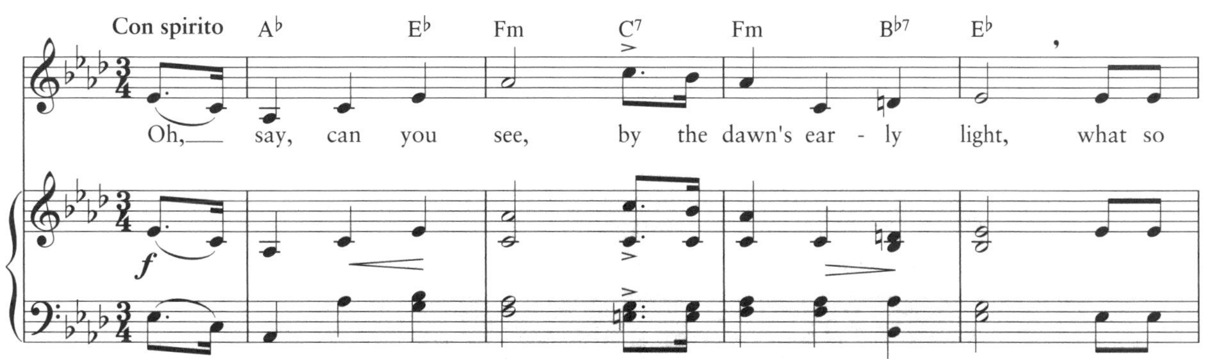
Con spirito
A♭ E♭ Fm C7 Fm B♭7 E♭
Oh, say, can you see, by the dawn's ear - ly light, what so
f

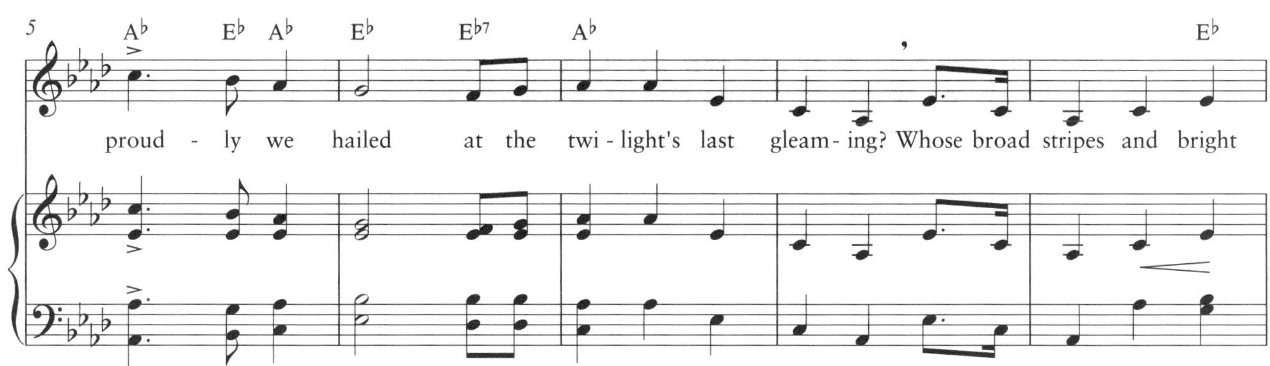
5
A♭ E♭ A♭ E♭ E♭7 A♭ E♭
proud - ly we hailed at the twi - light's last gleam - ing? Whose broad stripes and bright

10
Fm C7 Fm B♭7 E♭ A♭ E♭ A♭ E♭ E♭7
stars through the per - il - ous fight, o'er the ram - parts we watched, were so

PART TWO

Traditional Songs

15
A♭ E♭7
(,)
gal - lant - ly stream - ing? And the rock - et's red glare, the bombs burst - ing in
20
A♭ E♭ A♭ E♭ E♭7 A♭ Fm B♭7 E♭
air, gave proof through the night that our flag was still there. Oh,
25
A♭ D♭ F7 B♭m B♭7 A♭ E♭ E♭7
say, does that star - span - gled ban - ner yet wave o'er the
29
A♭ E♭ A♭ Fm B♭ A♭ E♭7 A♭
(,)
land of the free and the home of the brave.
ff

O Canada!

(French)

Ô Canada! Terre de nosaïeux, [o kanada tɛɾe də nozajø]	**O Canada! Land of our forefathers,**
Ton front‿est ceint de fleurons glorieux! [tõ frõte sɛ də flœɾõ glɔrjø]	**Your brow is wreathed with garlands glorious!**
Car ton bras sait porter l'épée, [kɑɾ tõ bɾa sɛ pɔɾte lepeə]	**Though your arm knows how to bear the sword**
Il sait porter la croix! [il sɛ pɔɾte la krwa]	**It knows how to bear the cross!**
Ton‿histoire‿est‿une‿épopée [tõnistwaretynepopeə]	**your history is an epic**
Des plus brillants exploits. [de ply bɾilãzeksplwa]	**of the most brilliant exploits.**
Et ta valeur, de foi trempée, [e ta valœr də fwa trãpeə]	**And your valor, in faith steeped,**
Protégera nos foyers‿et nos droits. [proteʒera no fwajeze no drwa]	**Will protect our homes and our rights**

O Canada!

National Anthem

Words by His Hon. R. Stanley Weir, D. C. L.
Recorder of Montreal
(1856–1926)

Canada
Music by C. Lavallée
(1842–1891)
Harmonized by G. A. Grant-Schaefer
(1872–1939)

For background and performance notes, see page 50.

Maestoso ♩ = 84
1
mf

5
f

9
E♭ B♭ Cm B♭ E♭ A♭ B♭sus B♭
O Can - a - da! Our home and na - tive land!
O Can - a - da! Ter - re de nos aï - eux,
mf

13
E♭ F7 B♭ Cm B♭ F7 B♭
True pa - triot love in all thy sons com - mand. With
Ton front est ceint de fleur - ons glo - ri - eux! Car ton

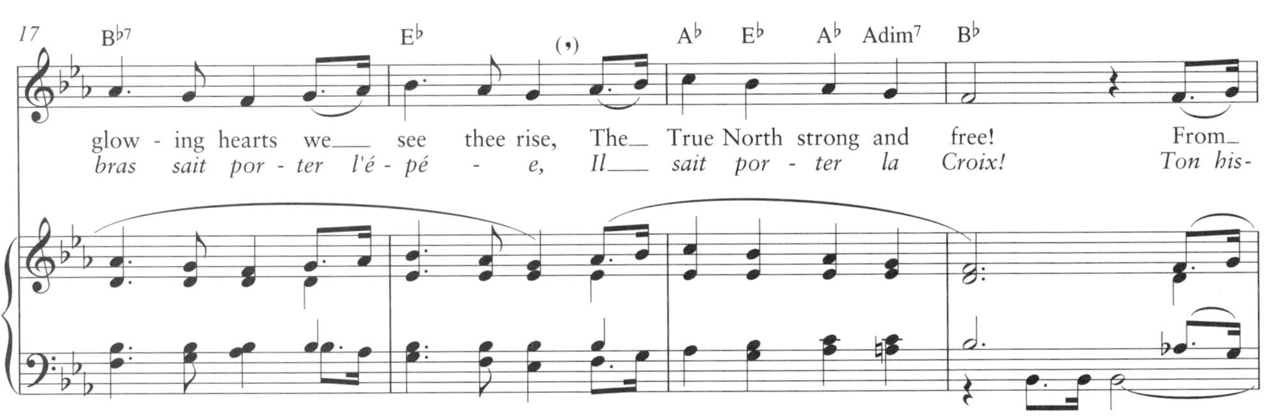
17
B♭7 E♭ (,) A♭ E♭ A♭ Adim7 B♭
glow - ing hearts we see thee rise, The True North strong and free! From
bras sait por - ter l'é - pé - e, Il sait por - ter la Croix! Ton his-

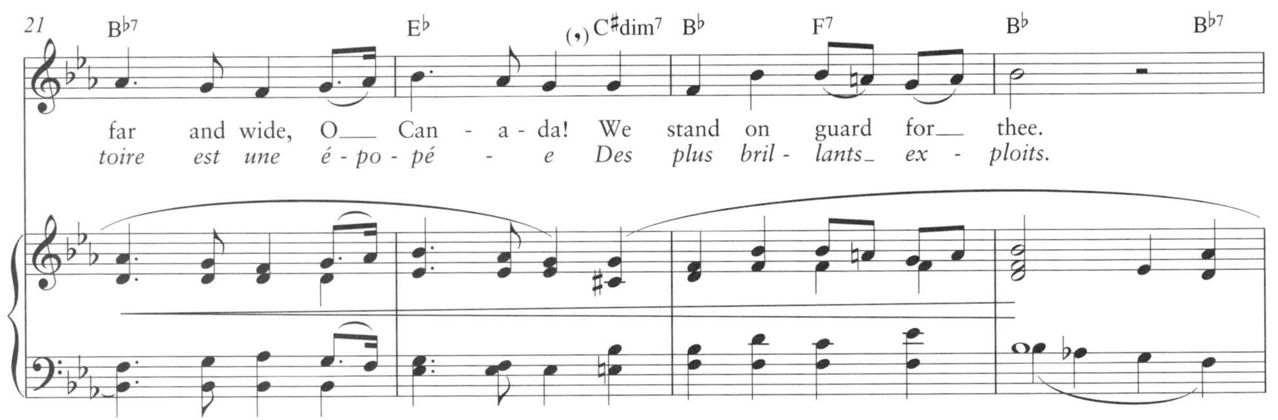
21
B♭7 E♭ (,) C♯dim7 B♭ F7 B♭ B♭7
far and wide, O Can - a - da! We stand on guard for thee.
toire est une é - po - pé - e Des plus bril - lants ex - ploits.

Chorus ad lib.
25
E♭ B♭ Cm Fm Fm/E♭ B♭
God keep our land glo - rious and free!
Et ta va - leur, de foi trem - pée,
f

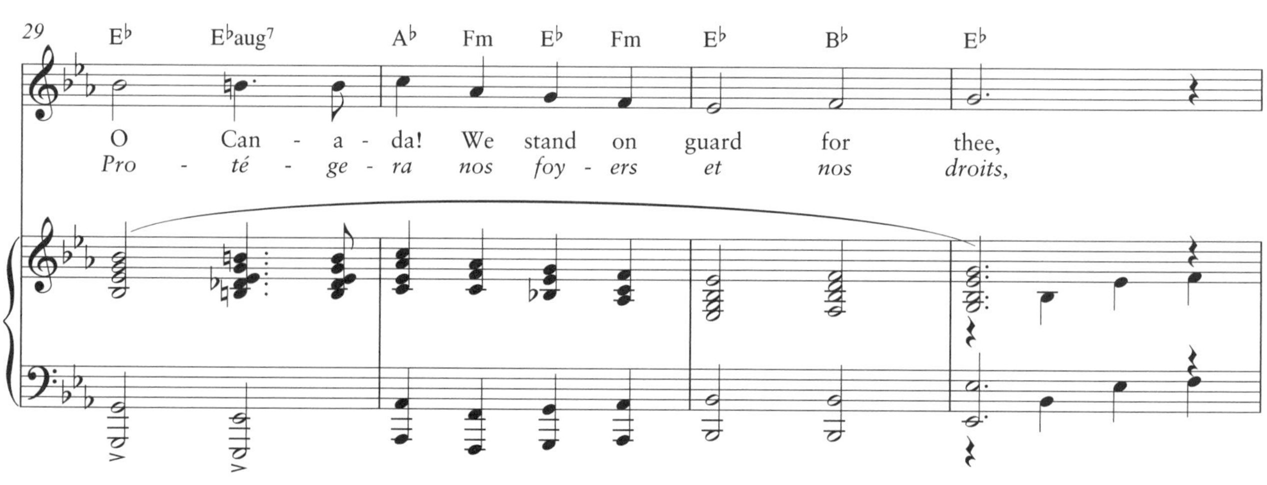
29
E♭ E♭aug7 A♭ Fm E♭ Fm E♭ B♭ E♭
O Can - a - da! We stand on guard for thee,
Pro - té - ge - ra nos foy - ers et nos droits,

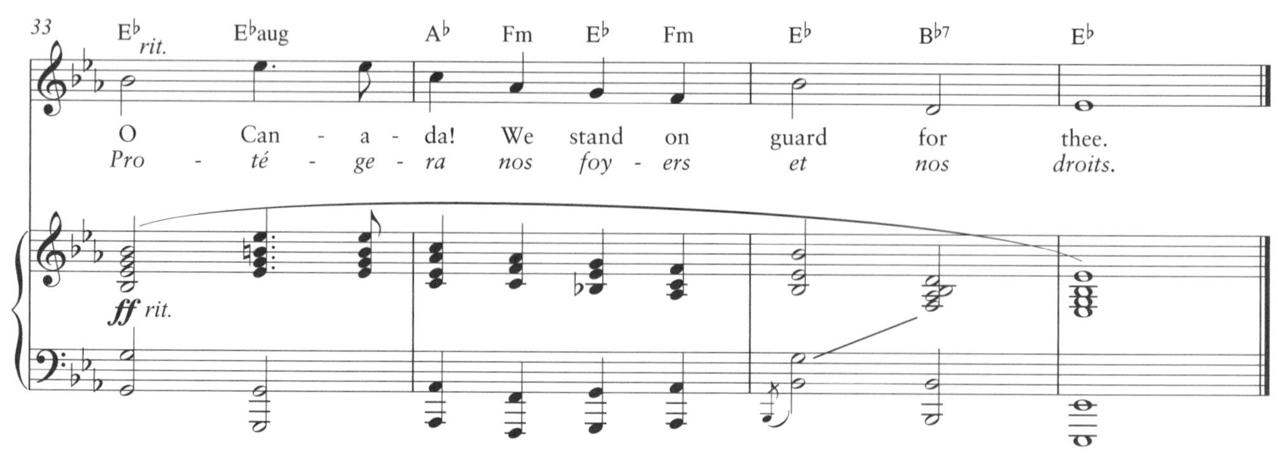
33
E♭ rit. E♭aug A♭ Fm E♭ Fm E♭ B♭7 E♭
O Can - a - da! We stand on guard for thee.
Pro - té - ge - ra nos foy - ers et nos droits.
ff rit.

Popular Songs

Theater Songs

Americans love musical theater. From Broadway blockbusters to off-Broadway sleepers, community theater to bus-and-truck touring productions, dinner theater to the local high school drama clubs—musicals are here to stay.

In the late 1800s America's theaters and music halls were filled with imported operettas (Gilbert and Sullivan, Franz Lehar) and bawdy British musical comedies. After the turn of the century George M. Cohan captured the audience's attention with uniquely American musicals like *Little Johnny Jones* in 1904.

Musical theater grew in popularity after World War I when theater audiences were humming the tunes of Jerome Kern, George Gershwin, and Cole Porter. The golden period of American musical theater is considered to be the twenty-year period from Rodgers and Hammerstein's *Oklahoma!* of 1943 to Harnick and Bock's *Fiddler on the Roof* in 1964. Other classic musicals from this era include Rodgers and Hammerstein's *The Sound of Music,* Irving Berlin's *Annie Get Your Gun,* Cole Porter's *Kiss Me, Kate,* Frank Loesser's *Guys and Dolls,* Lerner and Loewe's *My Fair Lady,* Meredith Willson's *The Music Man,* and Leonard Bernstein's *West Side Story.* All of these successful stage musicals were later turned into successful movie musicals, a trend recently revived when stage hits *The Phantom of the Opera, Rent, Sweeney Todd,* and *Jekyll & Hyde* were recreated as film musicals.

The popularity of stage and movie musicals waned during the Vietnam war, but musicals by Stephen Sondheim (*Sweeney Todd, Company, Into the Woods*) and England's Andrew Lloyd Webber (*Cats, The Phantom of the Opera*) filled Broadway theaters in the 1980s.

Today's musical theater cannot be so easily defined, because the lines of distinction between musical theater and opera are blurring to give us "opera/musical theater." More than ever, Broadway performers must be "triple-threats," equally competent in singing, dancing, and acting. Recent Broadway and off-Broadway shows range from revivals (*A Chorus Line, The Apple Tree, 110 in the Shade*) to rock musicals (*Rent; tick, tick . . . BOOM!*) to original pop-style musicals (*Jekyll & Hyde*) and musical dramas (*Les Misérables, Parade*).

A new twist is turning successful movies into stage musicals, such as *Legally Blonde: The Musical, The Color Purple, The Producers, Hairspray, The Full Monty,* and Disney's *Mary Poppins* and *The Little Mermaid.* No stylistic stone has been left unturned. One of the longest-running hits of the decade is *MAMMA MIA!,* which features middle-aged women dressed in spandex belting out tunes by the 1970s Swedish pop group, ABBA. Maybe we haven't come so far from vaudeville, after all.

Film and Television Songs

The newest types of songs are those written for film and TV. They appear in live and animated children's shows like *Sesame Street,* in film scores like *Titanic,* and in movie musicals like *Moulin Rouge.* Movie musicals include songs borrowed from the stage version as well as new pieces. Some movies and television shows, like *That 70's Show,* recycle music from the time period. Original songs for film and TV usually fall into one of three categories:

1. Broadway-style songs (*Prince of Egypt, Lion King*)
2. Pop-style songs (*Titanic,* James Bond theme songs, songs from TV's *Grey's Anatomy*)
3. Period-style songs that invoke the historical time period (film version of Jane Austen's *Pride and Prejudice,* Shakespeare films)

Some movies use more than one version of the same song. For example, in Disney's *Pocahontas,* Broadway actress Judy Kuhn sings "Colors of the Wind," and pop singer Vanessa Williams sings the same song under the closing credits. Regardless of the style, movie and TV songs have great appeal and can reach a wide audience through DVD rentals, CD soundtrack sales, and iTunes downloads.

Popular and Jazz Standards

Jazz, blues, pop, and standards are all variations of popular or nonclassical styles of music. They are not so easily differentiated because there is a lot of crossover between the genres. However, here is a nutshell summary of each.

Jazz, according to the late great Louis Armstrong, "is music that's never played the same way once." While there is no strict definition of jazz, this homegrown twentieth-century American music form has two key elements: improvisation and swing rhythm. Swing can be loosely defined as anything that propels the music forward: accents, free rhythm, and especially uneven short notes instead of "straight" eighth notes.

Jazz originated in New Orleans in 1917 and quickly spread to Chicago, New York, Memphis, and Kansas City. Its popularity transcends race, region, country, gender, and generations. Some important jazz musicians include Louis Armstrong, Duke Ellington, the Dorsey brothers, Benny Goodman, Billie Holiday, Charlie Parker, Miles Davis, Count Basie, John Coltrane, Ornette Coleman, and Wynton Marsalis.

Blues refers generally to music in a melancholy state. Originally, blues was a black American folk song tradition that influenced jazz and twentieth-century music. "Blues notes" (flatted 3rd, 5th, 7th notes in a major scale that give it a melancholy mood), pitch bending, and improvisation are all part of the style. A contemporary offshoot of the blues is rhythm and blues, or R&B.

Famous blues singers include Charley Patton, Lightnin' Hopkins, Mamie Smith, Ma Rainey, B. B. King, and more recently Nina Simone. Jazz great Duke Ellington wrote many instrumental and vocal blues.

Pop songs are usually contemporary favorites, are commercially successful, climb the Top 40 pop charts, and dominate the radio airwaves. The global interest in pop music has never been greater, as evidenced by the popularity of television shows like "American Idol." Today's pop stars and vocal groups typically have a very short shelf life. Does anyone remember Milli Vanilli, Hanson, and the Spice Girls?

Popular singers and pop groups occasionally transcend their time. Songs by the Beatles are among the best examples of timeless pop standards. The Beatles were the most popular and successful rock group in history ever, selling more recordings than any other band. Their original songs, written by Paul McCartney and John Lennon in the 1960s, ranged from sweet love ballads to edgy songs of rebellion.

Standards, or jazz standards as they are often called, can be loosely defined as songs that were popular from 1920 to about 1955. These include songs made famous by singers like Frank Sinatra, Rosemary Clooney, Bing Crosby, Tony Bennett, Sarah Vaughan, Ella Fitzgerald, and Mel Torme. Composers include Cole Porter, Hoagy Carmichael, Irving Berlin, and George Gershwin.

Music of this bygone era is surprisingly popular on today's college campuses. Part of the popular appeal is freedom of personal expression—the songs don't have to be sung exactly the same each time. Use the standards in the *The Singing Book* collection to experiment with your own improvisation. Keep the lyrics and tune relatively intact while making changes with rhythm, dynamics, and tempo. This is a more conservative type of improvisation than jazz. If you have any recordings of this music, compare the sung version to the actual written music and you will find many small differences. The tune and rhythm are only guidelines for some artists.

Someone Like You, from *Jekyll & Hyde—The Musical* (p. 136)

The character Lucy sings this song near the end of Act I of Frank Wildhorn's mad scientist musical, based on the Robert Louis Stevenson novel, *Strange Case of Doctor Jekyll and Mr. Hyde.* Lucy is trapped in a life of poverty and prostitution and believes that the kind and handsome Dr. Jekyll will lead her to a better life. "There'd be a new way to live, a new life to love, if someone like you found me!" Before the tragic ending, Lucy and Dr. Jekyll's fiancée, Emma, sing of their love for the same man in the showstopper duet, "In His Eyes." Another popular song from *Jekyll & Hyde,* "This Is the Moment," has been widely performed at beauty pageants and high school graduations, and was sung by Jennifer Holliday for President Clinton's inauguration. Wildhorn's songs are written in a style that makes them appealing to pop and crossover artists, including Trisha Yearwood, Patti LaBelle, Whitney Houston, and Wildhorn's ex-wife, Broadway star Linda Eder.

In 1999, Frank Wildhorn became the first composer since the 1980s reign of Sondheim and Lloyd Webber to have three musicals playing simultaneously on Broadway: *Jekyll & Hyde, The Civil War,* and *The Scarlet Pimpernel.* A second spooky offering, *Dracula—the Musical,* was a flop, but Wildhorn is hoping to repeat *Jekyll & Hyde*'s success with a new musical, *Mary Shelley's Frankenstein.*

Suggested recordings of "Someone Like You" (iTunes):

Genre: *Soundtrack* □ Christiane Noll: ***Jekyll & Hyde—The Musical: Original Broadway Cast Recording,*** 1997, Warner

Genre: *Vocal* □ Linda Eder: ***It's Time,*** 1997, Atlantic Recording

⏩If you like this song, take a look at "This Is the Moment" from *Jekyll & Hyde*

I Move On, from the film *Chicago* (p. 140)

Catherine Zeta-Jones and Renée Zellweger sing this Academy Award-nominated song under the closing credits of *Chicago,* the 2002 Oscar-winning movie based on the 1975 Broadway musical. Songwriter John Kander and lyricist Fred Ebb intended to insert the new song after "Nowadays" but finally decided that "I Move On" was too strong to be anything but an epilogue to the tale of Roxie Hart and Velma Kelly. Both the movie and the stage musical are set in the Roaring '20s, where murderess showgirls Roxie and Velma try to win fame and avoid the death penalty.

Kander and Ebb also wrote the hit Broadway musicals *Cabaret* and *Kiss of the Spider Woman.* In a radical departure from the sunny musicals of Rodgers and Hammerstein and Lerner and Loewe in the 1950s and 1960s, Kander and Ebb embraced sexuality and explored the darker side of human nature. Whether in Nazi Germany (*Cabaret*) or a Chicago jailhouse, survival under difficult or surreal situations is a common Kander and Ebb theme. "I'm out of dreams and life has got me down, I don't despair. . . . I just move on." After the death of Fred Ebb on September 11, 2004, John Kander made the decision to go forward with four incomplete Kander and Ebb musicals: *Curtains* (a comic whodunit), *All About Us* (based on Thornton Wilder's *The Skin of Our Teeth*), *The Visit,* and *The Minstrel Show,* which Kander describes as a "vicious" look at racial injustice in the Depression era.

Suggested recordings of "I Move On" (iTunes):

Genre: *Soundtrack* □ Catherine Zeta-Jones and Renée Zellweger: ***Chicago: Music from the Miramax Motion Picture,*** 2003, Sony

Genre: *Karaoke* □ ***Contemporary Female Pop, Vol. 5,*** 2006, Sound Choice

⏩If you like this song, take a look at "All That Jazz" from Chicago

ANYTHING YOU CAN DO, FROM *ANNIE GET YOUR GUN* (P. 145)

This musical battle of the sexes is sung by sharpshooters Annie Oakley and Frank Butler in a fictionalized version of their lives as stars of *Buffalo Bill's Wild West* show. Annie and Frank declare that each can do *anything* better than the other. In the original 1946 version of *Annie Get Your Gun* starring Ethel Merman, Annie comes to the conclusion that "You Can't Get a Man with a Gun." She lets Frank win to salve his male ego. In the 1999 revival, starring Bernadette Peters and later Reba McEntire, the ending was updated to reflect the modern times. The contest ends in a tie!

Annie Get Your Gun includes many memorable tunes by Irving Berlin, including "I've Got the Sun in the Morning," "The Girl That I Marry," and "There's No Business Like Show Business."

Suggested recordings of "Anything You Can Do" (iTunes):

GENRE: *Soundtrack* □ Barry Bostwick and Judy Kaye: ***Annie Get Your Gun: 1995 Studio Cast,*** First Complete Performance of the Lincoln Center Edition, 1996, Jay

GENRE: *Soundtrack* □ Howard Keel and Judy Garland: ***Irving Berlin in Hollywood,*** 1999, Rhino/Wea

GENRE: *Karaoke* □ ***Mixed Showtunes & TV Themes, Vol. 3,*** 2006, Sound Choice

⏩If you like this song, take a look at "There's No Business Like Show Business" from *Annie Get Your Gun*

WAND'RIN' STAR, FROM *PAINT YOUR WAGON* (P. 155)

Disillusioned fortune hunter Ben Rumson sings this song when the gold runs out in a mining town during the California gold rush of 1853. However, "Wandr'in' Star" can be sung by any restless soul who longs to see what better things life has to offer down the road. Frederick Loewe and Alan Jay Lerner, creators of the 1953 musical *Paint Your Wagon,* followed their own wandering stars.

Loewe was trained in classical music like his father, a Viennese opera singer, and, no doubt, Lerner's family expected him to stay in the family business (Lerner's department stores). They struck their own musical gold with hit Broadway musicals *Brigadoon, My Fair Lady, Gigi,* and *Paint Your Wagon.* Lerner and Loewe's stage musicals were later made into movies, and the 1969 movie version of *Paint Your Wagon* starred Lee Marvin as Ben Rumson.

Suggested recordings of "Wand'rin' Star" (iTunes):

GENRE: *Soundtrack* □ James Barton: ***Paint Your Wagon,*** original Broadway cast recording, 1951, rel. 1990, RCA Victor Broadway

GENRE: *Vocal* □ Bryn Terfel: ***If Ever I Would Leave You,*** 1998, Deutsche Grammophon

GENRE: *Karaoke* □ ***Karaoke Pop: Open Sesame,*** 2006, Charly

⏩If you like this song, take a look at "They Call the Wind Maria" from *Paint Your Wagon*

GOODNIGHT, MY SOMEONE, FROM *THE MUSIC MAN* (P. 159)

The song "Goodnight, My Someone" introduces us to the straight-laced character of Marian the Librarian. Marian is giving a piano lesson to young Amaryllis. While the girl plays her simple piano tune, we see a tender side of the teacher as Marian dreamily sings to the evening star.

Did you know that "Goodnight, My Someone" uses the same melody as "Seventy-Six Trombones"? By altering the tempo and the meter, Willson transformed a sweet waltz into a stirring march.

The Music Man was Meredith Willson's first and most enduring musical. Willson grew up in Mason City, Iowa, and later built his musical career in New York City where he was principal flutist with the New York Philharmonic and wrote music for radio shows. Willson told many stories of his childhood, and the Broadway composer Frank Loesser convinced him that Iowa would make a great setting for a musical. Willson's characters were based on composites of real "stubborn" Iowans he knew. The character of Marian, however, is based on Willson's mother.

Suggested recordings of "Goodnight, My Someone" (iTunes):

GENRE: *Soundtrack* □ ***The Music Man,*** rel. 2006, Studio Group

GENRE: *Soundtrack* □ Jessica Molaskey: ***Make Believe,*** 2004, PS Classics

Highly recommended: the DVD film version with Shirley Jones

⏩If you like this song, take a look at "Till There Was You" from *The Music Man*

Ten Minutes Ago, from *Cinderella* (p. 163)

The songwriting team of Richard Rodgers and Oscar Hammerstein II created some of the most beautiful and enduring songs on Broadway. The lovely waltz "Ten Minutes Ago" is sung by Prince Charming, and later Cinderella, as the two reflect on how quickly circumstances can change when you meet the right person.

Rodgers and Hammerstein's hit shows include *Oklahoma!, The Sound of Music, Carousel,* and *South Pacific*. Richard Rodgers's songwriting legacy is carried on by his daughter Mary Rodgers Guettel (*Once Upon a Mattress*) and grandson Adam Guettel, composer of *The Light in the Piazza,* which won six Tony Awards in 2005.

Suggested recordings of "Ten Minutes Ago" (iTunes):

Genre: *Soundtrack* □ Alfredo Antonini, dir., and Julie Andrews: ***The CBS Television Production of Rodgers and Hammerstein's Cinderella,*** 1957, rel. 1999, Sony

Genre: *Soundtrack* □ John Green, dir., and Lesley Ann Warren: ***Cinderella,*** 1965 Television Cast, rel. 1993, Sony

Where Is Love?, from *Oliver!* (p. 167)

The young orphan Oliver sings this hauntingly beautiful song to the mother he never knew. However, the song works very well as a love ballad for either a man or a woman when performed outside the context of the show's story. Many hit songs in musicals were designed to stand alone. In fact, some composers, like Gershwin, would write songs for one show and then insert them in a completely different musical.

The 1963 stage musical *Oliver!* by Lionel Bart was based on Charles Dickens's Victorian novel *Oliver Twist*. Five years later it was made into a movie, and when the musical was revived in London in 1994, it was revised and re-orchestrated to make it more like the movie version.

Suggested recordings of "Where Is Love?" (iTunes):

Genre: *Country* □ Tom Wopat: ***The Still of the Night,*** 2000, Angel

Genre: *Jazz* □ Irene Kral: ***Where Is Love?,*** 1974, rel. 2003, Choice

⏩If you like this song, take a look at "As Long as He Needs Me" from *Oliver!*

Over the Rainbow, from the movie *The Wizard of Oz* (p. 169)

This universally appealing song was written for the 1939 Hollywood musical, *The Wizard of Oz*. In 2000 it was named the number one "Song of the Century." Oddly enough, this beautiful, inspirational ballad was actually cut from the film three times. In the story, young Dorothy Gale is scolded by her aunt, "Find a place where you won't get into any trouble." Crestfallen, Dorothy asks her dog, Toto, "Do you suppose there is such a place? There must be. It's far, far away, behind the moon, behind the rain."

Some film executives thought the song should be cut because it slowed down the movie's action and they didn't understand why the girl was singing in a barnyard. The music publisher complained that the middle of the song was too simple and the octave leap on "some-where" was unsingable. Fortunately, composer Harold Arlen and the film's producer Arthur Freed convinced the powers that be to leave the song in. It became Judy Garland's theme song and has been recorded by artists like country star Willie Nelson, jazz greats Sarah Vaughan and Ella Fitzgerald, blues singers Patti LaBelle and Eva Cassidy, and American Idol 2006 runner-up Katherine McPhee.

Suggested recordings of "Over the Rainbow" (iTunes):

Genre: *Soundtrack* □ Judy Garland: ***The Wizard of Oz (Soundtrack from the Motion Picture),*** rel. 2004, Turner Entertainment

Genre: *Vocal* □ Barbra Streisand: ***One Voice,*** 1987, rel. 1990, Sony

⏩If you like this song, take a look at "Come Rain or Come Shine" by Harold Arlen

Sing! from the TV show *Sesame Street* (p. 173)

This catchy tune by Joe Raposo is a popular song from the famous children's television

PART TWO

Popular Songs

show. The deeper message, however, may be intended more for self-conscious adults. Raposo urges everyone to simply "Sing!" and not to worry about what anyone else thinks. That is also the point of this book: to inspire a lifelong love for singing.

Suggested recordings of "Sing!" (iTunes):

GENRE: *Vocal* □ The Carpenters: ***From the Top,*** 1991, rel. 1994, A&M

⏩If you like this song, take a look at "Bein' Green" by Joe Raposo

SOMEWHERE OUT THERE, FROM THE FILM *AN AMERICAN TAIL* (P. 175)

This tender duet, from the Don Bluth animated film *An American Tail,* was nominated for an Academy Award in 1986. The film is the story of a family of Russian mice who immigrate to the United States. When young Fievel Mousekewitz is accidentally separated from his family at Ellis Island, he sings "Somewhere Out There." In another part of the city, "underneath the same big sky," little sister Tanya Mouskewitz joins in the song.

The song is often performed as a love duet and appears in several wedding song anthologies. The James Ingram/Linda Ronstadt version that played under the film's closing credits climbed to the top of the pop charts.

James Horner is an award-winning composer of film scores and movie songs. He also wrote "All Love Can Be" from *A Beautiful Mind,* and "My Heart Will Go On" from *Titanic.*

Suggested recordings of "Somewhere Out There" (iTunes):

Genre: *R&B* □ James Ingram and Linda Ronstadt: ***Forever More: The Best of James Ingram,*** 1999, Priva

GENRE: *Vocal* □ Kiri Te Kanawa: ***The Kiri Selection,*** 1992, EMI Classics

⏩If you like this song, take a look at "My Heart Will Go On" from *Titanic*

A TIME FOR US/UN GIORNO PER NOI, FROM *ROMEO AND JULIET* (P. 178)

"A Time for Us," also known as "The Romeo and Juliet Love Theme," was written thirteen years before singer Josh Groban was born. Groban's version, featured on his 2006 album, *Awake!,* is sung in Italian—with new lyrics by Alfredo Rapetti—to Nino Rota's 1968 melody. Rota's genius was his ability to write new music that captured the style, mood, and pageantry of the film setting's time period. His musical score for Franco Zefirelli's *Romeo and Juliet* evoked Shakespeare's Italy, and the signature song, "A Time for Us," is in the style of a courtly Baroque lute song. You can compare it to an original lute song, John Dowland's "Come Again, Sweet Love" on p. 217.

Nino Rota (1911–1979) was Italy's finest composer of film music and is best remembered as the creator of the score for the film *The Godfather.* He was a classically-trained composer who also wrote symphonies, chamber works, and an opera.

Suggested recording of "Un giorno per noi" (iTunes):

GENRE: *Vocal* □ Josh Groban: ***Awake!,*** 2006, Reprise

⏩If you like this song, take a look at "Verita" as sung by Josh Groban

YOU RAISE ME UP (P. 181)

Like much of the music of Norwegian composer Rolf Løvland, "You Raise Me Up" spans many styles and influences. Is it classical, Norwegian, or Irish traditional music? World music or new age? The composer will say only that "the music comes straight from the heart, and contains elements of all this." Løvland and Irish violinist Fionnuala Sherry are the lead performers of the group Secret Garden, whose 2001 album, *Once in a Red Moon,* featured "You Raise Me Up" as sung by Ireland's Brian Kennedy. The song received worldwide acclaim after it was recorded in 2003 by an up-and-coming young American singer named Josh Groban. "You Raise Me Up" is Groban's most popular song and is frequently performed at weddings, funerals, and high school graduations as a tribute to those who "raise me up to more than I can be." True to the song's international heritage, it has been recorded by more than a hundred artists, including The Irish Tenors' Ronan Tynan, Norwegian pop star Sissel, British opera singer Russell Watson, and music theater star Michael Ball.

Suggested recordings of "You Raise Me Up" (iTunes):

Genre: *Vocal* □ Josh Groban: ***Closer,*** 2003, Reprise/Wea

Genre: *Vocal* □ Sissel: ***My Heart,*** 2004, Decca

Genre: *Acoustic* □ Secret Garden: ***20th Century Masters: The Best of Secret Garden: The Millennium Collection,*** 2004, Deutsche Grammophon

⏩If you like this song, take a look at the inspirational song "Wind Beneath My Wings"

Be Who You Were Born to Be (p. 185)

"Be Who You Were Born to Be" was written by Lucinda Drayton and Andrew Blissett of the hit British group Bliss. Both have been practicing Yogis for 10 years, a lifestyle that infuses their music with purpose and inspiration. With "no more time to waste," the song's message is to "jump off that cliff and be who you were born to be." Bliss has been popular in the UK since the 1990s, and the group is finding an ever-growing audience in the U.S. through music downloads on iTunes and their website, blissfulmusic.com. Drayton and Blissett wrote the hit song "The Real Thing" with Toni Di Bart in 1994, and followed up with their debut album, "Suicidal Angel," which topped British charts. Irish singer Sinead O'Connor recently covered the 2001 Bliss song, "A Hundred Thousand Angels." This arrangement of "Be Who You Were Born to Be" by Scarlett Antaloczy is exclusive to *The Singing Book* and authorized by Lucinda Drayton.

Suggested recordings of "Be Who You Were Born to Be" (iTunes or blissfulmusic.com):

Genre: *New Age* □ Bliss: ***Bliss,*** 2003, Blissful Music

⏩If you like this song, take a look at Bliss's "A Hundred Thousand Angels"

True Colors (p. 190)

"True Colors," by Tom Kelly and Billy Steinberg, became more than a song for 1980s rock diva Cyndi Lauper—it became a mission. Lauper has long contributed her talents to charities and causes, from USA for Africa's 1984 "We Are the World" to headlining the 2004 Nobel Peace Prize concert in Oslo, Switzerland. In 2007, the inaugural True Colors Tour, featuring rock legends and current artists, traveled to fifteen U.S. cities. The tour was sponsored by the Human Rights Campaign to raise awareness against discrimination.

"True Colors" was a hit for Phil Collins in the 1990s and was released posthumously on Eva Cassidy's *American Tune* in 2003. "True Colors" has been the theme song for television commercials (including one for Kodak film) and a memorable 2007 Super Bowl advertisement for Dove soap's Campaign for Real Beauty sung by Layah Jane.

Suggested recordings of "True Colors" (iTunes):

Genre: *Rock* □ Cyndi Lauper: ***True Colors,*** 1986, rel. 1990, Sony

Genre: *Jazz* □ Wendee Glick: ***True Colors,*** 2005, Jazzy Plus

Genre: *Rock* □ Phil Collins: ***Hits,*** 1998, Atlantic Recording

⏩If you like this song, take a look at Cyndi Lauper's "Time After Time"

Don't Get Around Much Anymore (p. 195)

"Don't Get Around Much Anymore" is one of the most popular songs by legendary American jazz composer and performer Duke Ellington (1899–1974) and lyricist Bob Russell (1914–1970), whose other collaborations included "Do Nothin' Till You Hear From Me" and "I Didn't Know About You." Artists who have recorded "Don't Get Around Much Anymore" include Ellington, Nat King Cole, Ella Fitzgerald, and rocker Rod Stewart. A classic break-up song, the catchy melody is a contrast to the apparent apathy of the lyrics: "Been invited on dates. Could have gone, but who cares." The music seems to indicate that the jilted lover will soon be back in circulation.

Duke Ellington first trained as an artist and painter, but he became renowned as a musician and big band leader. Some of America's finest jazz players performed in the Duke Ellington Orchestra in the 1940s. Ellington was nominated for a Pulitzer Prize and received a Grammy Lifetime Achievement Award in 1968.

Suggested recordings of "Don't Get Around Much Anymore" (iTunes):

Genre: *Jazz* □ Duke Ellington: *The Essential Duke Ellington,* 2005, Sony

Genre: *Soundtrack* □ Harry Connick, Jr.: ***When Harry Met Sally,*** 1989, Sony

Genre: *Jazz* □ Ella Fitzgerald: ***Ella Fitzgerald Sings the Duke Ellington Songbook,*** rel. 1999, Polygram

⏩If you like this Ellington/Russell song, take a look at "Do Nothin' Till You Hear From Me"

Blue Skies, from *Betsy* (p. 198)

When the stock market crashed in 1929, the most popular song in America was Irving Berlin's optimistic "Blue Skies." Countless singers have covered this song (recorded it after its introduction) including Lyle Lovett, the Chanticleer vocal ensemble, and the android Data in the 2002 film *Star Trek: Nemesis.*

Irving Berlin (born Israel Baline in Russia) immigrated to United States with his family in 1893 and became one of America's great composers. Many of his 1,500 songs, including some written for film and stage, have become standards. Though "Blue Skies" stands on it own, it was interpolated first into a little-known Rodgers and Hart musical, *Betsy,* in 1926. In 1946 Berlin borrowed his own song and title for the movie musical *Blue Skies* with Bing Crosby and Fred Astaire.

Suggested recordings of "Blue Skies" (iTunes):

Genre: *Jazz* □ Rosemary Clooney: ***From Bing to Billie,*** 2004, Concord Jazz

Genre: *Jazz* □ Frank Sinatra: ***The Best of the Columbia Years, 1943–1952,*** rel. 1998, Sony

Genre: *Jazz* □ Tierney Sutton: ***I'm with the Band,*** 2005, Telarc

⏩If you like this song, take a look at the Irving Berlin song "Always"

When I Fall in Love (p. 200)

This song was used in the soundtrack of the 1993 romantic film *Sleepless in Seattle.* Critics and audiences loved the original and cover versions of the lush ballads and swing standards in this film. It is worth renting the DVD for the soundtrack alone. Celine Dion and Clive Griffin's duet version of Victor Young's "When I Fall in Love" rivals earlier recordings by Nat King Cole, Doris Day, and Lena Horne.

Composer Victor Young was a conservatory-trained musician who began his career as a classical composer and concert violinist. In the 1920s, however, he turned to popular and film music. Young wrote hundreds of award-winning film scores and songs as chief composer and arranger for Hollywood's Paramount Pictures Studios, until his untimely death at age 56.

Suggested recordings of "When I Fall in Love" (iTunes):

Genre: *Vocal* □ Nat King Cole: ***Lovesongs,*** rel. 2003, Capitol

Genre: *R&B/Soul* □ Natalie Cole: ***Everlasting,*** 1987, rel. 1991, Elektra/Wea

Genre: *Pop* □ Linda Ronstadt: ***Lush Life,*** 1984, rel. 1990, Elektra/Wea

⏩If you like this song, take a look at the Vincent Young song "I Don't Stand a Ghost of a Chance with You"

They Can't Take That Away from Me, from *Shall We Dance?* (p. 202)

It is hard to pin down a character for this popular song since it appeared in two movies and a stage show, and resides in the collective consciousness of the country. It serves as a "break-up" song for anyone who has ever been dumped in a romantic relationship and chooses to dwell on the good memories.

The song first appeared in the 1937 Fred Astaire/Ginger Rogers movie classic *Shall We Dance?* and later in the 1949 MGM film *The Barkleys of Broadway.* It was also featured in the 1994 "new" Gershwin Broadway hit *Crazy for You,* which Ken Ludwig loosely adapted from Gershwin's 1920s stage musical *Girl Crazy.* This enduring standard by George and Ira Gershwin has been performed by Frank Sinatra, Ella Fitzgerald, Peggy Lee, Fred Astaire, Rosemary Clooney, Bobby Short, and more recently, Michael Feinstein and Diana Krall. You can't take this song away from America!

Suggested recordings of "They Can't Take That Away from Me" (iTunes):

Genre: *Vocal* □ Frank Sinatra: ***Songs for Young Lovers,*** 1955, rel 1998, Capitol

Genre: *Vocal* □ Sarah Vaughan: ***Ken Burns JAZZ Collection:*** Sarah Vaughan, 2000, Polygram

Genre: *Jazz* □ Ella Fitzgerald: ***Pure Ella,*** 1998, Verve

⏩If you like this song, take a look at the Gershwin song "Someone to Watch Over Me"

Skylark (p. 206)

Many nostalgic and love songs use bird imagery. Larks, bluebirds, whippoorwills, doves, and skylarks carry love's message on their wings (see "L'hirondelle messagère," p. 98, and "Lungi," p. 212). "Skylark" was a very lucky bird for songwriter Hoagy Carmichael. It was one of his many popular songs that topped the Hit Parade in the 1940s.

When Carmichael was still relatively unknown, his earlier songs like "Lazy River" and "Georgia on My Mind" were already being recorded by Duke Ellington, Louis Armstrong, and others. In 1936 Carmichael headed for Hollywood, where he teamed with lyricists like Johnny Mercer and Frank Loesser to write and sing songs like "Skylark," "Stardust," and "Heart and Soul." He quickly became a star on stage, screen, and recordings. Audiences liked the Indiana-born composer's folksy "down-home" charm, much the way modern audiences are drawn to Garrison Keillor and *Prairie Home Companion.*

Suggested recordings of "Skylark" (iTunes):

Genre: *Pop* □ Tony Bennett: ***Fifty Years: The Artistry of Tony Bennett,*** 2004, Sony

Genre: *Jazz* □ k.d. lang, on ***Best of Smooth Jazz, Vol. 4: For Lovers,*** 1998, Warner/Wea

Genre: *Vocal* □ Rosemary Clooney: ***The Songbook Collection,*** 2000, Concord

⏩If you like this song, take a look at the Hoagy Carmichael song "Stardust"

Someone Like You

from *Jekyll & Hyde*

Words by
Leslie Bricusse

Music by
Frank Wildhorn

For background and performance notes, see page 129.

9
F
C/F
B♭/F
F
The past was hold - ing me, keep-ing life at bay.
And now I see a world I've__ nev - er seen be - fore.

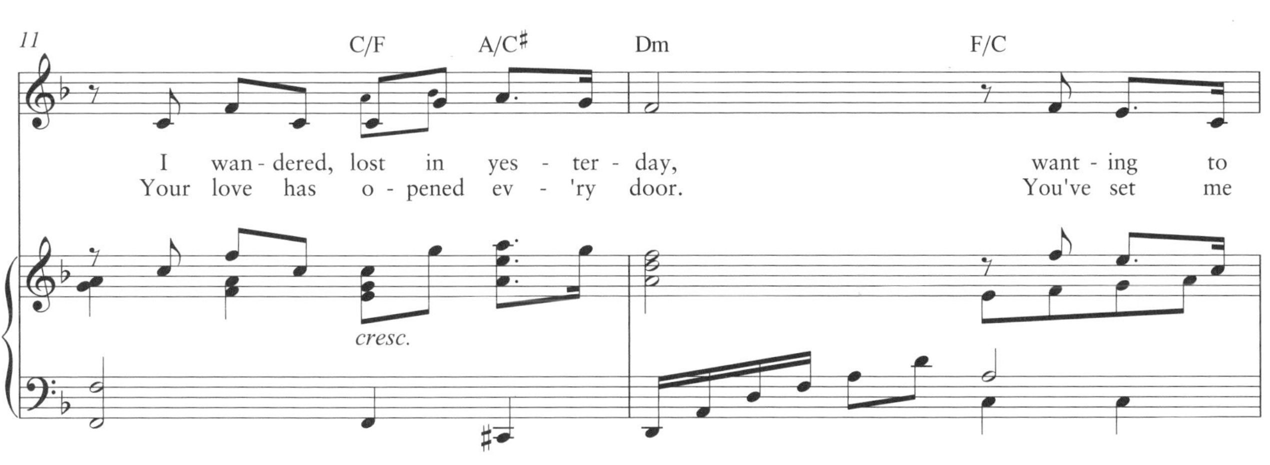
11
C/F
A/C♯
Dm
F/C
I wan-dered, lost in yes - ter - day, want - ing to
Your love has o - pened ev - 'ry door. You've set me
cresc.

13
B♭
Gm7
C7sus
C
F
fly, but scared to try. Then some-one like you found
free, now I can soar. For some-one like you found

16
Gm7
F
F/A
some - one like me, and sud - den - ly
some - one like me. You touched my heart.
18
B♭
Gm7♭5
F Dm7 Gm7
F Dm7 Gm7
noth - ing is the same. My heart's tak - en wing, and I feel so a - live, 'cause
Noth - ing is the same. There's a new way to live, a new way to love, 'cause
dim.
21
1.
F Dm7 Gm7 D♭/G♭
F
Em7
Em7/A A7
some-one like you found me.
24
2.
F Dm7 Gm7 C7sus
D♭
B/C♯
C♯7
some - one like you found me.
Oh,
molto rit.

26
F♯
G♯m7
some - one like you found some - one like me, and
f a tempo
28
F♯
F♯/A♯
B
G♯m7♭5
sud - den - ly nothing will ev - er be the same. My
30
F♯
D♯m
G♯7sus
A♯m
C♯/D♯
D♯7♭9
G♯m
heart's tak - en wing, and I feel so a - live, 'cause some - one like
p
much slower, freely
34
C♯7sus
F♯
Bmaj7
F♯
you loves me, loves me.
a tempo
rit.
pp

I Move On

from *Chicago*

Words by
Fred Ebb

Music by
John Kander

For background and performance notes, see page 129.

12
F♯7sus(♭9)
F♯7
F(♯5)
F(♭5)
E7(13)
I just move on.
15
A6/9
When
19
Amaj9
G♯7
A9/G
I can't find a sin - gle star That I can wish up - on
22
F♯7sus(♭9)
F♯7
F(♯5)
F(♭5)
E9
I just move on. I move on.

25
A6/9
I run so fast,
29
D9(♯11)
C♯m7
F♯m7
Bm7
E7sus
a shot - gun blast Can't hurt me not one bit.
(D.S.)
I'm out of dreams And life has got me down.
32
A(9)
D9(♯11)
C♯m7
F♯m7
I'm on my toes 'cause hea - ven knows. A
I don't des - pair. I don't go there. I
35
B9
Bm7
E7
C(♯9)/E♭
E9sus
mov - ing tar - get's hard to hit.
hang my bon - net out of town.
8va

38
C(#9)/E♭
E9sus
C(#9)/E♭
E9sus
So,
So,
(8)
41
Amaj9
G#7
A9/G
as I play in life's bal - let, I'm not the dy - in' swan,
there's no doubt I'm well cut out, To run life's mar - a - thon
44
to CODA
F#7sus(♭9)
F#7
F(#5)
F(♭5)
E9
A6/9
I just move on, I move on.
48
D.S. al CODA
Just when it seems

PART TWO

Popular Songs

Anything You Can Do

from *Annie Get Your Gun*

Words and Music by
Irving Berlin

For background and performance notes, see page 130.

9
Frank:
An - y - thing you can be, I can be great - er, Soon - er or lat - er I'm great-

12
Annie:
Frank:
Annie:
Frank:
Annie:
- er than you. No you're not. Yes I am. No you're not. Yes I am. No you're not.

15
Frank:
Yes, I am! Yes I am!
I can shoot a par-tridge with
f
mp

18
Annie:
a sin - gle car - tridge. I can get a spar-row with a bow and ar - row.

21
Frank:
I can live on bread and cheese.
Annie:
And on - ly that?
Frank:
Yes!
(optional tacet)
24
Annie:
So can a rat!
Frank:
An - y - thing you can sing, I can sing high - er,
27
Annie:
I can sing an - y - thing high - er than you.
Frank:
No you can't,
Annie:
Yes I can.
Frank:
No you can't,
30
Annie:
Yes I can.
Frank:
No you can't.
Annie:
Yes I can.
Frank:
No you can't.

PART TWO

Popular Songs

46
Annie: molto dim.
Frank:
can say soft - er. I can say an - y-thing soft - er than you. No you can't.
molto dim.

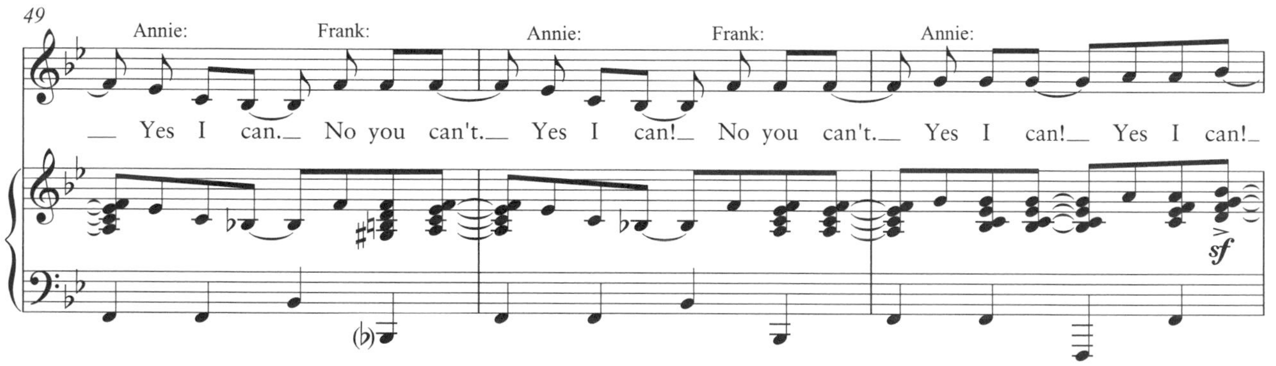
49
Annie: Frank: Annie: Frank: Annie:
Yes I can. No you can't. Yes I can! No you can't. Yes I can! Yes I can!
sf

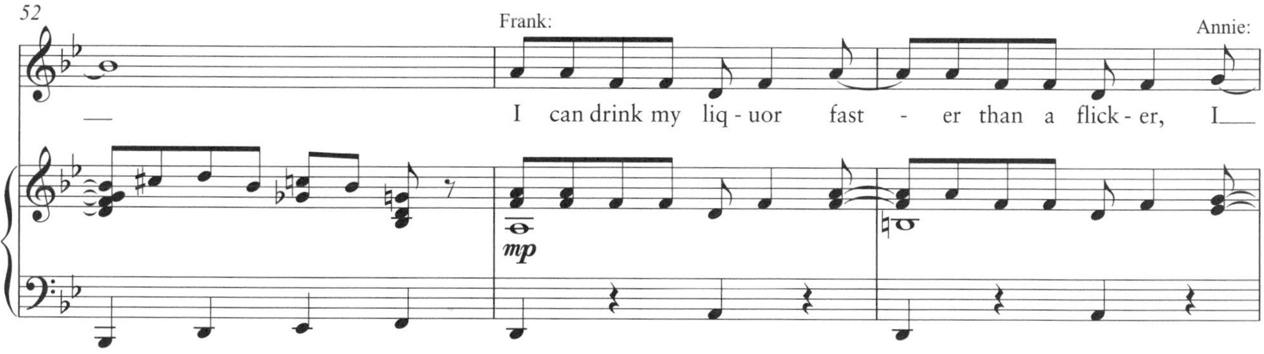
52
Frank:
Annie:
I can drink my liq - uor fast - er than a flick - er, I
mp

55
Frank:
can drink it quick - er and get e - ven sick - er, I can o - pen

PART TWO

Popular Songs

71

75
Freely
Frank:
Yes you can!
a tempo
can!
ad lib. repeat
a tempo
colla voce
mf
ff
mp

79
Annie:
An - y - thing you can wear, I can wear bet - ter, In what you wear I'd look bet-
mp

82
Frank:
Annie:
Frank:
Annie:
Frank:
- ter than you. In my coat? In your vest. In my shoes? In your hat. No you can't.

85
Annie:
Yes I can! Yes I can!
Frank:
An-y-thing you can say, I
3
f
mp

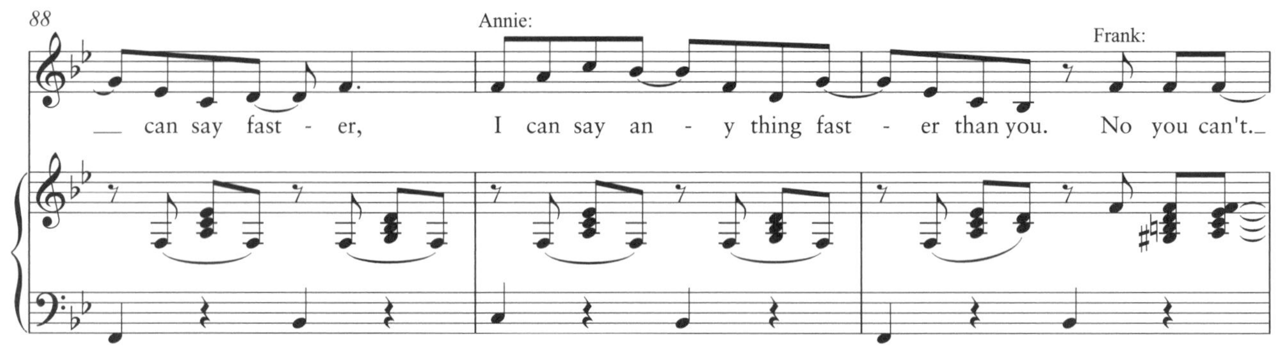
88
can say fast-er,
Annie:
I can say an-y thing fast-er than you.
Frank:
No you can't.

91
Annie:
Yes I can.
Frank:
No you can't.
Annie:
Yes I can!
Frank:
No you can't.
Annie:
Yes I can! Yes I can!
sf

94
Frank:
I can jump a hur-dle.
Annie:
I can wear a gir-dle.
Frank:
I
mp

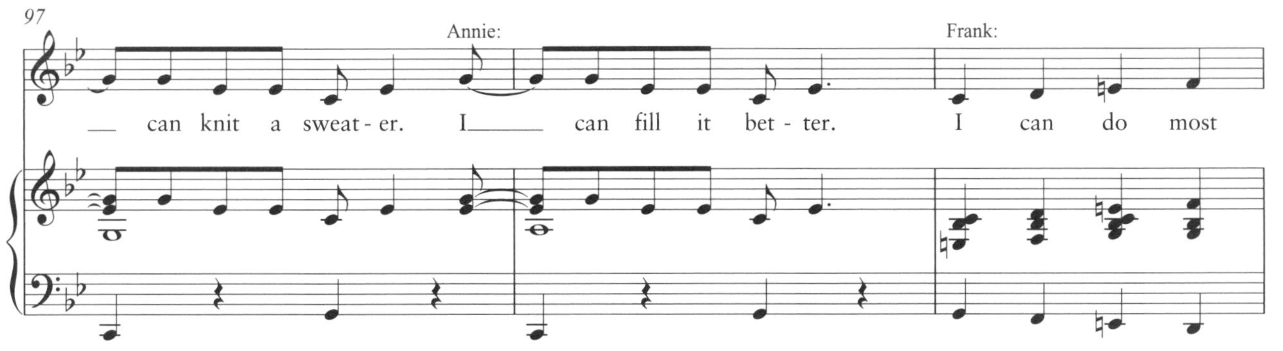
97
Annie:
Frank:
can knit a sweat-er. I can fill it bet-ter. I can do most

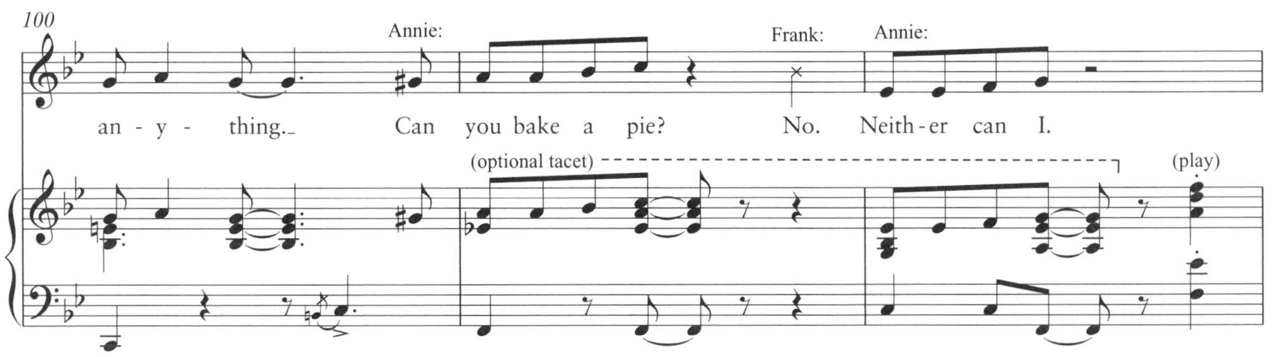
100
Annie:
Frank:
Annie:
an-y-thing. Can you bake a pie? No. Neith-er can I.
(optional tacet)
(play)

103
Frank:
Annie:
An-y note you can sing, I can sing sweet-er. I can sing an-y-thing sweet-
mp

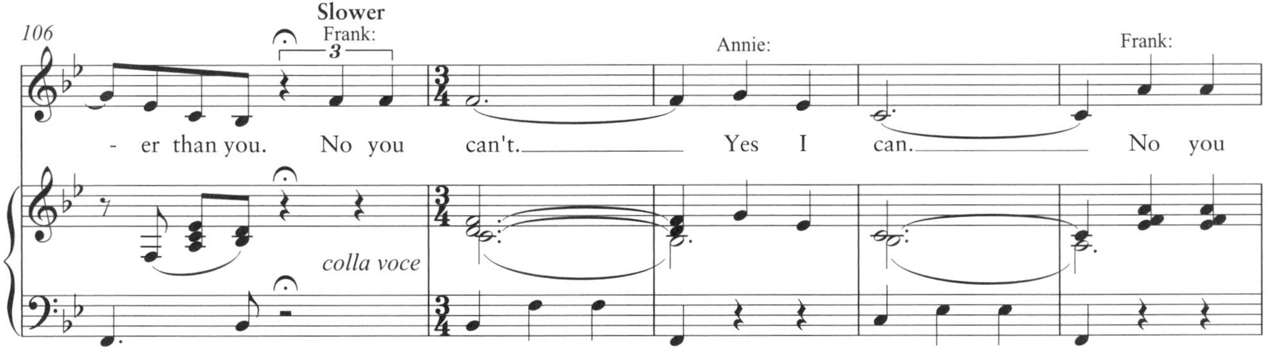
106
Slower
Frank:
Annie:
Frank:
-er than you. No you can't. Yes I can. No you
colla voce

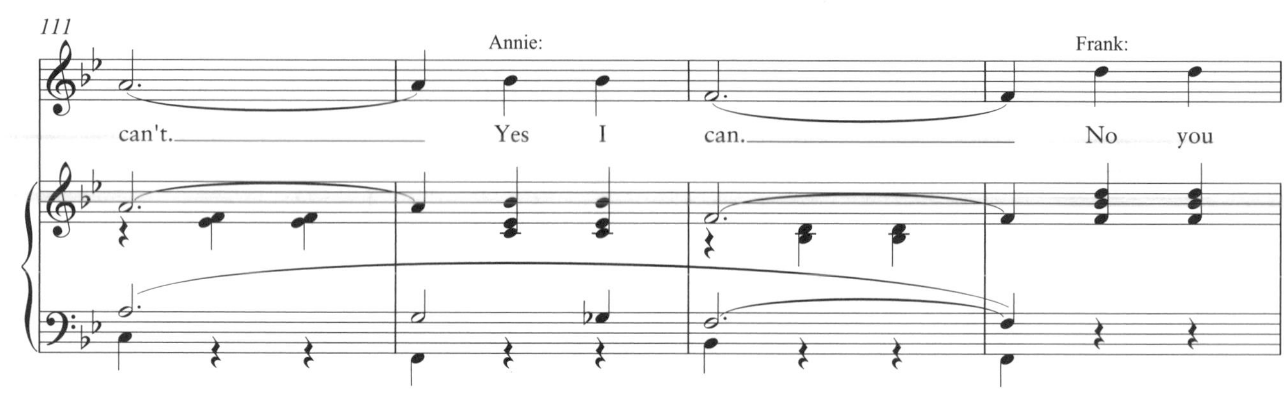
111
Annie:
Frank:
can't.
Yes I
can.
No you

115
Annie:
Frank:
Annie:
Frank:
can't. Yes I
can. No you
can't. Yes I
can. No you

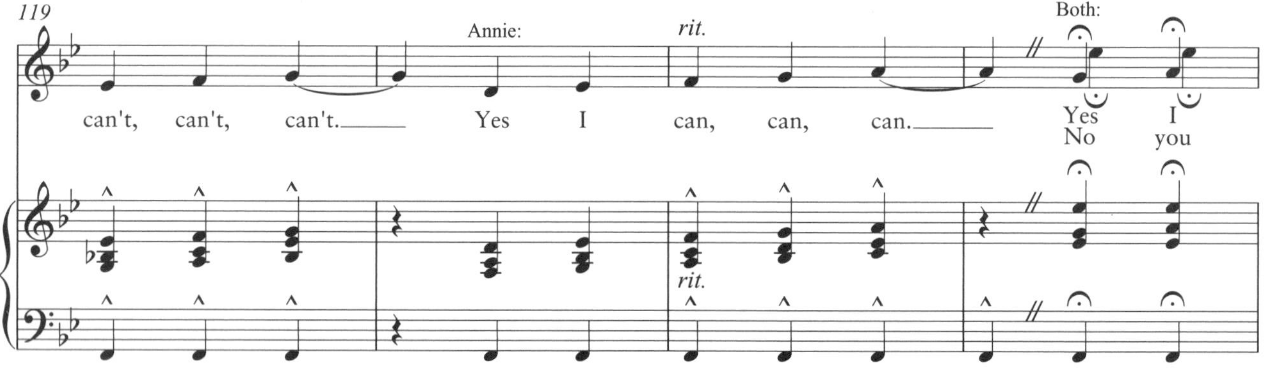
119
Annie:
rit.
Both:
can't, can't, can't.
Yes I
can, can, can.
Yes I
No you
rit.

123
can.
can't.
3
3
3

Wand'rin' Star

from *Paint Your Wagon*

Words by
Alan Jay Lerner

Music by
Frederick Loewe

For background and performance notes, see page 130.

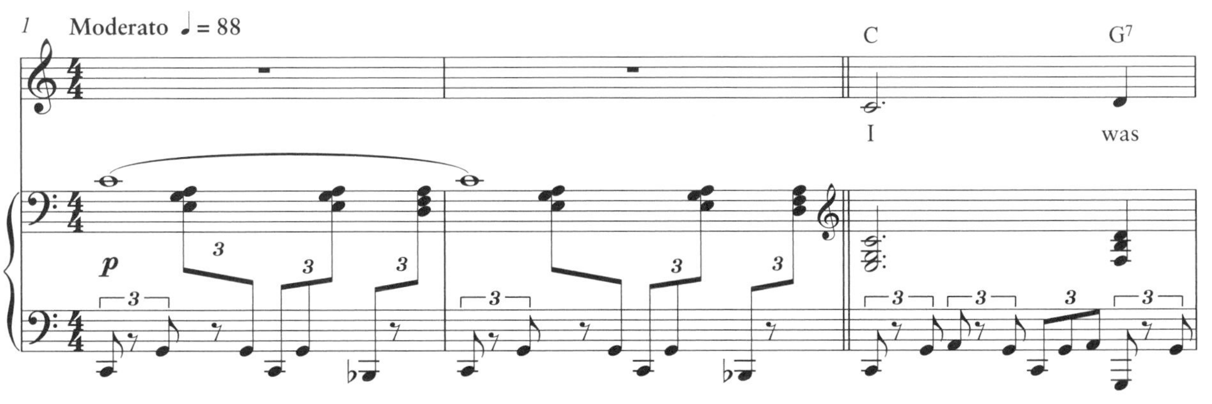

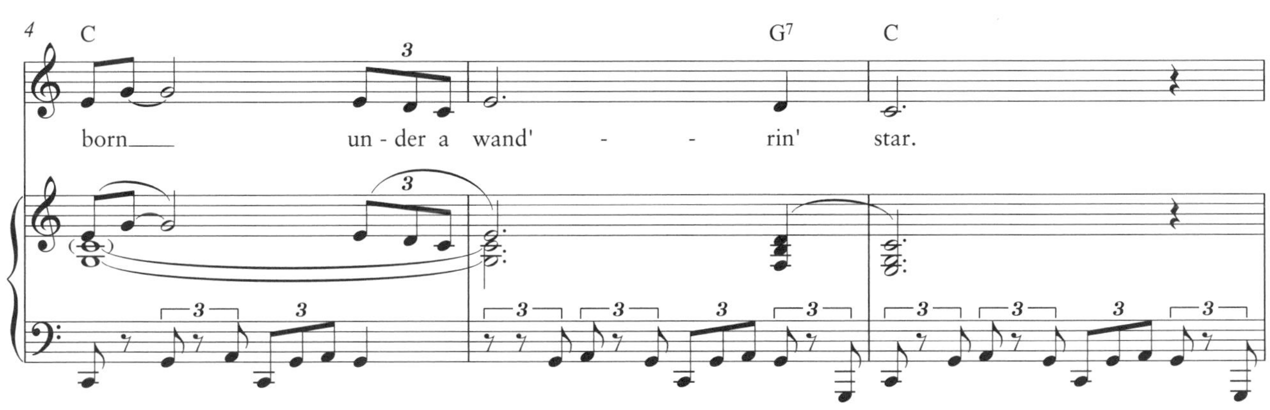

10
F
G7
F
star.
Wheels are made for roll - in',
Mules are made to pack. I
mf
13
C
Em
C♯dim
Am7
D7
Dm7
G7
C
G7
nev - er seen a sight that didn't look bet - ter look - in' back.
I was
16
C
G7
C
born
un - der a wand' - - rin'
star.
19
Em
Bm
Em
Mud can make you pris' - ner and the plains can make you dry.
Snow can burn your eyes but on - ly

22
Bm
Dm
Am
peo - ple make you cry.
Home is made for com - in' from, for dreams of go - in' to
f
25
Dm
Dm7
G7
C
G7
Which, with an - y luck will nev-er come true.
I
was
28
C
G7
C
born
un - der a wand' - - rin' star.
31
C
Am
I
was
born
un - der a wand' - - rin'

34
F G7 F
star. When I get to heav - en tie me to a tree, Or
37
C Em C♯dim Am7 D7 Dm7 G7 C G7
I'll be-gin to roam, And soon you know where I will be. I was
40
C Ddim Am Fm C
born un - der a wand' - rin' star, A wand' - rin',
44
F7 G7 C B♭7 C6 Dm7 C6
wand' - rin' star.

Goodnight, My Someone

from *The Music Man*

Words and Music by
Meredith Willson

For background and performance notes, see page 130.

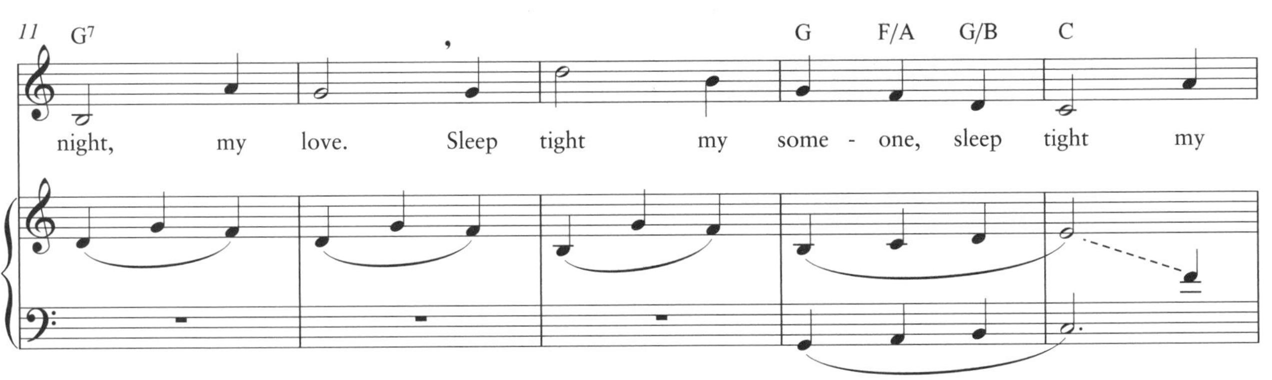

PART TWO

Popular Songs

Freely
16 Am7/E F/D G Am/C Gm7/C C7 B♭/F F E♭7(♯11) D7
love. Our star is shin - ing its bright - est light for good-
p
21 Gdim G D7 Gsus4 G G7 C
night, my love, for good - night. Sweet dreams be
26 C6 G7/F Adim/E♭ G/D G7/D A7/C♯ G7/D G F/G G7
yours, dear, if dreams there be; Sweet dreams to car - ry you
l.h.
31 C Am/C C G6 G6/B Am7 C7 C7(♯11) C7/G F F6
close to me. I wish they may, and I wish they

36 D7/F♯ Em/G F/G G7(♭9) C Dmaj/C Ddim/C C7
might. Now good - night, my some - one, good - night. True
8va
l.h.
41 F E/F F F♯aug F♯dim Gm7 D♯dim/G C7 Cdim C7 D/C C7
love can be whis - pered from heart to heart, when lov - ers are
46 C7aug F F E/F F F6 F F♯dim
part - ed they say. But I must de - pend on a
8va
l.h.
51 C/G poco rit. Am/G C G/D D G/D G D7/F♯ G F/G G7
wish and a star, as long as my heart does - n't know who you are. Sweet
poco rit.

Tempo I
57
C G7/F E♭dim G7/D A7/C♯ G7/D G7
dreams be yours, dear, if dreams there be. Sweet dreams to
pp
62
G F/A G/B Cdim C G Dm7 G7 Cmaj7 C7
car - ry you close to me. I wish they may, and I
67
F F♯dim G G7(♭9) C
ten.
wish they might. Now good-night, my some - one, good - night
ten.
ten.
colla parte
ten.
72
Cdim C/G G7 C
Good - night. Good - night.
l.h.
pp

Ten Minutes Ago

from *Cinderella*

Words by
Oscar Hammerstein II

Music by
Richard Rodgers

For background and performance notes, see page 131.

14
B7 Em Cm6 G/D A9
reel - ing, You gave me the feel - ing the room had no ceil - ing or
19
Am7/D D7 G D7sus/A D7
floor. Ten min - utes a - go, I met you, And we
25
G D7sus/A D7 G
mur - mured our how - do - you - do's, I want - ed to
30
B7 Em Cm6 G/D D7 G
ring out the bells and fling out my arms and to sing out the news.

36
F/G G7 C C/G F♯m7♭5/G G/B G/D
I have found her!* She's an an - gel with the
sf
41
Am7 D7 G(add9) F/G G7 C C/G F♯m7♭5/G
dust of the stars in her† eyes. We are danc - ing, we are
sf
47
G/B G/D A9/E A G A7 Am7/D D7
fly - ing And she's‡ tak - ing me back to the skies. In the
f
mp
53
G D7sus/A D7 G
arms of my love, I'm fly - ing o - ver moun-tain and mead - ow and

*him
†his
‡he's

59 D7sus/A D7 G B7 Em Cm6
glen And I like it so well, that for all I can tell, I may
65 G/D D7 Dm7 G7 C Am7
nev - er come down a - gain! I may nev - er come down to
71 Am7/D D7 1. G Em7 Am7 D7
earth a - gain. Ten
f sf mp
77 2. G A7♭5(♭9) D7 G
gain.
sf

Where Is Love?

from *Oliver!*

Words and Music by
Lionel Bart

For background and performance notes, see page 131.

18 B♭maj7 B♭m7 E♭7 A♭maj7 A♭ A♭6 A♭ Dm7 G7 C Dm7 G7
sweet "hel - lo" that's meant for on - ly me?
Who can say where she (he) may
Ev - 'ry night I kneel and
3
22 Cmaj7 C Cmaj7 C7 F G7 C C♯dim Dm7 G7
hide? Must I trav - el far and wide Till I am be-side the
pray, Let to-mor-row be the day When I see the face of
3
26 Cmaj7 Cm7 F9 B♭maj7 B♭6 Amaj7 A7(♭9) Dm7 Am
some - one who I can mean some-thing to? Where,
1. 2.
30 Dm7 G7(♭9) C Am Dm7 G7 C F6 Fdim Cmaj7 C6
Where Is Love? Love?
rit.

Over the Rainbow

from *The Wizard of Oz*

Words by
E. Y. Harburg

Music by
Harold Arlen

For background and performance notes, see page 131.

17
Cm
A♭7
F9
Fm7/B♭
E♭/B♭
lead - ing from your win - dow - pane to a place be - hind the
cresc.
21
Fm7/B♭
E♭/B♭
Fm7/B♭
B♭7
sun. just a step be - yond the rain.
Chorus
♩ = 84
25
E♭
Gm
E♭7
A♭
Gm7
Some - where o - ver the rain - bow way up high,
p - mf
29
A♭6
A♭m6
E♭/B♭
C7(♭9)
F7
E♭
there's a land that I heard of once in a lull - a - by.

33
E♭
Gm
E♭7 (,) A♭
Gm7
Some - where o - ver the rain - bow skies are blue,
37
A♭6
A♭m6
E♭/B♭
C7(♭9)
F7
E♭
and the dreams that you dare to dream real - ly do come true. Some
41
E♭
Fm7/B♭
B♭7/E♭
E♭6
day I'll wish up - on a star and wake - up where the clouds are far be - hind me, where
45
E♭
E♭6
E♭
F♯dim7
Fm6
B♭9(♯5)
trou - bles melt like lem - on drops, a - way, a - bove the chim - ney tops that's where you'll find me,

49
E♭ Gm E♭7 (,) A♭ A♭maj7 A♭7 Gm7 Edim7 A♭6 A♭m6
Some - where o - ver the rain - bow blue - birds fly. Birds fly
54
E♭/B♭ C7(♭9) , F7 Fm7/B♭ B♭7 E♭ B♭9 B♭7(♭9) E♭ B♭7(♭9)
1. 2.
o - ver the rain - bow, why then, oh why can't I? I?
rall.
58
A♭/E♭ E♭6 Fm7 B♭7/F
If
62
rit.
E♭ Fm7 , B♭7 E♭6
hap - py lit - tle blue - birds fly be - yond the rain - bow, why oh why can't I?
dim.
pp
l.h.
ten.

Sing!

from *Sesame Street*

Words and Music by
Joe Raposo

For background and performance notes, see page 131.

21
B♭maj9
B♭maj6
Cm7/B♭
F7
B♭maj9
B♭maj6
B♭
Sing! Sing a song. Make it sim - ple. to last your whole life
27
A♭/B♭
B♭7
E♭maj7
D7sus6
Gm7
long. Don't wor - ry that it's not good e - nough for an - y - one else to
32
C9
Cm7
F7
B♭
hear. Sing! Sing a song.
Optional
37
B♭maj9
B♭maj6
B♭maj9
B♭maj6
E♭maj7
E♭maj6
B♭maj9
La la la la la la la la la la la la la la la la la la.

Somewhere Out There

from *An American Tail*

Words by
Cynthia Weil

Music by
James Horner and Barry Mann

For background and performance notes, see page 132.

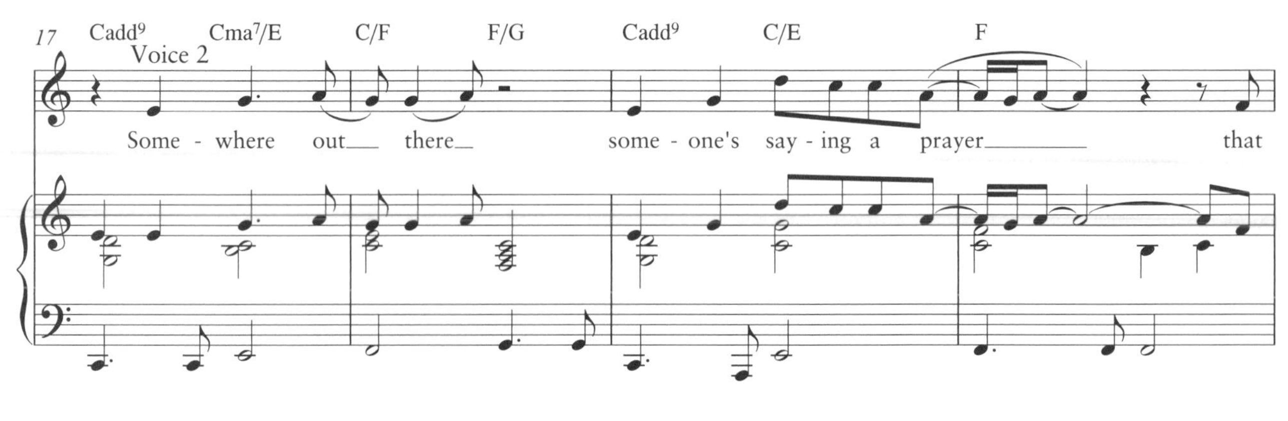
17
Cadd9 Cma7/E C/F F/G Cadd9 C/E F
Voice 2
Some - where out there some - one's say - ing a prayer that

21
Dm7 G/F Cm7 Am Dm7 C/E F/G C
Both
we'll find one a - noth - er in that big some - where out there. And

25
F G/F F G/F Fmaj7 G/F
e - ven though I know how ve - ry far a - part we are it helps to think we might be wish - in'

28
F G/F A♭ B♭/A♭ A♭ B♭/A♭
Voice 2
Voice 1
on the same bright star. And when the night - wind starts to sing a lone - some lul - la - by it

31
A♭
B♭/A♭ poco rit.
a tempo
G
helps to think we're sleep - ing un - der - neath the same big sky.
poco rit.
a tempo
34
C
Cmaj7/E
Fmaj9
F/G
C
C/E
F
Both
(Melody)
Some - where out there if love can see us through,
38
Dm
G/F
Em7
Am
poco rit.
F
G
then we'll be to - geth - er some - where out there, out where dreams come
poco rit.
Ped.
42
C
Cmaj7/E
C/F
G7sus
Cadd9
true.
a tempo

Un giorno per noi

A Day for Us

(Italian)

Un giorno sai, per noi verrà [un dʒɔrrno sai pɛrr noi verra*]	A day, you know, for us will come.
La libertà di‿amarci qui senza limiti [la libɛrrta diamarrtʃi kwi sɛntsa limiti]	The liberty of loving here without limit
E fiorirà il sogno‿a noi negato [e fjɔrira il sɔɲɔanɔi negato]	will blossom into the dream that was denied us.
Si svelerà l'amor celato‿ormai [si svelera lamorr tʃelatorrmai]	The love that was concealed will now be revealed.
Un giorno sai, per viverà [un dʒɔrrno sai pɛrr vivera]	A day, you know, to live
La vita che ci sfugge qui [la vita kɛ tʃi sfuddʒe kwi]	the life that escapes us here.
l'amore‿in noi supererà [lamɔreinnɔi superera]	The love in us will overcome
Gli‿ostacoli e le maree delle‿avversità [ʎiostakoli e le mare dɛlleavversita]	the obstacles and the tides of adversity
E ci sarà anche per noi nel mondo [e tʃi sara aŋke pɛrr nɔi nɛl mɔndo]	and there will also be for us in the world
Un tempo‿in cui l'amore vincerà [un tɛmpoin kwi lamore vintʃera]	a time in which love will triumph.

---

*Written double "r" is a prolonged rolled/trilled [rr].

A Time for Us / Un giorno per noi

from *Romeo and Juliet*

Words by Larry Kusik and Eddie Snyder
New lyrics by Alfredo Rapetti

Music by
Nino Rota

For background and performance notes, see page 132.

17
B♭ F Cm Gm A♭
time for us at last to see a life worth
gior - no sai per vi - ve rà la vi - ta
f
dim. poco
22
E♭ Dm Gm Dm E♭
while for you and me. And with our love through tears and thorns we will en-
che ci sfug - ge qui. L'a - mo-re in noi su - pe - re rà gli o-sta-co-
mp
27
Dm B♭ Cm Gm Dm E♭
dure as we pass sure - ly through ev'-ry storm. A time for us some day there'll be a
li e le ma - ree del le av - ver-si - tà. E ci sa-rà an-che per noi nel
32
Cm Dm Gm Dm Gm Gm
1. 2.
new world. a world of shin-ing hope for you and me. A time for me.
mon - do un tem - po in cui l'a - mo-re vin-ce - rà. Un gior-no rà.
dim.
rall.
p

You Raise Me Up

Words and Music by
Brendan Graham and Rolf Løvland

For background and performance notes, see page 132.

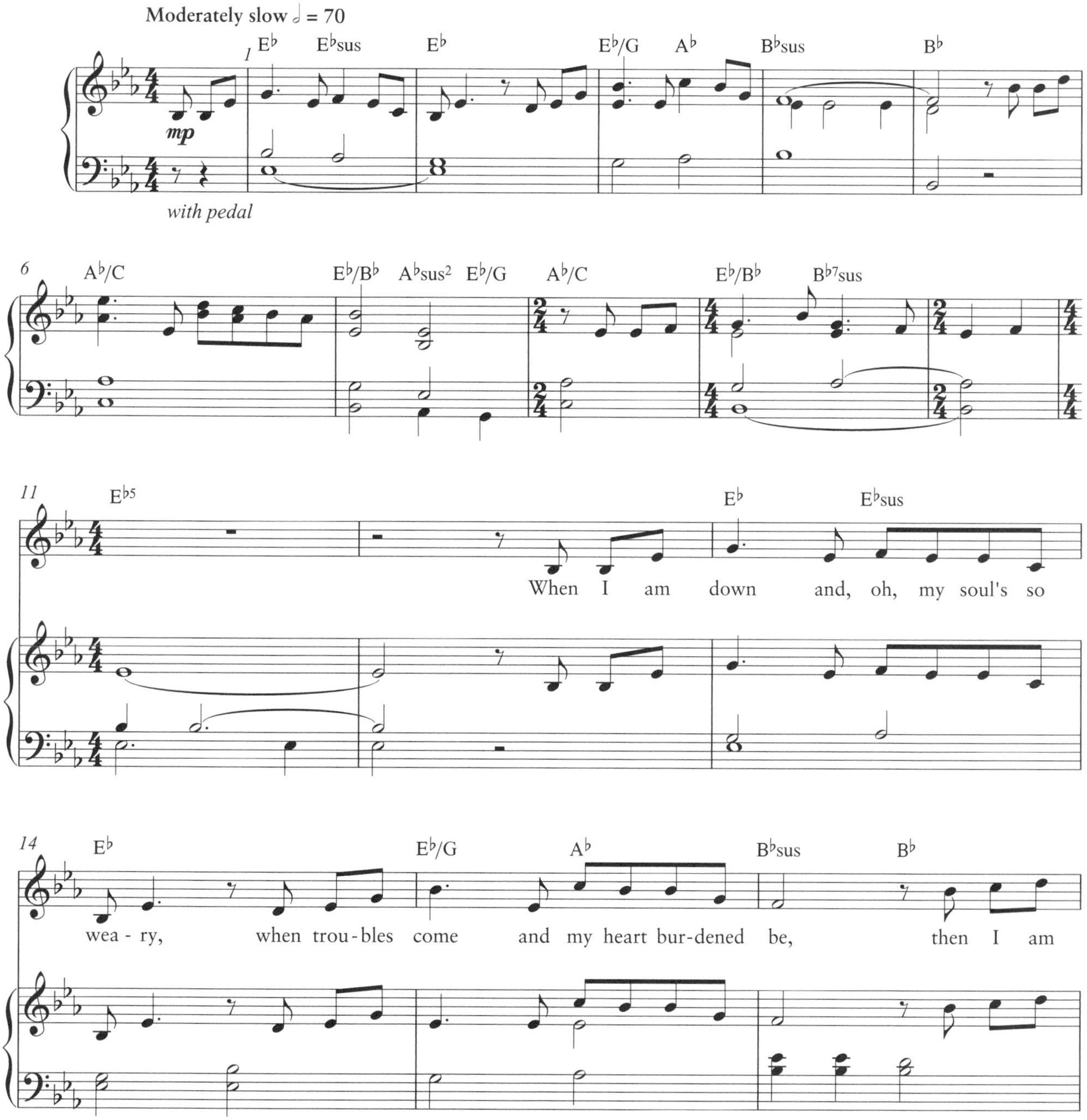

Moderately slow 𝅗𝅥 = 70

1 E♭ E♭sus E♭ E♭/G A♭ B♭sus B♭

mp

with pedal

6 A♭/C E♭/B♭ A♭sus2 E♭/G A♭/C E♭/B♭ B♭7sus

11 E♭5 E♭ E♭sus

When I am down and, oh, my soul's so

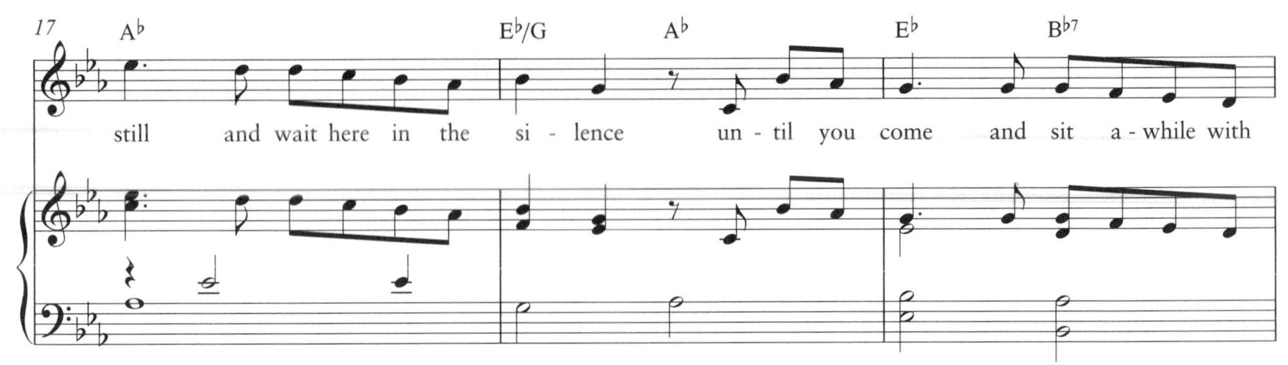
17
A♭
E♭/G
A♭
E♭
B♭7
still and wait here in the si - lence un - til you come and sit a - while with

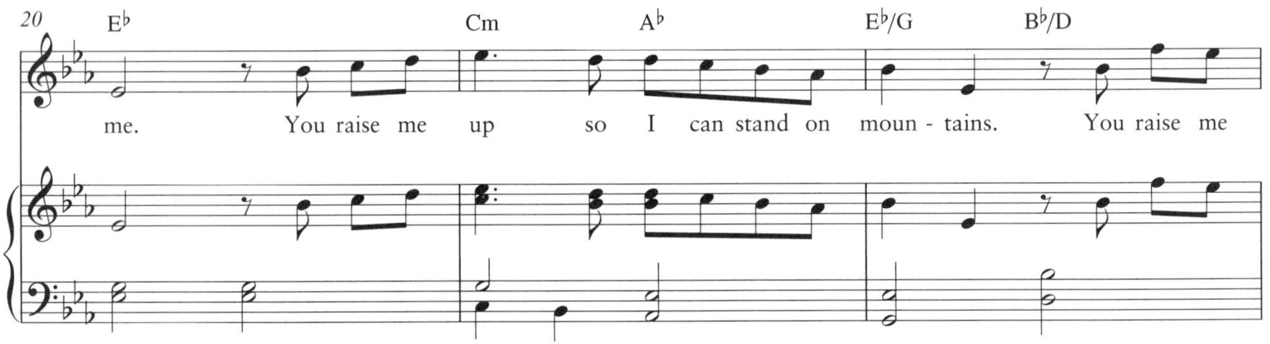
20
E♭
Cm
A♭
E♭/G
B♭/D
me. You raise me up so I can stand on moun - tains. You raise me

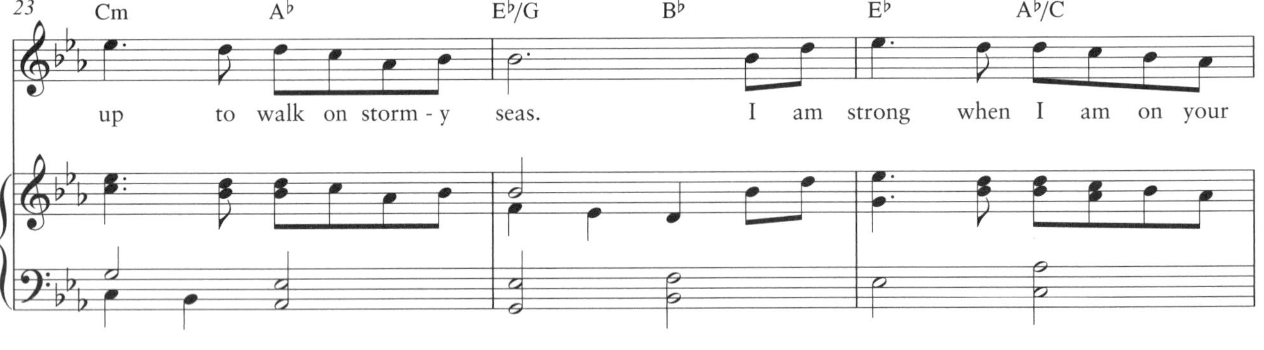
23
Cm
A♭
E♭/G
B♭
E♭
A♭/C
up to walk on storm - y seas. I am strong when I am on your

26
E♭/G
A♭
E♭/B♭
B♭7
E♭
shoul - ders. You raise me up to more than I can be.

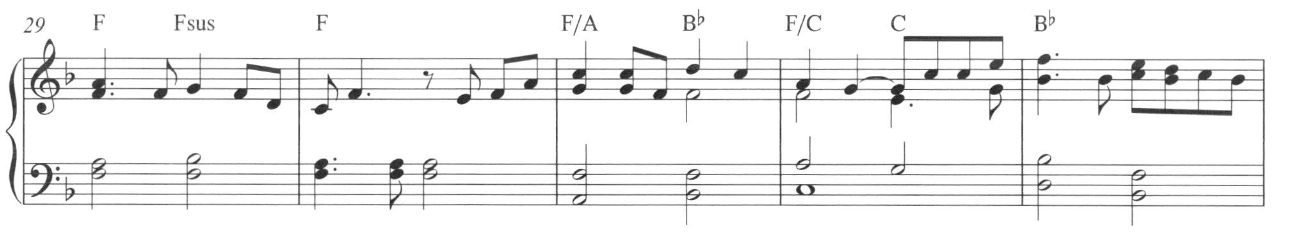

PART TWO

Popular Songs

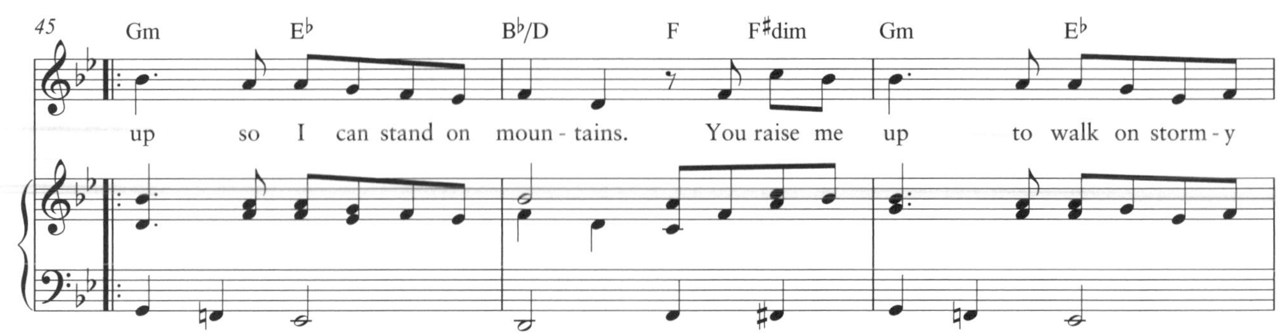
45
Gm E♭ B♭/D F F♯dim Gm E♭
up so I can stand on moun - tains. You raise me up to walk on storm - y

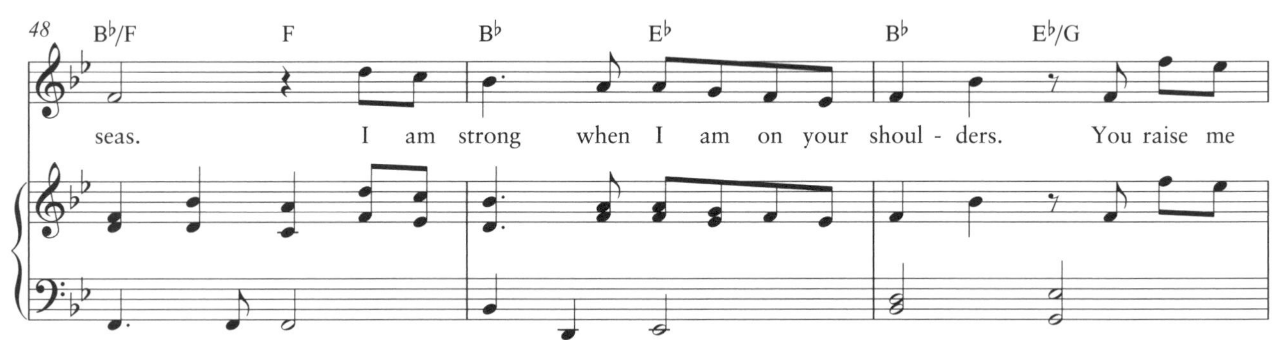
48
B♭/F F B♭ E♭ B♭ E♭/G
seas. I am strong when I am on your shoul - ders. You raise me

1.
2.
51
B♭/F F7 B♭ D/F♯ B♭/F F7
up to more than I can be. You raise me up to more than I can

54
Gm E♭ B♭/F F7sus F7 E♭/B♭ B♭
be. You raise me up to more than_ I can be.
p

Be Who You Were Born to Be

Words and Music by
Lucinda Drayton
Transcribed by Scarlett Antaloczy*

For background and performance notes, see page 133.

*Used by permission of Blissful Music, www.blissfulmusic.com, exclusively for *The Singing Book*.

PART TWO

Popular Songs

22
F
C
G
Fmaj7
shout and say I am the one 'Cuz there's been too much

27
Em7
Am
G
F
cry' - in and talk of be - ing free

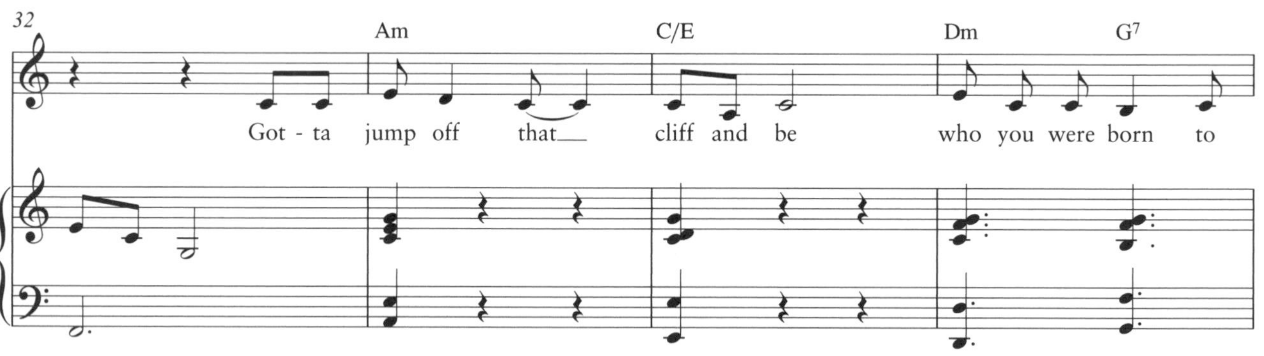
32
Am
C/E
Dm
G7
Got - ta jump off that cliff and be who you were born to

36
C
F
C
G7sus4
be.

Verse 2

Broad

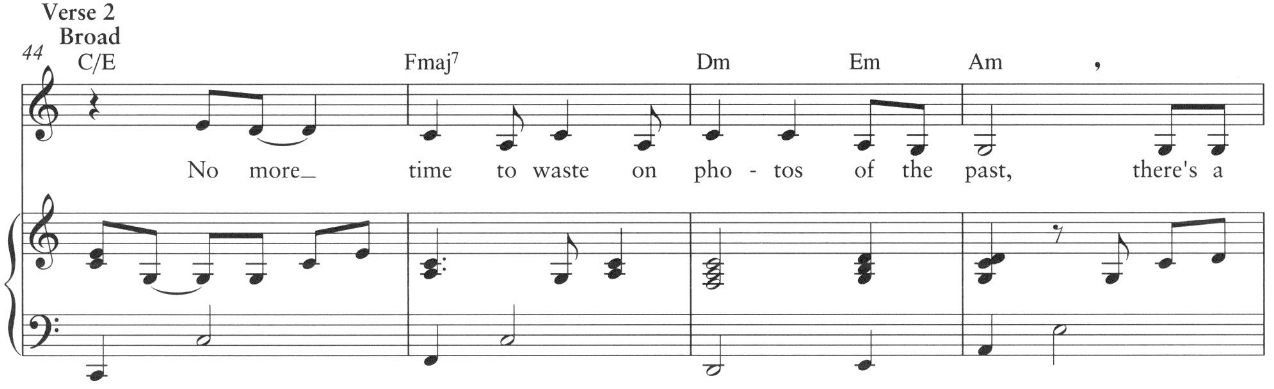

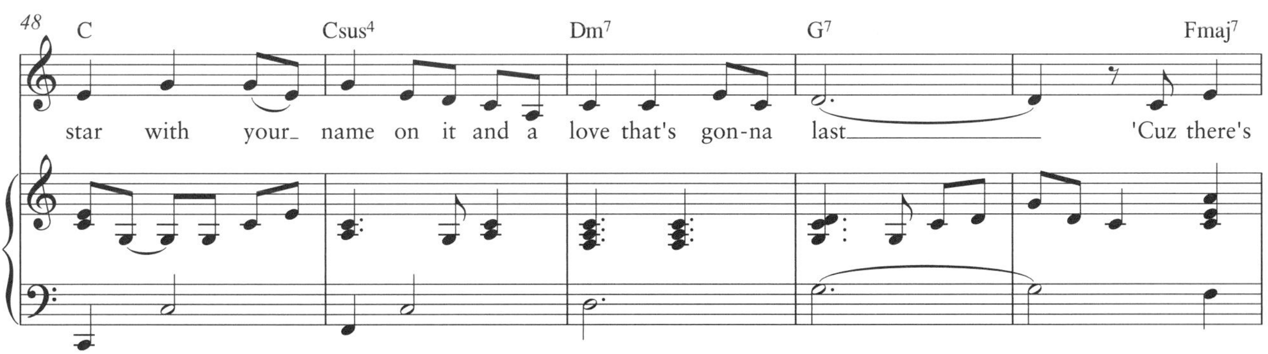

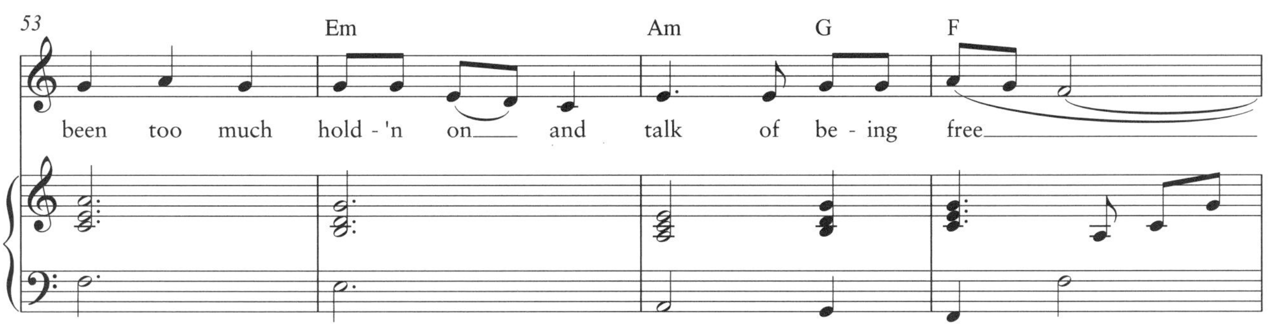

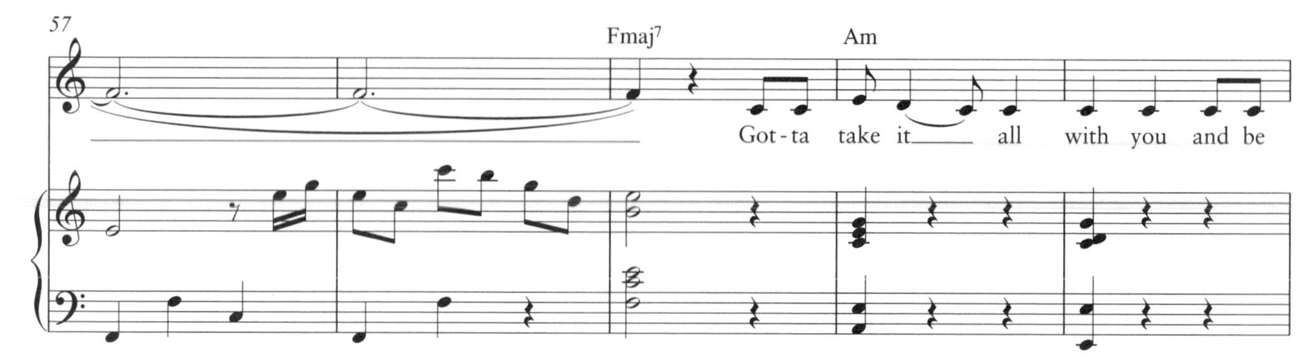
57
Fmaj7
Am
Got-ta take it all with you and be

62
Dm
G7
C
F
C
G7sus4
who you were born to be.

67
C
F
Dm
G
C
da da da da da da da da da Now I

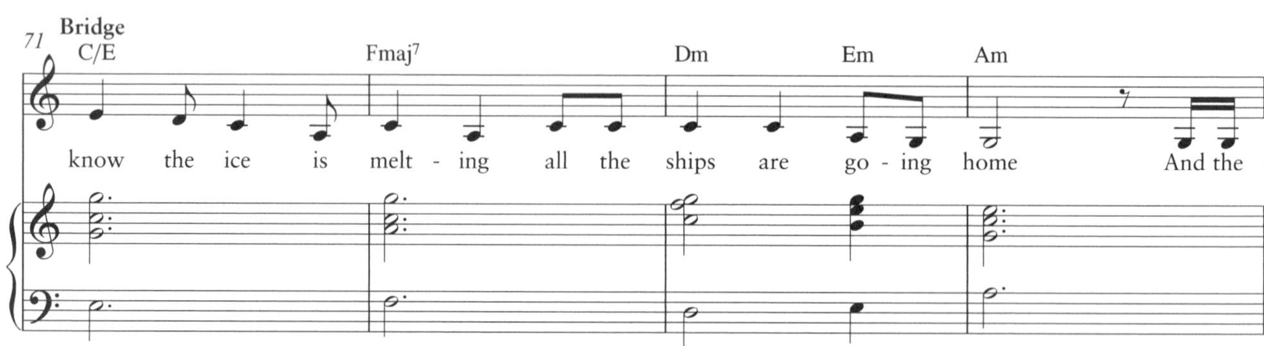
Bridge
71
C/E
Fmaj7
Dm
Em
Am
know the ice is melt - ing all the ships are go - ing home And the

75
G/B
C7sus4
Am
Em9
wind is get - ting cold - er and we feel more and more a - lone

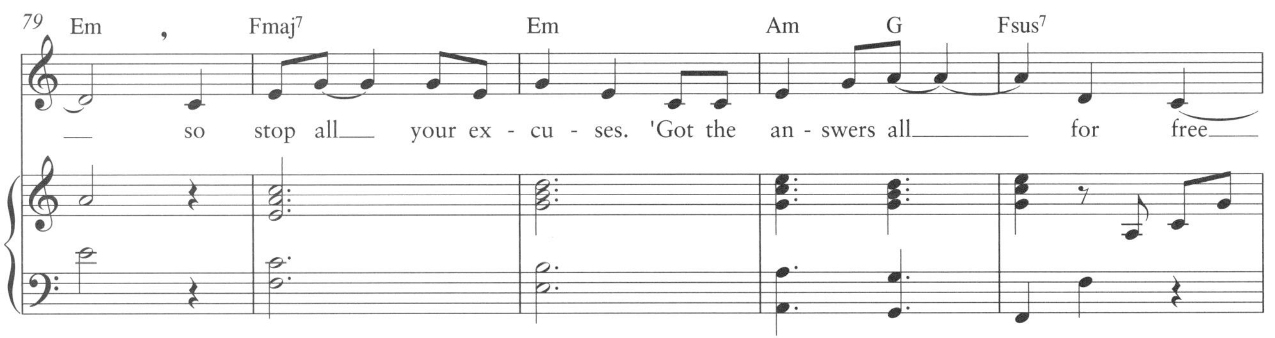
79
Em
Fmaj7
Em
Am
G
Fsus7
so stop all your ex - cu - ses. 'Got the an - swers all for free

84
Ad lib on repeat
Am
Em
Jump off that cliff and be
Sha - la la la la la

89
G7sus4
1., 2., 3.
C
4.
C
D/C
C6
who you were born to be. be.
Sha - la la la la la

PART TWO

Popular Songs

True Colors

Words and Music by
Billy Steinberg and Tom Kelly

For background and performance notes, see page 133.

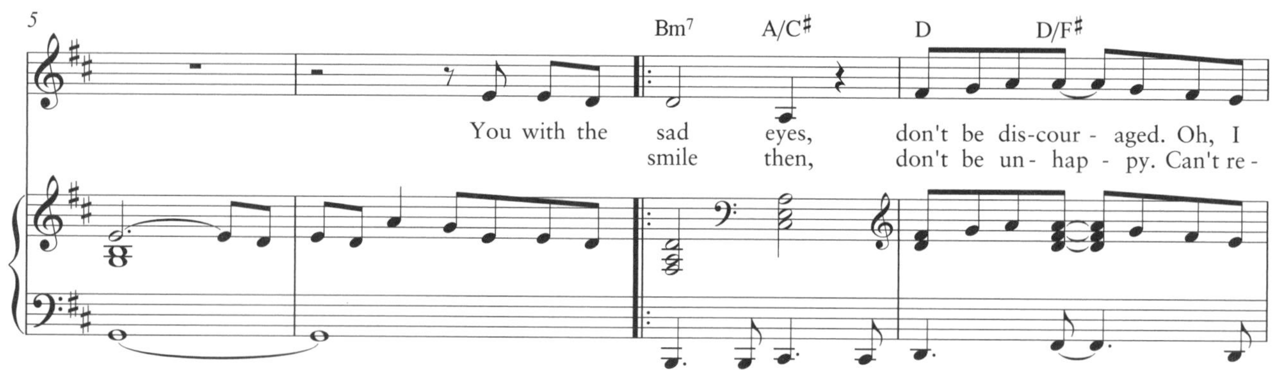

12
D/F♯ G Bm7 A Em7/D D
you can lose sight of it and the dark-ness in-side you makes you feel so small. But I
tak-in' all you can bear, just call me up be-cause you know I'll be there. And I'll
see your
15
G D A G D
true col - ors shin - in' through. I see your true col - ors and
18
G A G D G Bm
that's why I love you. So, don't be a - fraid to let them show. Your
21
Em7/D D
to Coda
Em7/D D Asus A
true col - ors, true col - ors are beau - ti - ful, ooh, like a

24
1.
Bm7 A/C♯ D G Bm7 A/C♯ D Gsus2
rain - bow. Show me your
28
2.
Bm7 A/C♯ D D/G Bm7 A/C♯ D A/C♯ A
rain - bow.
32
Gadd2 Bm7 A/C♯ D D/F♯
Such sad eyes. Take
36
G Bm7 A6 D Em7
cour-age now and re - al - ize. When this world makes you cra - zy and you're

39
D/F♯
Gadd2
Bm7
A
Em7/D
D
D.S. al Coda
tak - in' all you can bear,
just call me up be-cause you know I'll be there. And I see your
Coda
42
Em7/D
D
Em7/D
D
A
true col - ors, true col - ors are shin - in' through. I see your
45
G
D
G
A
G
D
true col - ors and that's why I love you. So, don't be a - fraid, Just
48
F♯7♭9
Bm7
Em7/D
D
Em7/D
D
let them show. Your true col - ors, true col - ors,

51
Em7/D
D
A
true_ col - ors are beau-ti - ful, beau-ti - ful like a rain - bow.

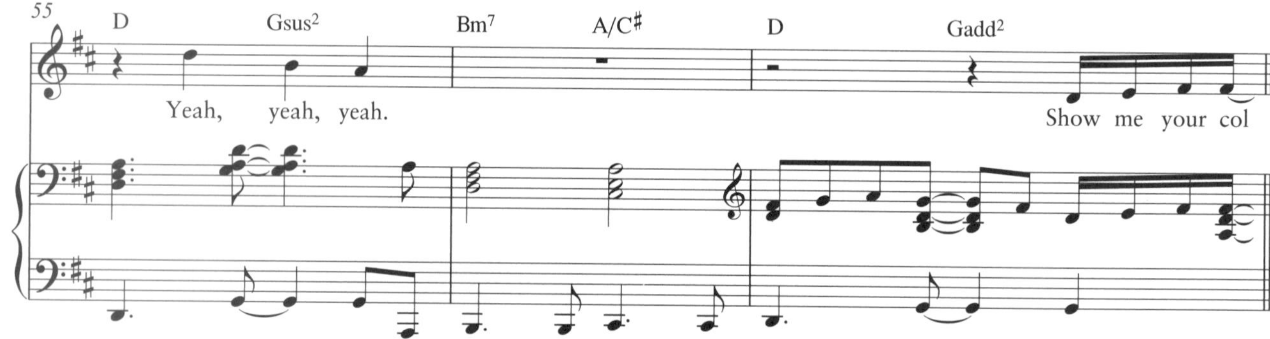
55
D
Gsus2
Bm7
A/C♯
D
Gadd2
Yeah, yeah, yeah. Show me your col

58
Bm7
A/C♯
D
Gadd2
Bm7
A/C♯
- ors. Show me_ rain - bow._

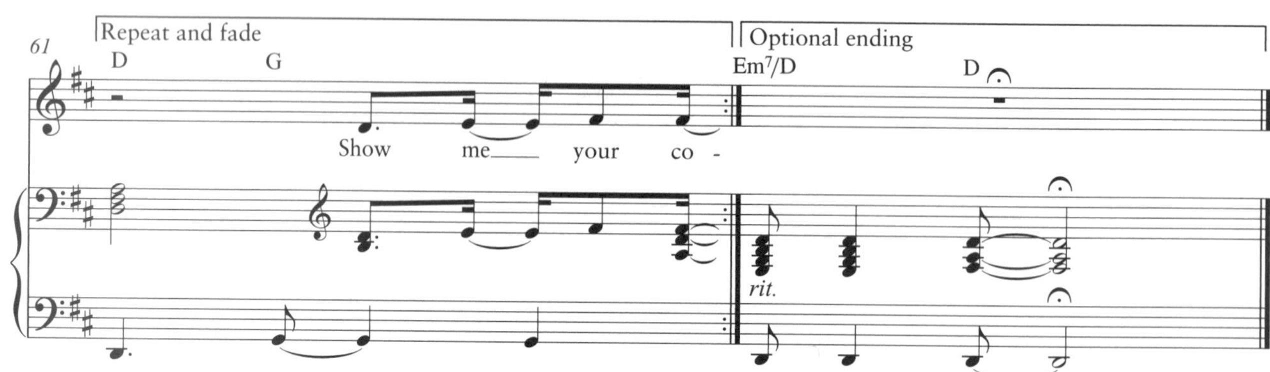
Repeat and fade
Optional ending
61
D
G
Em7/D
D
Show me_ your co -
rit.

Don't Get Around Much Anymore

Words and Music by
Duke Ellington and Bob Russell

For background and performance notes, see page 133.

PART TWO

Popular Songs

Chorus
14
C
A9
Am7
dance, heard they crowd-ed the floor. Could-n't bear it with-out
18
D9
G7
C6
— you,_ don't get a-round much an - y - more. Thought I'd vis - it the
22
C
A9
Am7
club, got as far as the door. They'd have asked me a-bout
26
D9
G7
C
— you,_ don't get a-round much an - y - more._

30
F
Fm
Em7
C
C7
C7(♯5)
F
Dar - ling, I guess my mind's more at ease. But nev - er-the - less,
mf
35
Am6
B7
Em
B
G7
C
why stir up mem-o - ries? Been in - vit - ed on dates,
39
A9
Am7
D9
might have been but what for? Aw - f'lly dif-f'rent with - out you,
43
G7
1.
C
2.
C
don't get a-round much an-y - more. Missed the Sat - ur-day more.
mf
p

Blue Skies

from *Betsy*

Words and Music by
Irving Berlin

For background and performance notes, see page 134.

16
Bm7(b5) G Eb(#5) F Bb9 C7 F
(even)
noth-ing but blue - birds all day long.
21
Bbm F Bbm F Bbm F
Nev-er saw the sun shin-ing so bright, nev-er saw things go-ing so right. No-tic-ing the days
26
Bbm F Bbm F C7 F A7 D A(#5) A
Swing
hur-ry-ing by; when you're in love, my how they fly. Blue days, all of them
31
F Bm7(b5) G Eb(#5) F Bb9 C7 F
gone, noth-ing but blue skies from now on.

When I Fall in Love

Words by
Edward Heyman

Music by
Victor Young

For background and performance notes, see page 134.

17
Fm7 C7(♭9) Fm Fm7 B♭/D B♭7 E♭
man - y moon - light kiss - es seem to cool in the warmth of the sun. When I give my
3
22
B♭7 E♭ C7(♯5) C7 Fm
heart it will be com - plete - ly, or I'll nev - er give my heart;
28
A♭dim E♭/G A♭ C7 Fm A♭m6 E♭/B♭
And the mo - ment I can feel that you feel that way too is when I fall in
34
Fm7 B♭7 E♭ G♭dim Fm7 B♭7(♭9) E♭ A♭9 C♭9 E♭
1. 2.
love with you. you.

They Can't Take That Away from Me

from *Shall We Dance?*

Lyrics and Music by
George Gershwin and Ira Gershwin

For background and performance notes, see page 134.

13
Am7 D7 G6 Am7 D7 Gmaj7 G6 G
mel - o - dy ling - ers on. They may take you from me, I'll
17
Am7 D7 Gm A♭ A♭(♯5) Edim7 Fm B♭/D Edim7
miss your fond ca - ress. But though they take you from me, I'll still pos -
Refrain (not fast)
Swing
21
F7/C B7(♭5) B♭7 A♭ B♭11 E♭6 B♭6 E♭ G♭dim7
ess: The way you wear your hat, The way you sip your tea,
poco marcato
slowly with warmth
mp - mf
25
B♭7sus4 B♭7 Fm7 B♭11 B♭m E♭ B♭7(♯5) Gm7(♭5) Cm D7(♭5) Gm7(♭5)
The mem'-ry of all that No, no! They
mf

29
A♭ Fm C9 F7 A♭ B♭11 E♭6 B♭6 E♭ G♭dim7
can't take that a-way from me! The way your smile just beams, The way you sing off key,
mp
33
B♭7sus4 B♭7 Fm7 B♭11 B♭m E♭ B♭7(♯5) Gm7(♭5) Cm D7(♭5) Gm7(♭5)
The way you haunt my dreams, No, no! They
mf
37
A♭ Fm B♭7sus4 B♭7 E♭6 E♭ Gm C7 D7(♭5) Gm C7 D7(♭5)
can't take that a-way from me! We may nev-er, nev-er meet a-gain On the
con calore
41
Gm Em7(♭5) A7(♯5) A7sus4 D7 Gm C7 D7(♭5) Gm Gm7(♭5) C7
bump-y road to love, Still I'll al-ways, al-ways keep the mem'-ry

PART TWO

Popular Songs

PART TWO

Popular Songs

Skylark

Words by
Johnny Mercer

Music by
Hoagy Carmichael

For background and performance notes, see page 135.

10
A♭ Fm7 B♭7 E♭6 B♭7 E♭ A♭
wait - ing to be kissed? SKY - LARK, Have you seen a val - ley
13
E♭ Gm A♭ E♭ A♭ E♭
green with Spring, Where my heart can go on jour-ney - ing,
3
16
F7 B♭7 E♭ B♭7 E♭
3
O - ver the sha - dows and the rain, to a blos - som cov - ered lane? And in your
3
19
A♭ E♭6 Fm7 E7 E♭7 A♭maj7 E♭dim A♭6 D♭7
3
lone - ly flight, Have - n't you heard the mu - sic in the night,
3

22
C7 Ddim C7 Fm Fm7 Fdim D♭ Fm E♭7 A♭7
— Won - der - ful mu - sic, Faint as a "will o' the wisp," Craz - y as a loon,
3 3
25
G A7 D7 G B♭7 E♭6 B♭7
Sad as a gyp - sy ser - e - nad - ing the moon. (Oh,) SKY - LARK,
28
E♭ A♭ E♭ Gm A♭ E♭ A♭ E♭
— I don't know if you can find these things, But my heart is rid - ing on your wings,
32
F7 B♭7 E♭ B♭7
1. E♭ B13 B♭13
2. E♭ E6 E♭6
— So, if you see them an - y - where, Won't you lead me there? there?

Art Songs and Arias

Art Songs

When you look at how old some of these art songs are it is easy to think they belong in a museum. Great works of art are hung in museums so that everyone can enjoy them, and they are so expensive that most of us would never be able to own an original. We have to stick with reprints. However, unlike visual art, original "art" music can be sung and repeated forever. This is the great tradition we have in art music, especially the great songs of composers such as Schubert, Schumann, Brahms, Fauré, Debussy, and others. Museum-quality American art song writers include Copland, Barber, Ives, and Rorem. Their songs live today because of the universal appeal of the music and the message.

Art songs differ from folk song and popular music in several ways:

1. Art songs are written down by composers trained musically rather than being passed on by oral tradition like folk songs. Some popular composers do write their music; however, many pop and rock songwriters create the music "by ear" and rely on other musicians to faithfully *transcribe* (write out) the music.
2. Art songs are usually performed as written, with little deviation except for historically appropriate ornaments. The duty of the singer of art song is to interpret the musical message of the poet and the composer. Folk songs, pop songs, and especially jazz and standards rely more on the singer's ability to improvise, "stylize," and personalize a song.
3. Art song recitals (concerts) are typically performed without amplification in small to medium-size recital halls. This is why trained singers learn to sing with energized voices that can fill large spaces. Microphones and electronically amplified instruments help pop and rock musicians play to huge crowds in clubs or outdoor arenas. While jazz and standards vocalists also use microphones, they typically play to smaller, more intimate venues.
4. Composers of art song and musical theater consider words and music to be of equal importance. However, art song composers often set famous poetry by such well-known poets as Shakespeare, Emily Dickinson, and the great German and French poets Goethe, Heine, and Verlaine. Ideally, art songs are sung in the original language of the poet. Classically trained singers study Italian, German, French, and sometimes other languages and usually provide English translations of the foreign texts in programs so that the audience can follow the story or mood. Folk music and popular music is usually sung in the vernacular, or local, language.
5. Art songs are usually compositions for solo voice and piano. When other instruments are added or used instead of a piano, the compositions are called

chamber music. Folk singers may perform with just a guitar while popular singers may perform with piano or electronic keyboards, back-up singers, and an entire band.

These distinctions are not set in stone and there is increasing crossover (fusion) between art music and popular styles today. Many classically trained song composers (like David Baker and Davide Zannoni) also have jazz training and some of their art songs have a definite jazz flavor. Other contemporary art song composers (like Richard Pearson Thomas) infuse their art songs with Celtic and folk-like melodies. Libby Larson's *Cowboy Songs* and *Songs from Letters (Calamity Jane)* incorporate traditional elements of Americana. Still other composers like John Kander ("A Letter from Sullivan Ballou") write for both the concert hall and the Broadway stage.

Arias

Operatic arias are sung at points in an opera where the story line slows down to express emotion. Arias are designed to magnify the mood or the conflict the character is feeling. "I love you" sung on an extremely high note is far more dramatic than if it is simply spoken. This is why "opera buffs" are so passionate about opera—it gives them a real buzz. Many non-singers will gladly pay a fortune to see an opera anytime they have the chance.

Operas are big theatrical productions that demand big voices most of the time. Opera singers have to sing, usually with no microphone, over orchestras that may have 100 instrumentalists. This is why they spend years working on their voices.

Every opera has a story and each aria is part of that story. Therefore, singers need to know the context of the arias they sing. Oratorios, like Handel's *Messiah* (see "He Shall Feed His Flock like a Shepherd," p. 238), are similar to opera; however, they use biblical texts or tell a sacred story. Operas and oratorios also include recitatives (declamatory sections that move the story along), duets, and other ensembles (see *Hansel and Gretel* duet, p. 254), and chorus numbers.

COME AGAIN, SWEET LOVE (P. 217)

This song was published in John Dowland's *First Book of Songes or Ayres* in 1597. It was so popular that it was reprinted six times. He followed this success with a second and third book of airs. During Dowland's time "songs" and "airs" (or "songes" and "ayres") were used interchangeably to mean song. (*Note:* Though they are spelled similarly, an "air" is not the same thing as an "aria.")

Dowland lived in England during the time of Shakespeare and his songs were written for voice and lute, a stringed instrument that is a forerunner to today's guitar. Since the singer and the lutenist were often the same person, the texture of the accompaniment is kept light and unobtrusive so the singer can easily be heard. As Dowland wrote in the dedication for his First Book, "to the sweetness of instrument applies the lively voice of man, expressing some worthy sentence or excellent poem." The arrangement in this book is for piano and voice and if a guitarist is available the effect is even better.

Suggested recordings of "Come Again, Sweet Love" (iTunes):

GENRE: *Classical* □ Barbara Bonney: ***Fairest Isle,*** 2001, Decca

GENRE: *Classical* □ Jakob Lindberg and Rogers Covey-Crump: ***Dowland: The First Booke of Ayres,*** 1994, Bis

⏩If you like this song, take a look at the Dowland lute song "Goe Crystall Teares"

THE ANGLER'S SONG (DUET) (P. 219)

This fishing song by Henry Lawes, the leading English composer during the reign of Charles I, was first published in Izaak Walton's classic guide *The Compleat Angler* in 1653. Walton's best-selling book, which has been reprinted more than 300 times, tells the idyllic story of a fisherman, a hunter, and a fowler as they travel the river Lea in the spring. The story is sprinkled with illustrations, woodcuts, and practical fishing advice as well as writer's quotations and several songs. The singers in "The Angler's Song" rationalize that since life is just a "hodge-podge of bus'ness, and money, and care," you might as well go fishing! Interestingly, the music for Lawe's song was printed with the bass part upside down to allow the two singers to face each other while they sang.

Henry Lawes and his younger brother William Lawes (1602–1645) wrote more than 500 songs and set many texts by famous poets and playwrights, including Thomas Carew and John Milton. True to the musical taste of the time, the Lawes brothers wrote songs of courtly love, nymphs, and Arcadian shepherds. When William was killed in the Battle of Chester, Henry dedicated "A Pastoral Elegie: Cease you jolly shepherds" to his memory.

Suggested recording of "The Angler's Song" (CD):

Genre: *Classical* □ Robin Blaze: ***Henry and William Lawes: Songs,*** 2006, Hyperion

Suggested recordings of other Henry Lawes songs (iTunes):

Genre: *Classical* □ Paul Hillier and Nigel North: ***The Rags of Time: 17th c. English Lute Songs and Dances,*** 2002, Harmonia Mundi

⏩If you like this Henry Lawes song, take a look at the William Lawes song "Gather ye rosebuds while ye may"

Donzelle, fuggite (p. 221)

This aria or "canzone" (Italian for song) by Francesco Cavalli was probably inspired by Greek and Roman mythology. The maidens in "Donzelle, fuggite" are warned to run away from provocative beauty. If the look of love penetrates your heart, you will be wounded by its darts!

Like many outstanding song composers, Cavalli was himself a fine singer. He knew how to write expressive vocal lines to interweave with the instrumental lines. This is a "da capo" aria in ABA form, which means that the beginning and ending part are the same, with a contrasting, slower middle section. It is standard for the singer to add some *ornaments* (embellished notes) on the repeat of the A section. Cavalli wrote more than forty mostly forgotten Italian operas that contain arias in this style.

Suggested recording of "Donzelle, fuggite" (CD)

Genre: *Classical* □ Ezio Pinza: ***Early Italian Songs,*** 1993, Pearl

⏩If you like this song, take a look at the Cavalli aria "Fortunato mio cor"

Selve amiche, ombrose piante (p. 225)

Italian composer Antonio Caldara wrote hundreds of sacred and secular compositions and was one of the most famous composers of the Baroque era. "Selve amiche" is an *arietta* (little aria) from a long-forgotten opera, and, like many of Caldara's arias, it stands alone today as a concert or studio song. A special feature of this song is the use of a compositional technique called *melisma,* in which one word or syllable is set to several notes. Caldara uses 13 notes for the word "core" to show the unsteady nature of the singer's heart. Arie Antique of the seventeenth and eighteenth centuries, such as Caldara's "Selve amiche" and "Sebben crudele" have been voice lesson standards since they were collected and edited by Alessandro Parisotti (1853–1913) in the late 1800s. One hundred years later, John Glenn Paton edited a collection of these popular songs with an eye for historical accuracy and Baroque-style accompaniments. The songs that appear in the standard *24 (or 26) Italian Songs and Arias* have also received fresh new treatments in recordings by opera and pop singers (see "Star vicino," p. 229, arranged by Scarlett Antaloczy).

Suggested recordings of "Selve amiche" (iTunes):

Genre: *Classical* □ Cecilia Bartoli: ***Arie Antique,*** 1992, Decca

Genre: *Classical* □ Theresa Berganza: ***Brava Berganza!,*** rel. 2005, Deutsche Grammophon.

Genre: *Classical* □ Dimitri Hvorostovsky: ***Portrait,*** 2006, Decca

⏩If you like this song, take a look at the Caldara song "Alma del core"

Star vicino (p. 229)

For years, "Star vicino" has been wrongly attributed to composer Salvatore Rosa; most recent editions list the composer as "Anonymous." The unknown composer has left us with one of the simplest and most beautiful of the surviving Arie Antique (see "Selve amiche," p. 225). Scarlett Antaloczy's fresh new arrangement of this aria is in the style of crossover artists Josh Groban and Sarah Brightman. "Star vicino" is a *strophic* song, meaning that both verses of text are set to the same music (unlike the *da capo* form of "Donzelle, fuggite"). It is up to the singer to *ornament,* or embellish, the second verse by adding extra notes. In this song, the singer delights in being near the one he or she idolizes, then, in verse two, despairs at the thought of being parted from the loved one. The composer uses *melismas* (see "Selve amiche," p. 225) to emphasize the words "vago" (attractive) and "d'amore" (of love.)

Suggested recording of "Star vicino" (iTunes):

GENRE: *Classical* □ Sumi Jo: ***La Promessa,*** 1998, Erato

Alternate recording of "Star vicino" (CD):

GENRE: *Classical* □ James Rainbird: ***The Sublime Treble Voice of James Rainbird,*** rel. 2004, Priory

⏩If you like this song, take a look at the Arie Antique song "Tu lo sai" by Giuseppe Torelli

LUNGI (P. 233)

For nearly one hundred years, the songs of Paolo Tosti (1846–1916) have remained popular with tenors from Enrico Caruso to Placido Domingo to Andrea Bocelli. The lyrics of "Lungi," by Giosuè Carducci, are of a higher literary quality than most of the *sentimental songs* of the late 1800s; Carducci based his text on Heinrich Heine's famous romantic German poem "Auf Flügeln des Gesanges" (by Felix Mendelssohn; available online as a bonus song). Paolo Tosti was a trained singer and voice teacher in his native Italy before he traveled to London in his twenties, where he was appointed singing master to the royal family in 1880. Tosti became a British citizen in 1906 and was knighted "Sir" Francesco Paolo Tosti by King Edward VII. In addition to his Italian *melodia,* Tosti wrote many English songs, such as "Good-bye" (not to be confused with his "Addio," which also means "good-bye"). By the turn of the century, Tosti's song sheets were on nearly every middle- and upper-class parlor piano in England and America. So many copies were printed that today it is relatively easy to find Tosti songs in bins of old sheet music at antique stores. If you are lucky, you might even find the 1912 ragtime parody tune titled "Mr. Tosti, Why Did You Write 'Good Bye'?"

Suggested recording of "Lungi" (CD):

GENRE: *Classical* □ Renato Bruson: ***Tosti: Romanze su Testi Italiani,*** rel. 2006, AMG

Suggested recordings of other Tosti songs (iTunes):

GENRE: *Classical* □ Andrea Bocelli: ***Sentimento,*** 2003, Decca

GENRE: *Classical* □ Ben Heppner: ***Ben Heppner Sings the Songs of Paulo Tosti,*** 2003, Deutsche Grammophon

GENRE: *Classical* □ Enrico Caruso: ***Italian Songs,*** rel. 2002, BMG

⏩If you like this song, take a look at "Serenata" by Paulo Tosti

HE SHALL FEED HIS FLOCK (ARIA AND RECITATIVE) FROM *MESSIAH* (P. 238)

The alto solo from Handel's oratorio *Messiah* "recites" or announces God's healing miracles, then sings tenderly of the good shepherd's care. This is an example of a "recitative" paired with an "aria." The first part is in a rather speech-like singing style. The second part is beautifully and lyrically sung, with a warm expressive tone.

Most people are familiar with the "Hallelujah Chorus" from *Messiah,* even if they haven't heard the entire work. *Messiah* is regularly performed in America, especially at Christmas time. In Handel's time, however, *Messiah* wasn't just a holiday offering. People flocked to the performances as if it were a modern-day Broadway hit. Handel, who was born in Germany, originally wrote *Messiah* in English. When he wrote it, he had been living in England for nearly thirty years—a German composer writing Italian opera and English oratorio in London.

Suggested recordings of "He Shall Feed His Flock" (iTunes):

GENRE: *Classical* □ Anna Sophie von Otter: ***Handel: Messiah,*** 1988, Deutsche Grammophon

GENRE: *Classical* □ Marian Anderson: ***The RCA Victor Vocal Series: Marian Anderson,*** pre-1972, rel. 1989, RCA

⏩If you like this song, take a look at the alto aria "O Thou That Tellest Good Tidings to Zion," from *Messiah*

ICH LIEBE DICH (P. 241)

This *Lied* (German song) is also known as "Zärtliche Liebe" ("Tender Love") and is probably the most famous of Ludwig van Beethoven's

(1770–1827) 65 solo songs. Students who are only familiar with Beethoven's loud, heroic, orchestral music are often surprised at the sweetness and simplicity of the Lieder that he wrote for singers to perform at home with the "new" pianoforte (the piano in Beethoven's time was a status symbol of middle-class wealth, much like today's iPod and home theater systems). For the text of this *haus musik* (house music), Beethoven chose a poem of enduring love and commitment: "I love you in the morning and in the evening, through times of joy and times of weeping." The song is a prayer that God will "protect and keep us both." This song works equally well performed by a man or woman, and there are many recordings available by famous singers such as Fritz Wunderlich and Kirsten Fladstad. An excellent modern recording of "Ich liebe dich" can be heard on the opening track of Finnish soprano Karita Mattila's *Wild Rose* CD. Musical America (www.musicalamerica.com) named Mattila their 2005 Musician of the Year, claiming that with the beauty of a movie star and the charisma of a rock star, Mattila "renews an aging art form and drives the public into frenzies."

Suggested recordings of "Ich liebe dich" (iTunes):

Genre: *Classical* □ Karita Mattila: ***Wild Rose,*** 2005, IMG

Genre: *Classical* □ Fritz Wunderlich: ***The Arts of Fritz Wunderlich,*** rel. 2005, Deutsche Grammophon

Genre: *Classical* □ Kirsten Flagstad: ***The Early Recordings, 1914–1941,*** rel. 1995, Simax

⏩If you like this song, take a look at the Beethoven song "Der Kuss" (The Kiss)

If You've Only Got a Moustache (p. 245)

In "If You've Only Got a Moustache," Stephen Collins Foster (1826–1864) and lyricist George Cooper reveal to men that the secret to success with women is to grow facial hair! Foster wrote nearly 300 songs, which have become an important part of our American history and are still popular today. To keep up with the demand for new songs, Foster wrote a variety of sentimental songs (such as "Jeannie with the Light Brown Hair" and "Beautiful Dreamer"), laments (such as the online bonus song "Gentle Annie"), songs of hope (such as "There's a Good Time Coming"), and some very funny songs like "There Are Plenty of Fish in the Sea" and "My Wife is a Most Knowing Woman." Most of Stephen Foster's songs are about people and places in the American south. However, this composer of "Oh, Susanna!" certainly didn't come from Alabama with a banjo on his knee. He was born in Pennsylvania and wrote most of his songs in Pittsburgh. Foster's controversial "negro" songs about the pre–Civil War South ("Old Folks at Home," "Camptown Races," "Massa's in de Cold, Cold Ground"), written for minstrel shows, are now politically inappropriate unless considered in their historical setting.

Suggested recordings of "If You've Only Got a Moustache" (iTunes):

Genre: *Classical* □ Jan de Gaetani and Gilbert Kalish: ***Songs by Stephen Foster,*** 2005, Rhino Entertainment

Genre: *Classical* □ Douglas Jimerson: ***Stephen Foster's America,*** 2004, AmeriMusic

⏩If you like this song, take a look at the Foster song "There Are Plenty of Fish in the Sea"

O Mistress Mine (p. 248)

"O mistress mine, where are you roaming?" is the song of Feste, the clown, in the second act of William Shakespeare's comedy *Twelfth Night*. Shakespeare's famous text has been set to music by many prominent British and American composers, including Ralph Vaughan Williams, Amy Beach, Peter Warlock, Erich Korngold, Gerald Finzi, Percy Grainger, Roger Quilter, Theodore Chanler, and Sir Arthur Sullivan. Sir Charles Villiers Stanford (1852–1924) wrote *The Clown's Songs from Twelfth Night*, Op. 65, which includes "O Mistress Mine," "Come away, death," and "The rain it raineth every day." The theme of "O Mistress Mine" is *carpe diem*—life is short and we must live for the pleasures of the moment. "Present mirth has present laughter. What's to come is still unsure."

Note the melodic leaps up and down on the words "sing both high and low" and the sudden impulsive *forte* and *sforzando* (loud and strongly accented) on the command "Then come kiss me, sweet and twenty." Stanford was an Irish-born composer and music teacher who was knighted in 1902 for his valuable contributions to British music. Stanford's music, often overshadowed by that of his former students—Vaughan Williams, Gustav Holst, and John Ireland, of the Royal College of Music and Cambridge University—has seen a resurgence in recent years.

Suggested recordings of "O Mistress Mine" by Stanford and other composers (iTunes):

GENRE: *Classical* □ Stephen Varcoe: ***Stanford Songs, Vol. 1,*** 2000, Hyperion

GENRE: *Classical* □ Emma Kirkby: ***Amy Beach: Chanson d'amour,*** 2002, Bis ("O Mistress Mine" by Amy Beach from ***Three Shakespeare Songs,*** Op. 37)

GENRE: *Classical* □ Bryn Terfel: ***Silent Noon,*** 2005, Deutsche Grammophon ("O Mistress Mine" by Roger Quilter from ***Three Shakespeare Songs,*** Op. 6)

⏩ If you like this song, take a look at the Stanford song "Windy Nights"

EL MAJO TIMIDO (P. 251)

A young girl waits every night for the handsome, timid boy who comes to her window. Will he have the courage to speak to her this time? Alas, no! As soon as he sees her, he runs away—again! The text by Fernando Periquet is somewhat ambiguous, so it is up to the singer to decide if she is truly amused by this nightly escapade, or if she is being sarcastic.

The composer, Enrique Granados, was born in the Catalonian province of Spain. He studied music in Paris and then returned to Barcelona to become one of the most famous Spanish composers. Many of his songs are short and playful, with a guitar-like pattern in the piano accompaniment.

Suggested recordings of "El majo timido" (iTunes):

GENRE: *Classical* □ Teresa Berganza: ***Brava Berganza!: A Birthday Tribute,*** rel. 2005, Deutsche Grammophon

GENRE: *Classical* □ Victoria de los Ángeles: ***Ars Musicae de Barcelona,*** rel. 1999, EMI

GENRE: *Classical* □ María Lluïsa Muntada: ***Enric Granados: Integral de l'obra per a veu i piano,*** 1996, Lleida

⏩ If you like this song, take a look at the Granados song "El majo discreto"

EVENING PRAYER (DUET), FROM *HANSEL AND GRETEL* (P. 254)

In the first act of Humperdinck's fairy tale opera by the Brothers Grimm, the two children, Hansel and Gretel, are lost in the woods. As night descends they find a spot to sleep in the forest and pray that the angels will watch over them.

This lovely duet has been sung all over the world as a bedtime prayer and is included on some lullaby recordings. Though the opera's story has some gruesome elements, like abandoning children in the woods and threatening to bake them into cookies, it remains a favorite with adults and children. Perhaps it is because of Humperdinck's folk-like music; the colorful characters of the Witch, the Sand Man, and the Dew Fairy; or simply because we know how the story ends.

Suggested recordings of "Evening Prayer" (iTunes):

GENRE: *Classical* □ Andreas Delfs, dir.: ***Hansel and Gretel*** by Engelbert Humperdinck. Milwaukee Symphony Orchestra, 2006, Avie

GENRE: *Classical* □ Wendy Loder: ***Yestertime Songs for Children,*** 2001, Wendy Loder

⏩ If you like this song, take a look at the Dew Fairy's song from Act III of ***Hansel and Gretel***

SUMMERTIME, FROM *PORGY AND BESS* (P. 256)

The character of Clara has only a supporting role in Gershwin's famous folk opera, yet she gets the best song. "Summertime" is a lullaby that Clara sings to her baby in Act I, and then again as a "reprise" (repeated section) in Act II. Finally, in a very poignant scene after Clara and her husband Jake have drowned in the river, the character of Bess sings "Summertime" to the newly orphaned baby.

Gershwin suggested to DuBose Heyward that they collaborate on an opera after reading Heyward's novel *Porgy.* Heyward wrote the *libretto* (the script) for the opera and some of the song texts, including "Summertime." This tender lullaby has been recorded by thousands of classical, jazz, pop, and folk singers around the world. The Houston Grand Opera soundtrack (which won a Tony award and two Grammys) is generally considered the definitive recording of the complete opera.

Suggested recordings of "Summertime" (iTunes):

GENRE: *Classical* □ Clamma Dale: "Summertime" from ***Porgy and Bess.*** Houston Grand Opera, rel. 1985, BMG

GENRE: *Classical* □ Anna Moffo: "Summertime" on ***Classical Music Library, Vol. 8: American Classics,*** 2005, Readers Digest

GENRE: *Classical* □ Billie Holiday, "Summertime" on ***The Great Songs of George Gershwin,*** 1958, Sony

⏩If you like this song, take a look at "My Man's Gone Now" from ***Porgy and Bess***

OH, BETTER FAR TO LIVE AND DIE, FROM *THE PIRATES OF PENZANCE* (P. 259)

THE SUN, WHOSE RAYS ARE ALL ABLAZE, FROM *THE MIKADO* (P. 263)

During London's Victorian era, lyricist William S. Gilbert teamed up with composer Arthur A. Sullivan to create a highly successful series of *operettas* (comic light operas), which are still performed frequently in England and the United States. Some of the most popular Gilbert and Sullivan operettas performed by the famed D'Oyly Carte Opera Company included *The Pirates of Penzance, The Mikado, The Yeomen of the Guard,* and *H.M.S. Pinafore.* The plots are comical and convoluted, with stock characters such as a young heroic tenor, a sweet soprano ingénue, a pair of villains (contralto and baritone), and a character to stop the show with a hilarious patter song (see the online bonus patter song, "Modern Major General"). In *The Pirates of Penzance,* the Pirate King extols the virtues of a life of crime with, "Oh, better far to live and die under the great black flag I fly." Gilbert and Sullivan's Pirate King is similar to Barrie's Captain Hook in *Peter Pan* and Johnny Depp's Captain Jack Sparrow in the recent *Pirates of the Caribbean* films.

The Pirate King is successful because he is clever. Not so the heroine Yum Yum in *The Mikado.* Think Elle Woods in *Legally Blonde* or Phoebe in the sitcom *Friends*. What Yum Yum lacks in intelligence, however, she makes up for with beauty and charm. Her lovely ballad pays homage to the beauty of nature and her own loveliness on her wedding day: "I am a child of nature, and take after my mother."

Suggested Gilbert and Sullivan recordings (iTunes):

GENRE: *Classical* □ Isidore Godfrey, dir.: "Oh, better far to live and die" from ***Gilbert & Sullivan: Highlights and Overtures.*** D'Oyly Carte Opera and Orchestra, rel. 2004, Avid

GENRE: *Classical* □ Valerie Masterson: "The sun, whose rays are all ablaze" from ***The Ultimate Gilbert & Sullivan Collection.*** Royal Philharmonic Orchestra, Royston Nash, dir. 1998, Decca

⏩If you like these songs, take a look at "Poor Wand'ring One" (from ***The Pirates of Penzance***) and "When I Was a Lad" (from ***H.M.S. Pinafore***)

TOI, LE COEUR DE LA ROSE (*AIR DE L'ENFANT*) (P. 267)

In Maurice Ravel's (1875–1937) fantasy opera *L'enfant et les sortilèges* (The Child and the Spells), an unruly boy throws a temper tantrum, breaking his toys and disrespecting his mother. As punishment, the boy must stay in his room without any supper, where the furniture, stuffed animals, and toys come to life to reprimand the naughty boy. The beautiful storybook princess, torn from a page in the boy's favorite fairy tale, appears in the room to sing farewell to the boy. Saddened, he sings the lovely, simple song, "Toi, le coeur de la rose" ("You, the heart of the rose"). This song is also known as "Air de l'enfant" ("Song of the child") and is generally considered to be Ravel's tribute to the composer Jules Massenet (1842–1912).

Modern audiences may be reminded of a similar story by another Maurice—Maurice Sendak, who wrote and illustrated the popular children's book "Where the Wild Things Are." In 1999, the New York City Opera staged a production of Ravel's *L'enfant et les sortilèges* on a set designed by Maurice Sendak.

Suggested recordings of "Toi, le couer de la rose" (iTunes):

GENRE: *Classical* □ André Previn, dir.: ***L'Enfant et les sortilèges,*** by Maurice Ravel. London Symphony Orchestra, 1999, Deutsche Grammophon

GENRE: *Classical* □ Lorin Maazel, dir.: ***L'Enfant et les sortilèges,*** by Maurice Ravel. Berlin Philharmonic, 1997, Deutsche Grammophon

⏩If you like this song, take a look at the Ravel song "Chanson française"

THE HIPPOPOTAMUS (P. 270)

For years the humorous satirical songs of the English songwriting team Flanders and Swann existed only on stage and in live recordings of their hit revue *At the Drop of a Hat*. The show was enormously popular with London theatergoers in the late 1950s and early 1960s. Swann admits that "so-called composer that I was, I never wrote any [of the songs] down. Michael improvised [lyrics] when he felt like it, constantly improving and altering. I varied the accompaniments and laughed anew as the jokes grew. Most of the music remained in my mind." Public demand for printed versions of Flanders and Swann's songs was high, but Flanders insisted that their performances couldn't be written down. It was only after her father's death in 1975 that Claudia Flanders convinced Donald Swann to preserve "The Hippopotamus" and other songs for future generations. In the foreword to *The Songs of Michael Flanders and Donald Swann* (1977, second edition 1996) Swann writes, "The songs can be taken from these pages, and can grow again in your, the player's hands, with your or another's voice. Each singer will do what he pleases, and so he should."

Suggested recording of "The Hippopotamus" (iTunes):

GENRE: *Classical* □ John Lithgow: ***Singing in the Bathtub***, 1999, Sony

⏩If you like this song, take a look at Flanders and Swann's "The Gnu Song"

COME READY AND SEE ME (P. 273)

"Come Ready and See Me" is American composer Richard Hundley's (b. 1931) best-known song. The poem is by Hundley's close friend, James Purdy, who also wrote "Waterbird." "Come Ready and See Me" is frequently sung by women; however, tenor David Park's recent recording proves that it can also be a haunting ballad for a man. Almost anyone can relate to the experience of longing for the return of a loved one ("come ready and see me before it's too late . . . before the years run out.") The few Hundley songs available have been staples in the voice studio for decades, and artists such as Park, Paul Sperry, and Fredericka Von Stade have performed them regularly in recitals, even though until recently there were very few recordings and limited publication of his songs. Accessibility of Hundley's lesser-known art songs should now ensure their places in the voice studio and recital hall. In *Song: A Guide to Art Song Style and Literature*, Carol Kimball writes that Richard Hundley is one of only twelve composers (including Samuel Barber and Aaron Copland) recognized as a "standard American composer for vocalists" by the International American Music Competition sponsored by Carnegie Hall and the Rockefeller Foundation. Hundley's melodic style—a crossover between art music and American musical theater/cabaret—was ahead of its time in the 1970s, when much art music was deliberately dissonant and avant-garde. Hundley led the way for many contemporary art-song composers, including Lori Laitman, Ricky Ian Gordon, Richard Pearson Thomas, and Ben Moore.

Suggested recording of "Come Ready and See Me" (CD):

GENRE: *Classical* □ David Parks and Read Gainsford: ***Under the Bluest Skies: Songs of Richard Hundley***, 2007, David Parks

"Come Ready and See Me" is also available as a free audio file at www.richardhundley.com.

⏩If you like this song, take a look at the Hundley song "Waterbird"

Come Again, Sweet Love

Words and Music by John Dowland
(1563–1626)

For background and performance notes, see page 210.

PART TWO

Moderate ♩ = 88
1. Come a -
2. Come a -

gain, Sweet love doth now in - vite Thy
gain, That I may cease to mourn Thro'

Art Songs

grac - es that re - frain To do me due de - light, To see,
thy un - kind dis - dain; For now, left and for - lorn, I sit,
pp

cresc.
11
(,)
(,)
— to hear, — to touch, — to kiss, — to die —
— I sigh, — I weep, — I faint, — I die —
cresc.
14
— With thee a - gain in sweet-est sym - pa - thy, To see, —
— In dead - ly pain and end - less mis - er - y, I sit, —
17
(,)
(,)
— to hear, — to touch, — to kiss, — to die —
— I sigh, — I weep, — I faint, — I die —
20
rall.
— With thee a - gain in sweet - est sym - pa - thy.
— In dead - ly pain and end - less mis - er - y.
rall.

The Angler's Song
(Duet)

Words by Isaak Walton
(1593–1683)

Music by Henry Lawes
(1596–1662)

For background and performance notes, see page 210.

*alternate text

Donzelle, fuggite

Damsels, run away

(Italian)

Donzelle, fuggite procace beltà! [dontsɛlle, fuddʒitte prrokatʃe belta]	**Damsels, run away from provocative beauty!**
Fuggite, fuggite, fuggite! [fuddʒitte fuddʒitte fuddʒitte]	**Run away, run away, run away!**
Se lucido sguardo vi pénetra‿il core, [se lutʃido zgwarrdo vi penɛtrrail kɔre]	**If seductive glances penetrate your heart,**
Lasciate quel dardo del perfido‿amore, [laʃate kwel darrdo del perrfidoamore]	**Escape [Cupid's] arrow of perfidious love**
Che‿insidie scaltrite tramando vi sta! [keinsidje skaltrrite trramando vi sta]	**that attempts to trap you!**

Donzelle, fuggite

(Damsels, Run Away!)

Words and Music by Francesco Cavalli
(1602–1676)
Arranged by Cynthia Lee Fox

For background and performance notes, see page 211.

18
Fug - gi - te, fug - gi - te, fug - gi - te! Don - zel - le fug - gi - te pro -

24
2nd time to Coda
ca - ce bel - tà!

29
Se lu - ci - do sguar - do vi pén - e - tra il

34
co - - - - - re, las -

39
cia - te quel dar - do del per - fi - do a - mo - re, che in si - die scal -

44
tri - te tra - man - do vi sta!

49
D.S. al CODA
Don -

54
CODA

Selve amiche, ombrose piante

Forest friendly

(Italian)

Selve amiche, ombrose piante [sɛlve amike ɔmbrrɔze pjante]	**Forest friendly, shady plants**
fido‿albergo del mio core. [fidoalbɛrrgo dɛl mio cɔre]	**Faithful shelter of my heart**
chiede‿a voi quest'alma‿amante [kjɛdea vɔi kwɛstalmamante]	**This soul loving asks of you**
qualche pace al suo dolore [kwalke patʃe a suo dɔlɔre]	**Some peace from its sadness**

PART TWO

Selve amiche, ombrose piante

(Kindly forest)

Arietta

Music by Antonio Caldara
(1670–1736)

For background and performance notes, see page 211.

Art Songs

13
fi - do al - ber - - - - - - go del mio co - -
(,)
17
- re, chie - de a voi que - st'al - ma a - man - te
p
p
21
cresc.
qual - che pa - ce, qual - che pa - ce al suo do - lo - - - re,
cresc.
25
cresc.
assai
f rit.
qual - che pa - ce, qual - che pa - ce al suo do - lo - - re.
cresc.
assai
f rit.

29
p
Sel - ve a - mi - che, om - bro - se pian - te, fi - do al - ber - go
p
32
del mio co - - - - re, fi - do al - ber - -
35
rit.
tr
- - - - - - go del mio co - - - -
rit.
38
- re.
f a tempo
rit. assai.

Star vicino

To Be Near

(Italian)

Star vicino‿al bell'idol che s'ama [starr vitʃinoal bɛllidol ke sama]	To be near the beautiful idol that one loves
è‿il piu vago diletto d'amor [eilpju vago dilɛtto damorr]	is the most vague delight of love.
Star lontano dal ben ke si brama [starr lontano dal ben kɛ si brama]	To be far away from the beloved who is desired
è d'amore‿il più vivo dolor [e damoreilpju vivo dolor]	is the most vital sadness of love.

Star vicino

Anonymous, c. 1600
Contemporary arrangement by Scarlett Antaloczy

For background and performance notes, see page 211.

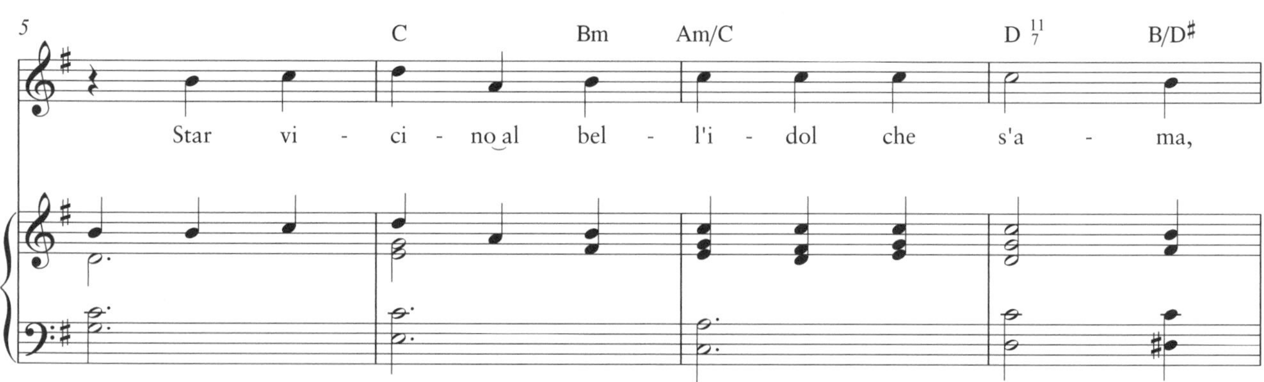

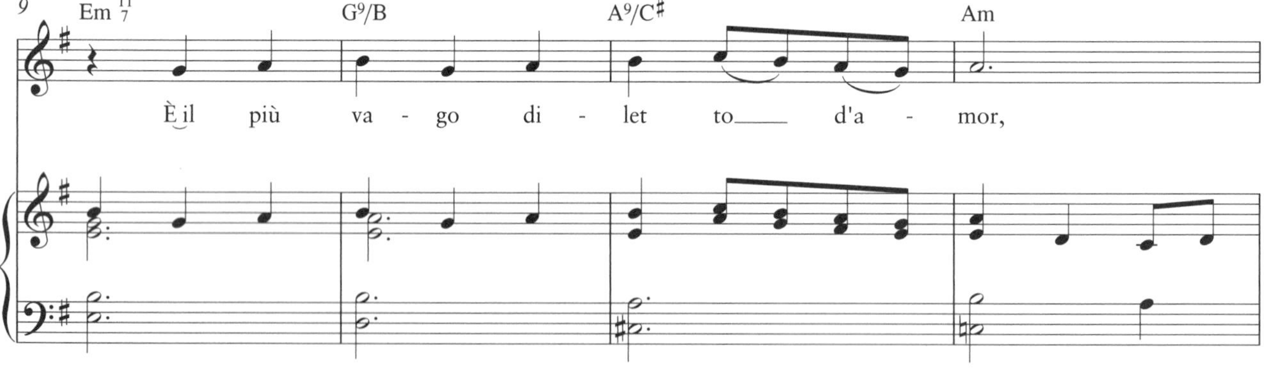

13
D7sus4
G
G/F♯
C/E
G/D
G9/C
G/B
È il più va - - - - - - - - -
17
Am
Gmaj7/B
Gmaj7
Cmaj♯11 7
Cmaj7
- - - go di - let to d'a - mor.
rit.
21
a tempo
mf
l.h. melody
Star lon -
26
C
Bm
Am/C
D11 7
B/D♯
E11 7
ta - no dal ben che si bra - ma, È da -

30
G9/D
A9/C♯
Am
D7sus4
mo - re il più vi - vo dor - lor.
È da
34
G
G/F♯
C/E
G/D
G9/C
G/B
Am
mo - - - - - - - - - - - - -
38
Gmaj7/B
Gmaj7
Cmaj♯11 7
G
G/F♯
C/E
G/D
re il più ri - vo do - lor.
mf
42
G9/C
G/B
Am
D
G
rit.
p dim.
pppp

Lungi

Long (far away)

(Italian)

Lungi, lungi, sull'ali del canto [lundʒi lundʒi sullali dɛl cɑnto]	Away, away on the wings of song
di qui lungi recare‿io ti vo' [di kwi lundʒl rekɑreio ti vo]	I wish to carry you away.
Là, nei campi fioriti del santo Gange, [la nei kampi fjɔriti dɛl sɑnto gɑndʒe]	There in the flourishing banks of the holy Ganges
un luogo bellissimo io so. [un lwogo bɛllissimo io so]	I know a beautiful place,
Ivi rosso‿un giardino risplende [ivi rɔssoun dʒɑrrdino risplɛnde]	A red, resplendent garden.
Della luna nel cheto chiaror. [dɛlla luna nɛl keto kjɑrɔrr]	In the quiet moonlight
Ivi‿il fiore del loto ti‿attende, [ivil fjɔre dɛlloto tiattɛnde]	The lotus flowers await,
o soave sorella die fior. [o soɑve sɔrellɑ di fjɔrr]	Oh gentle flower sisters.
Le viole bisbiglian vezzose, [le vjɔle bisbiʎɑn vɛttsoze]	The violets whisper,
guardan gli‿astri su alto passar; [gwɑrrdan ʎɑstrri su ɑlto pɑssɑrr]	Gaze at the stars that pass high
E fra loro si chinan le rose odorose novelle‿a cantar [e frrɑ loɾo si kinɑn lɛ rrose odoroze novɛlleakɑntɑrr]	And bend between them the fragrant rose stories and sing.
O, che sensi d'amore di calma [o ke sɛnsi dɑmɔre di kɑlmɑ]	Oh that sense of calm love
beveremo nell'aure colà [bevɛremo nɛllɑure kolɑ]	Drinks endlessly.
Sogneremo, seduti a‿una palma. [soɲeremo sedutiɑuna palmɑ]	We dream under a palm tree,
Lunghi sogni di felicetà [luŋgi soɲi di fɛlitʃitɑ]	Long dreams of happiness.

— *translation adapted from "Auf Flügeln des Gesanges" by Heinrich Heine.*

Lungi

(Far Away)

Words by
Parole di Giosuè Carducci
(1835–1918)
based on "Auf Flügeln des Gesanges"
by Heinrich Heine

Music by
Francesco Paolo Tosti
(1846–1916)

For background and performance notes, see page 212.

10
cresc.
ros - so un giar - di - no ri - splen - de Del - la lu - na nel che - to chia
cresc.
13
rit.
pp
a tempo
ror: I - vi il fio - re del lo - to ti at - ten - de, o so -
rit.
pp
a tempo
16
a - ve so - rel - la dei fior, I - vi il fio - re del lo - to ti at -
19
pp
rit.
ppp
ten.
a tempo
ten - de, o so - a - ve so - rel - la dei fior.
a tempo
pp
col canto
p
pp

22
p
Le vi-
26
p
o - le bi - sbi - glian vez - zo - se, guar-dan gli a - stri su al - to pas-
29
(,)
p
sar; E fra lo - ro si chi - nan le ro - se o - do - ro - se no - vel - le a can
33
sentito
tar. O, che sen - si d'a-mo - re di cal - ma, Be - ve - re - mo nel - l'au - re co-

37
rit.
pp
a tempo
là! Sogne-re-mo, se-du-ti a u-na pal-ma. Lunghi so-gni di fe-li-ci-
rit.
a tempo
pp
41
tà, So-gne-re-mo, se-du ti a u-na pal-ma. Lun-ghi
pp
pp
44
ppp
ten.
rit.
a tempo
so-gni di fe-li-ci-tà, se-du-ti a u-na
rit.
a tempo
p
col canto
p
47
rit.
pal-ma, So-gne-re-mo.
pp rit.
col canto
ppp
rit.

PART TWO

Art Songs

He Shall Feed His Flock

from *Messiah*

Music by George Frideric Handel
(1685–1759)

For background and performance notes, see page 212.

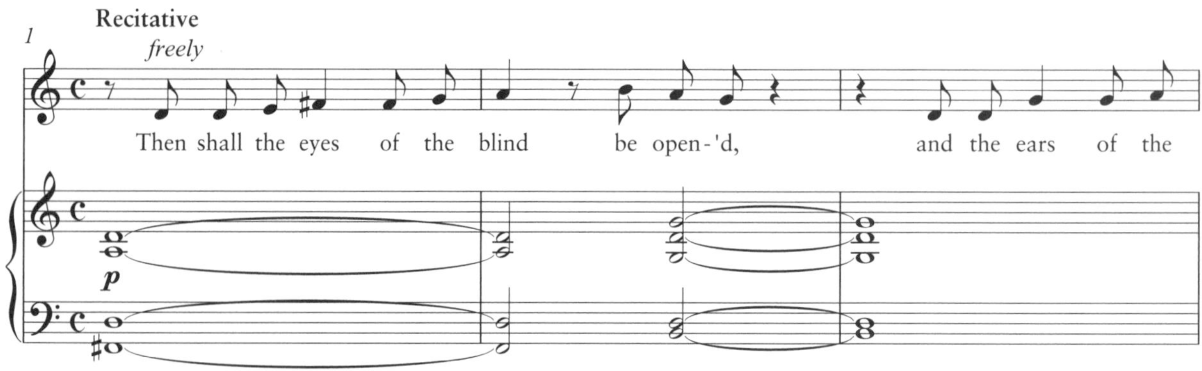

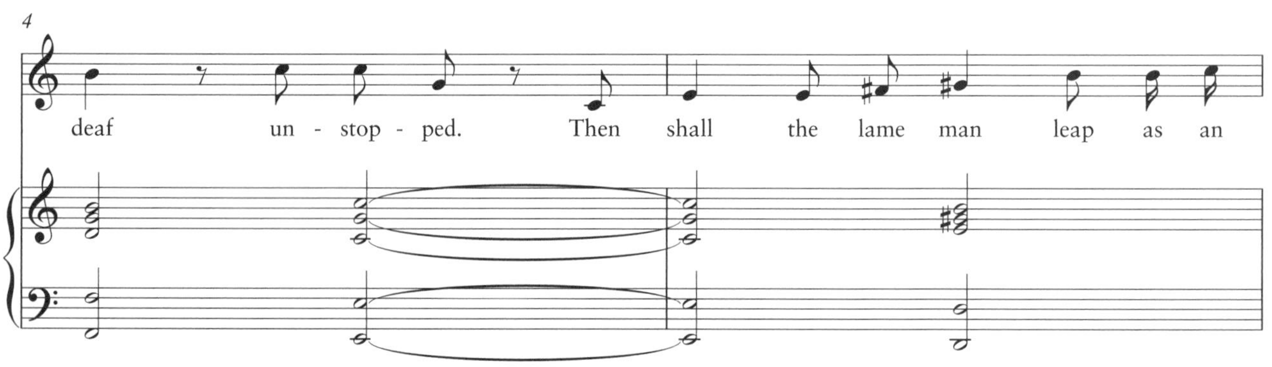

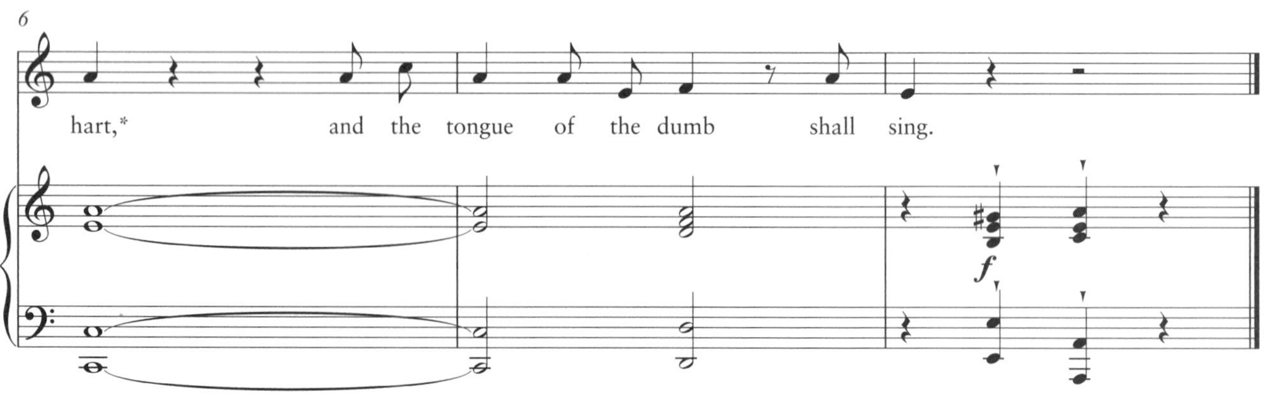

*deer

Aria
♩. = 140
p
He shall feed His flock like a shep - herd, and
He shall ga - ther the lambs with His arm, with His arm,
cresc.
He shall feed His flock like a shep - herd, and
p

13
(,)
,
He shall ga - ther the lambs with His arm,
with His arm,
cresc.
16
and car - ry them in His bo - som, and
p
19
(,)
,
,
gen - tly lead those that are with young, and gen - tly lead those, and
22
(,)
gen - tly lead those that are with young.

Ich liebe dich (Zärtliche Liebe)

I Love You (Tender Love)

(German)

Ich liebe dich, so wie du mich, [ɪç libə dɪç zo vi du mɪç]	I love you as you love me,
am Abend und am Morgen [am ɑbend ʊnd am mɔrgən]	In the evening and in the morning.
noch war kein Tag, wo du und ich [noç vɑɾ kɑin tɑk vo du ʊnt ɪç]	There never was a day where you and I
nicht theilten uns're Sorgen. [nɪçt tɑiltən unsɾə zɔɾgən]	Did not share our cares.
Auch waren sie für dich und mich [ɑʊx vɑɾən zi fyɾ dɪç ʊnt mɪç]	Also, for you and me
getheilt licht zu ertragen, [gətɑilt lɪçt tsu ɛɾtragən]	This sharing was light to endure.
Du tröstetest im Kummer mich, [du trøstətɛst ɪm kʊmmer mɪç]	You comforted me in distress.
ich weint' in deine Klagen, [ɪç vɑint ɪn dɑinə klɑgən]	I wept in your complaint,
Drum Gottes Segen über dir [drum gɔttəs zegən ybər diɾ]	That God's blessing be over you,
du meines Lebens Freude, [du mɑinəs lebəns fɾɔidə]	You, my life's joy.
Gott schütze dich, erhalt dich mir, [gɔtt ʃytsə dɪç ɛɾhɑlt diç miɾ]	God protect you and keep you,
schütz' und erhalt' uns beide [ʃyts ʊnt ɛɾhɑlt ʊns bɑidə]	Protect and keep us both.

Ich liebe dich (Zärtliche Liebe)

WoO 123 *(Herrosee)*

Words and Music by Ludwig van Beethoven
(1770–1827)

For background and performance notes, see page 212.

Andante ♩ = 84
Ich lie - be dich, so wie du mich, am A - bend und am Mor - gen, noch
p

war kein Tag, wo du und ich nicht theil - ten uns' - re Sor - gen.
mf

Auch wa - ren sie für dich und mich ge -
p

13
theilt leicht zu— er - tra - gen, du trö - ste - test im Kum - mer mich, ich—
17
weint' in dei - ne Kla - gen, in dei - ne Kla - gen. Drum
f
p dolce
21
Got - tes Se - gen ü - ber dir du mei - nes Le - bens
cresc.
p
24
Freu - de, Gott— schü - tze dich, er - halt' dich mir, schütz'
f

27
dim.
p
f
und er - halt' uns beide, Gott schü - tze dich, er -
dim.
p
30
halt' dich mir, schütz' und er - halt' uns
dim.
33
bei - de, er - halt', er - halt' uns bei - de, er - halt' uns
cresc.
f
37
bei - - - de.

If You've Only Got a Moustache

Words by
George Cooper

Music by Stephen C. Foster
(1826–1864)

For background and performance notes, see page 213.

With spirit ♩. = 72
8va

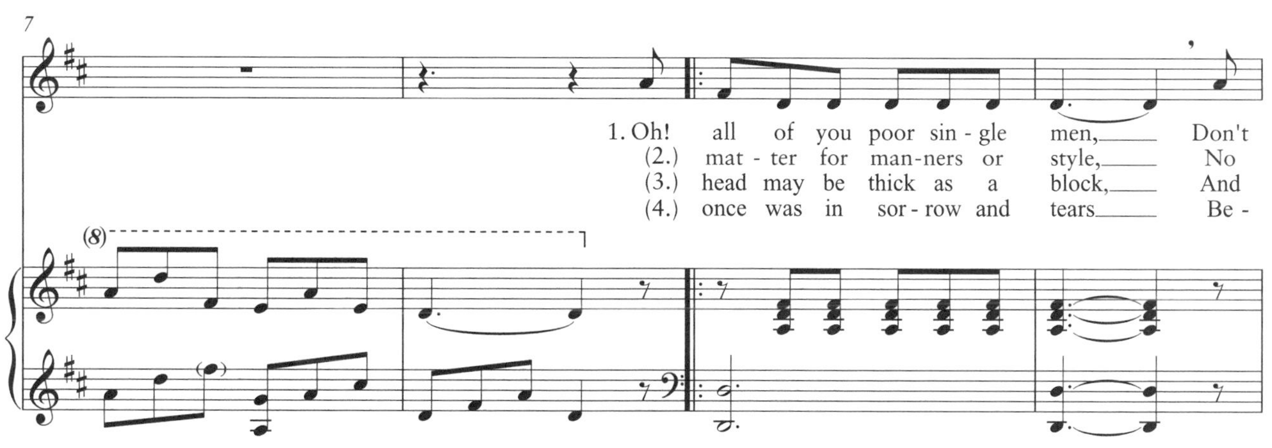
1. Oh! all of you poor sin - gle men, Don't
(2.) mat - ter for man-ners or style, No
(3.) head may be thick as a block, And
(4.) once was in sor - row and tears Be -
(8)

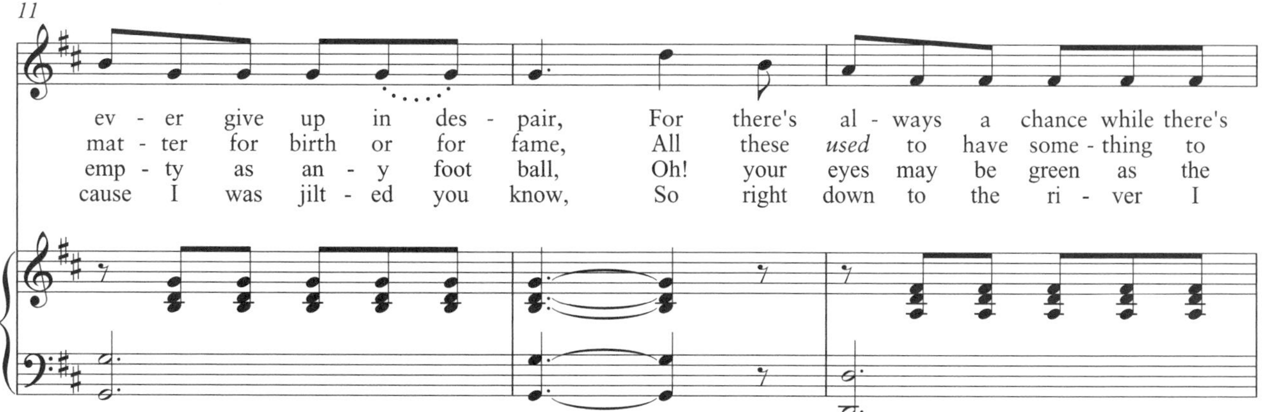
ev - er give up in des - pair, For there's al - ways a chance while there's
mat - ter for birth or for fame, All these used to have some - thing to
emp - ty as an - y foot ball, Oh! your eyes may be green as the
cause I was jilt - ed you know, So right down to the ri - ver I

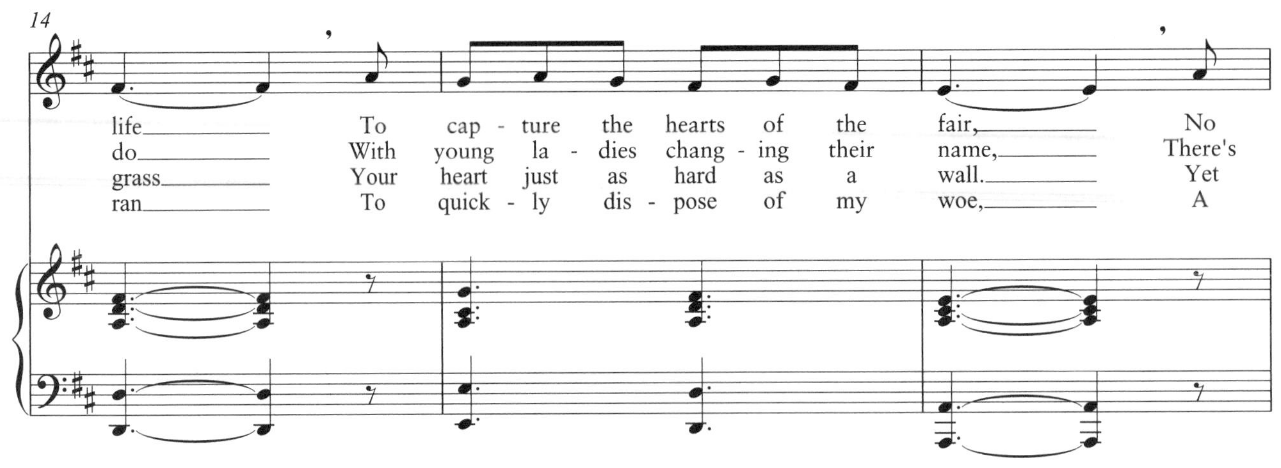
14
life_ To cap - ture the hearts of the fair,_ No
do_ With young la - dies chang - ing their name,_ There's
grass_ Your heart just as hard as a wall._ Yet
ran_ To quick - ly dis - pose of my woe,_ A

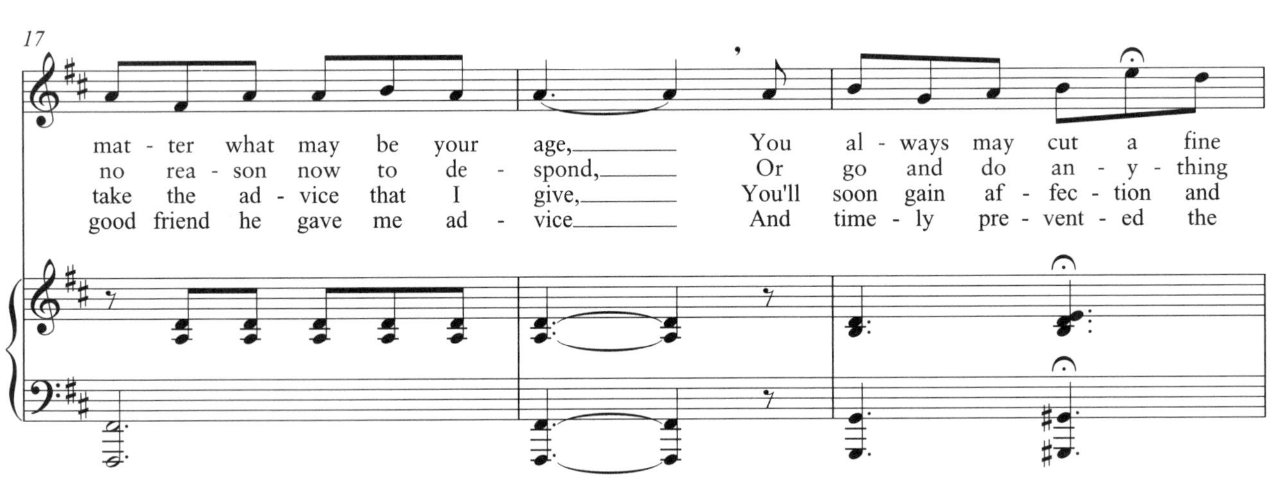
17
mat - ter what may be your age,_ You al - ways may cut a fine
no rea - son now to de - spond,_ Or go and do an - y - thing
take the ad - vice that I give,_ You'll soon gain af - fec - tion and
good friend he gave me ad - vice_ And time - ly pre - vent - ed the

20
dash,_ You will suit all the girls to a hair_ If you've
rash,_ For you'll do though you can't raise a cent,_ If you'll
cash,_ And will be all the rage with the girls,_ If you'll
splash,_ Now at home I've a good wife and ten heirs,_ And all

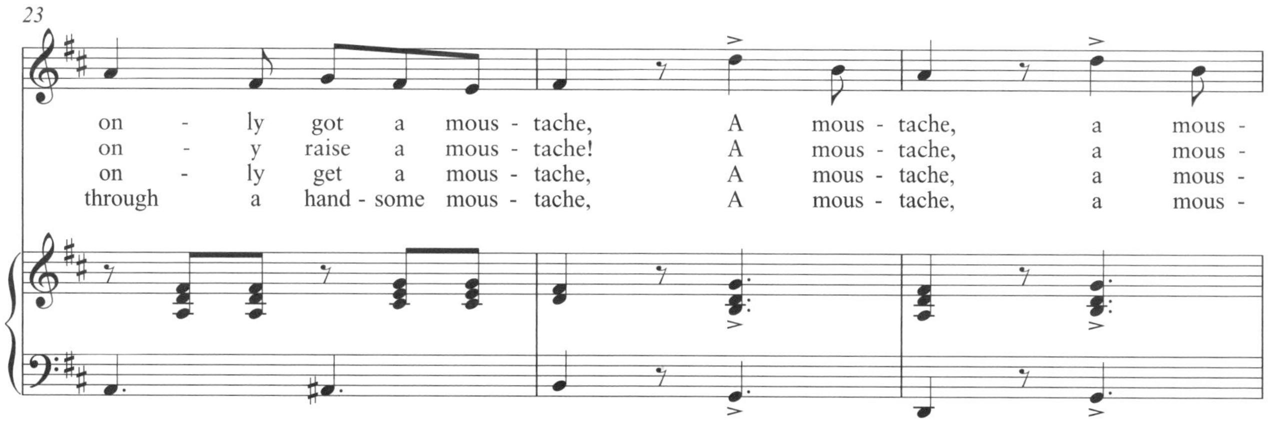

PART TWO

Art Songs

PART TWO

Art Songs

O Mistress Mine

from *Twelfth Night*

Words by
William Shakespeare
(1564–1616)

Music by
Sir Charles Villiers Stanford
(1852–1924)

For background and performance notes, see page 213.

13
cresc.
fur - ther, pret-ty sweet - ing; Jour-neys end in lo - vers
cresc.
17
f
meet - ing, Ev - 'ry wise man's son doth
21
mp
know. What is
mf
p
25
f
p
love? 'Tis not here - af - ter; Pre-sent mirth hath pre-sent laugh - ter; What's to
p

29
cresc.
come is still un - sure: In de -
cresc.
33
f
sf
lay there lies no plen - ty; Then come kiss me,
36
rall.
sweet and twen - ty, Youth's a stuff will not en -
mf
rall.
40
dure.
f

El majo timido*

The Timid Suitor

(Castillian Spanish)

Llega‿á mi reja y me mira** [ʎega mi rreha i me miɾa]	**He arrives at my window and looks at me**
por la noche un majo [poɾ la notʃe un maxo]	**Each and every night, a majo.**
que‿en cuanto me ve y suspira se [ken kwanto me βe i suspiɾa se]	**Then, as soon as he sees me and sighs,**
vá calle abajo. [βa kaʎe aβaxo]	**He goes down the street.**
¡Ay! que tío más tardio! [ai ke tio mas taɾðio]	**Oh, that man is so slow!**
Si asi se pasa la vida, [sijasi se pasa la βiða]	**If this is the way he spends his life,**
Estoy divertida. [estoi diβeɾtiða]	**I am entertained.**

**majo* is an untranslatable word for a handsome young man.
**In Castillian Spanish, double ll is pronounced [ʎ], as in "million."

El majo timido

(The Timid Suitor)

Words by Fernando Periquet

Music by Enrique Granados (1867–1916)

For background and performance notes, see page 214.

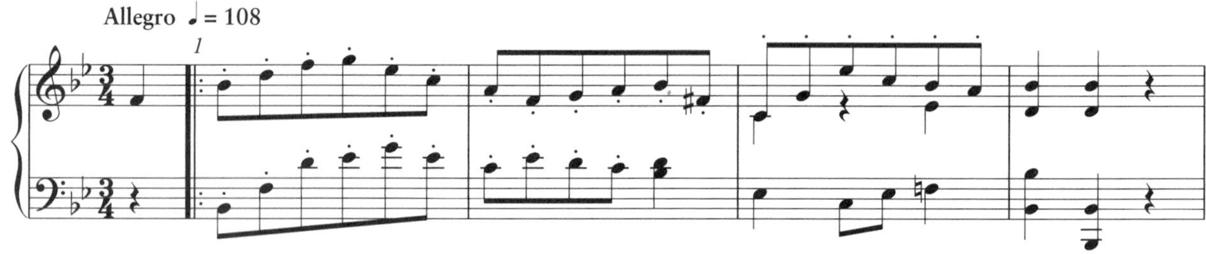
Allegro ♩ = 108
1

5
Lle-ga á mi re - ja y me mi - ra por la no - che un ma - jo

9
que, en cuan-to me ve y sus - pi - ra se vá ca - lle a - ba - jo.
13
¡Ay qué tí - o más tar - dí - o!
17
¡Si a sí se pa-sa la vi - da es - toy di - ver - ti - da!
21

PART TWO

Evening Prayer

from *Hansel and Gretel*

Music by Engelbert Humperdinck
(1854–1921)

For background and performance notes, see page 214.

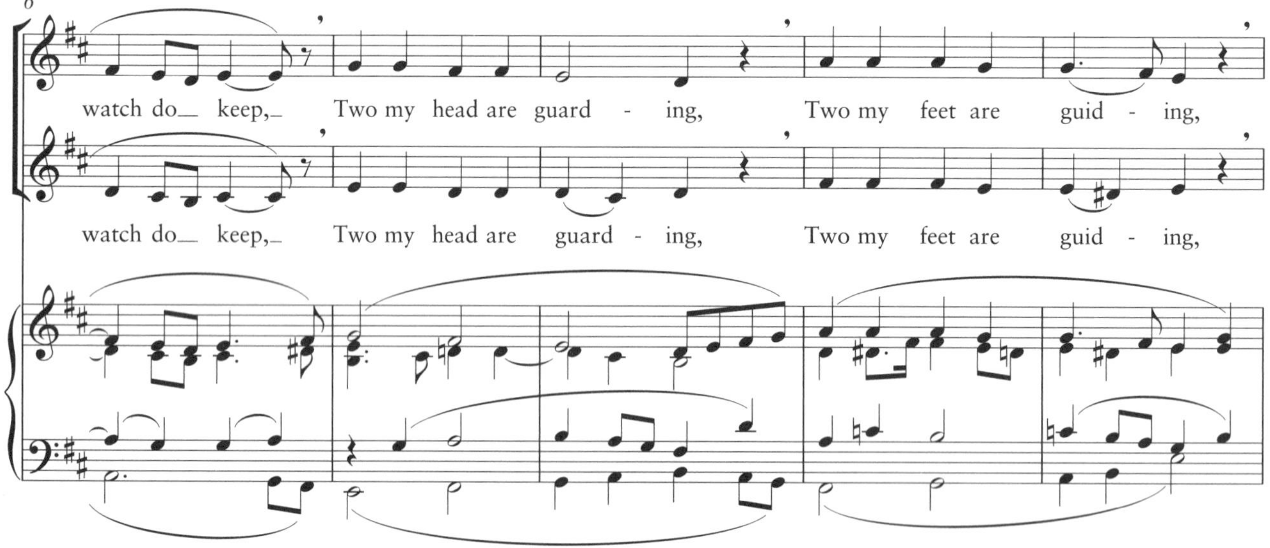

Art Songs

11
Two are on my right hand, Two are on my left hand, Two who warm - ly
Two are on my right hand, Two are on my_ left hand,
poco cresc.
16
cov - er, Two who o'er me hov - er, Two to whom 'tis giv - en To
cresc.
(,)
Two who warm-ly cov - er, Two who o'er me hov - er, Two who guide my
cresc.
21
poco rit.
Tempo
guide my steps to Hea - - ven.
(,)
steps to Hea - - ven.

Summertime

from *Porgy and Bess*

Words by DuBose Heyward
(1885–1940)

Music by George Gershwin
(1898–1937)

For background and performance notes, see page 214.

a tempo
14
C G7 C C6 C7 Fm6 Gm6 Fm6 Gm6
high. Oh, yo' dad-dy's rich, An yo' ma is good-
mf
r.h.
18
Fm6 Gm6 Fm6 B♭7 A♭ Fm B♭ E♭9sus
look - in', So hush, lit-tle ba - by, don' you
3
22
Fm B♭9(♭5) Fm6 Gm6/F B♭9 B♭9(♭5) (no 3rd)
poco animato
poco rit.
cry. One of these
8va
poco animato
poco rit.
Tempo I
26
Fm6 Gm6 Fm6 Gm6 Fm6 Gm6 Fm6 Gm6 Fm6
morn - in's you goin' to rise up sing - in', Then you'll

30
B♭m7
B♭m7/D♭
B♭m7/F
F
C
G♭7
C
C6
C7
spread yo' wings an you'll take the sky.
But 'till that
3
34
Fm6
Gm6
Fm6
Gm6
Fm6
Gm6
Fm6
B♭7
morn - in' there's a noth - in' can harm you With
38
A♭
B♭m
B♭
E♭9sus
Fm
B♭
E♭9sus
mp
Dad - dy an' Mam - my stand - in' by.
42
A♭
A♭m/D♭
G♭
C7(add A)
Fm
Fm6
dim.
ten.
8va

Oh, better far to live and die

(Pirate King's Song)
from *The Pirates of Penzance*

Words by Sir William S. Gilbert
(1836–1911)

Music by Sir Arthur Sullivan
(1842–1900)

For background and performance notes, see page 215.

16
mo - nious part With a pi - rate head and a pi - rate heart!
ships,__ it's true, Than a well - bred mon - arch ought to do!
19
A - way to the cheat - ing
But ma - ny a king on a
22
world go you, Where
first - class throne, If he
cresc.
25
pi - rates all___ are well - to - do, But I'll be true to the
wants to call___ his crown his own, Must man - age some - how

28
rall.
song I sing, And live and die a Pi - rate King,
to get through More dir - ty work than ever I do,
rall.
31
a tempo
For I am a Pi - rate King!
a tempo
p
35
And it is, it is a glo - rious thing to be a Pi - rate
39
King
King! For I am a Pi - rate King.
Chorus
f
You are! Hur - rah for the Pi - rate
f

PART TWO
Art Songs

43
And it is, it is a glor - rious thing_ to be a Pi - rate
King!
p
47
King. Hur-rah for the Pi - rate
It is! Hur - rah for our Pi - rate King! Hur-rah for the Pi - rate
f
51
King!
King!
f

The sun, whose rays are all ablaze

from *The Mikado*

Words by Sir William S. Gilbert
(1836–1911)

Music by Sir Arthur Sullivan
(1842–1900)

For background and performance notes, see page 215.

9
But, fierce and bold, In fie - ry gold, He glo - ries all ef - ful - gent!

11
I mean to rule the earth, As he the sky— We
cresc.

14
real - ly know our worth, The sun and I!
I mean to rule the earth, As he the sky—We
dim.

17
rall.
a tempo
real-ly know our worth, The sun and I!
mf
p sostenuto

20
Ob - serve his flame, That pla - cid dame, The moon's ce - les - tial high - ness;
22
There's not a trace Up - on her face of dif - fi - dence or shy - ness:
24
She bor - rows light, That, thro' the night, Man - kind may all ac - claim her,
26
And, truth to tell, She lights up well, So I, for one, don't blame her.

PART TWO

Art Songs

28
Ah, pray make no mis - take,
p
30
We are not shy; We're ve - ry wide a - wake!
cresc.
32
The moon and I!
Ah, pray make no mis-take, We are not shy; We're
dim.
34
rall.
ve - ry wide a-wake! The moon and I.
rall.
mf

Toi, le coeur de la rose

You, the heart of the rose

(French)

Toi, le coeur de la rose [twa lə kœɾ də la rozə]	You, the heart of the rose
Toi, le parfum du lys blanc, [twa lə parfœ̃ dy lis blɑ̃]	You, the perfume of the white lily
Toi, tes mains et ta couronne, [twa te mɛ̃ e ta kuɾɔnə]	You, your hands and your wreath (crown)
Tes‿yeux bleus et tes joyaux [tezyø blø e te ʒwajo]	Your blue eyes and your jewels
tu ne m'as laissé, comme‿un rayon de lune, [ty nə ma lɛse kɔmœ̃ rajõ də lynə]	You did not leave me, like a ray of the moon
Qu'un cheveu d'or sur mon‿épaule [kœ̃ ʃəvø doɾ syr mõnepɔl]	That a golden hair on my shoulder
Un cheveu d'or et les debris d'un rève [œ̃ ʃəvø doɾ e le dəbri dœ̃ rɛvə]	A golden hair and the debris of a dream

---

Toi, le coeur de la rose

(Air de l'enfant)

Words by
Sidonie-Gabrielle Colette
(1873–1954)

Music by
Maurice Ravel
(1875–1937)

For background and performance notes, see page 215.

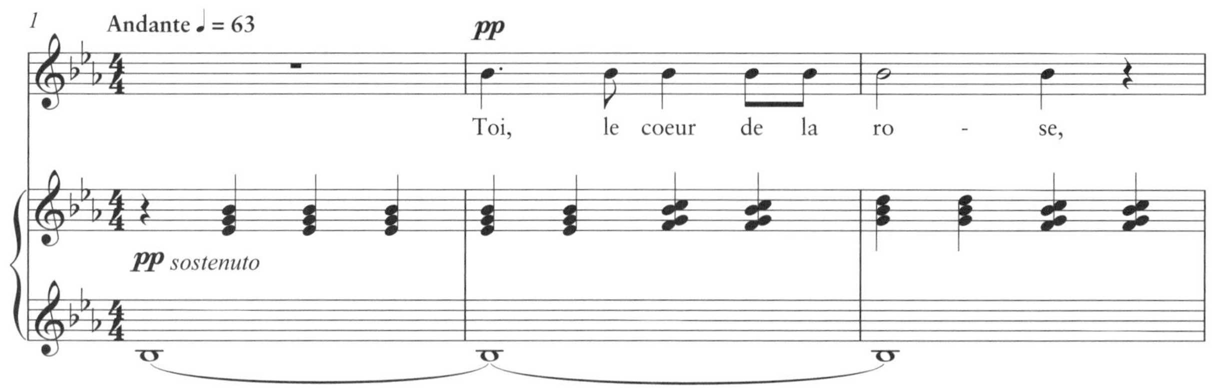

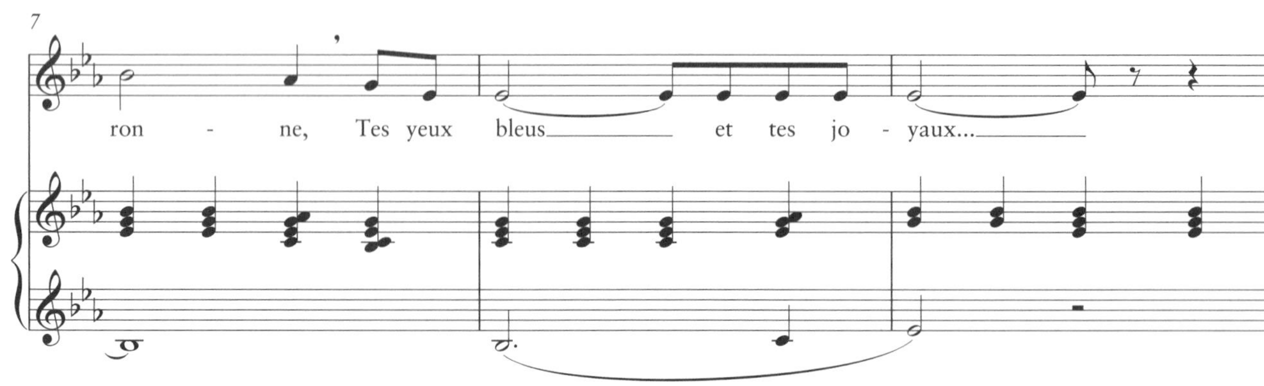

10
p
Tu ne m'as lais - sé, comme un ra - yon de lu - ne, Qu'un che - veu d'or sur mon é -
p
13
più p
pau - le, Un che - veu d'or...
più p
16
pp
et les dé - bris d'un rè - ve...
pp
19

The Hippopotamus

Words by Michael Flanders
(1922–1975)

Music by Donald Swann
(1923–1994)

For background and performance notes, see page 216.

16
lay By the light of the e - ven - ing star. A -
vice, Came tip - toe - ing down to her love. Like
scene That en - sued by the Sha - li - mar side? They
21
way on the hill - top sat comb - ing her hair His fair Hip - po -
thun - der the fo - rest re - e - choed the sound Of the song that they
dived all at once with an ear - split - ting splosh Then rose to the
26
po - ta - mine maid; The Hip - po - po - ta - mus was
sang as they met. His i - na - mo - ra - ta ad -
sur - face a - gain, A re - gu - lar ar - my of
31
no ig - no - ra - mus And sang her this sweet ser - e - nade:
just - ed her gar - ter And lift - ed her voice in du - et:
Hip - po - po - ta - mi All sing - ing this haunt - ing re - frain:

37 REFRAIN
Mud, mud, glo - ri - ous mud, Noth - ing quite like it for
43
cool - ing the blood! So fol - low me, fol - low, down to the hol - low And
49
1.2.
there let us wal - low in glo - - ri - ous mud!
55
3.
rit.
2. The
3. Now glo - - ri - ous mud!
mf
rit.
8vb

Come Ready and See Me

Words by James Purdy
(b. 1923)

Music by Richard Hundley
(b. 1931)

For background and performance notes, see page 216.

out, But you must haste on foot or by sky For
no one can wait for - ev - er Un-der the blu - est sky I
can't wait for - ev - er, For the years are
run- ning out.
mp
p
f
non rit.
legato con pedale sempre

25
mf
I'm wait - ing with a can - dle No
mf
28
mp
wind will blow out, But you must haste on
poco dim.
p
31
foot or by sky For no one can wait for - ev - er Un - der the
34
blu - est sky I can't wait for - ev - er,

38
For the years are run - ning out.
espr.
42
rall. - - meno mosso - - - - returning to tempo
I can't wait for - ev - er For the
rall. - - meno mosso - - - - returning to tempo
p
cresc.
mp
46
poco riten. tempo
years are run - ning out.
poco riten. tempo
cresc.
mf
50
dim.
p

PART THREE

How the Voice Works

The first part of this book is devoted to getting you involved in and enjoying the art of singing. The goal of this section is to help you understand the amazing process and precision with which your voice produces sound, and some of the logical reasons for using specific techniques. Included here is a discussion of elementary vocal anatomy, additional exercises, and "finding out for yourself . . ." sections.

The human voice is fascinating to study. The more we know about it, the more we marvel at all its possibilities for producing sound. As a singer, you need to have a working knowledge of the major parts of your voice. It will help you be sensible about using your voice and keep you from panicking when anything goes awry.

CHAPTER SEVEN

Muscles and Physical Alignment

While we are being sensible, it is also useful to be logical about the human body. What follow are some hints about how to read and think about the anatomy of the voice.

STRUCTURE

Every building has a blueprint and a skeletal structure. This is what keeps it from collapsing. The same is true of the human body. Always look at the skeletal structure first to give you vital clues to how the body functions. These clues will give you important information about possible movement and support for joints, including those in the vocal skeleton.

To get a good idea of how a joint can move, look at how cartilage and/or bones fit together. For example, bones with rounded ends usually fit into bones with concave ends—some shallow, some deep. By looking at their shapes you can begin to decide what possibilities of movement there are and where there might be restrictions. Next you can begin to look at where, logically, a muscle would need to be located to move that joint.

MUSCLES

Skeletal muscles create movement of the body—not ligaments and membranes. When a muscle contracts, a joint changes position. Any move we make takes a signal of intent from the brain. The message is then sent to the muscle via nerve fibers and it is given the equivalent of an electric charge. The muscle then shortens or contracts. When the brain stops sending the signal and the charge stops, the muscle relaxes. This will give you a clue about highly tense or nervous people who can never either sit or stand still. Being "wired" is a good way to describe these people. In the case of hyperactivity, the brain rarely stops sending messages to the muscles. The muscles remain partly contracted and take energy away from what you really want to do—in your case, sing. The body needs to replace tension with appropriate muscle use.

Muscles have to cross over joints and shorten or contract to move them. To determine the action of a muscle, you need to know where it is attached and in which direction the fibers are running. (You also need to know that muscles only contract to create an action. They do not push or expand.) By noting the direction of the fibers you can determine the direction of possible action of the muscle. Therefore, when you are looking at anatomical illustrations on a flat page, you can determine the action with a certain amount of logic rather than trying to memorize every muscle and its action. It is helpful to know that in general, muscles are named according to where they are located in the body, their shape, or their actions. Their Latin names are routinely used in texts, but don't let that deter you.

In order for muscles to contract and move a joint in one direction, muscles on the opposite side of the joint must relax. Sometimes muscles do not let go completely because they are still receiving a signal. When this happens, there is restriction of movement. A tug-of-war between opposing muscles creates muscular antagonism. When this kind of antagonism is used to stabilize a joint to help its performance, it is known as synergy. For example, when standing on one leg, the muscles on opposite sides of your thigh must help stabilize your hips. However, it is the unwanted antagonism that creates the problems. Using more muscles than you need when you are singing can make singing difficult for you, especially when a joint that needs flexibility becomes locked.

All this is a simple introduction and explanation for a very complex topic. For more information you can refer to anatomy books and Internet sites that have more detailed discussions of the human body.

PHYSICAL ALIGNMENT

Freeing your body and posture is not just for singing; it has a direct relationship to your physical balance, energy, health, voice, breathing, and image. The word *posture* conjures up memories of someone saying "Get your shoulders back and stand up straight." These verbal admonitions are given in great seriousness and with good intention, but they are not always very helpful, creating more problems than they solve. Many who are told to get their shoulders back as children poke their heads forward and tense their upper backs. You can walk down the street and easily pick out those people who may have been given that postural direction. Correcting posture means working with how it feels, not just verbal instructions.

A balanced, free, and flexible posture is fundamental to efficient vocal production and lovely voice quality. The alignment of the breathing mechanism—the chest, the voice box (larynx), and throat (resonator)—is the starting point for healthy singing. Correcting a voice without generating good postural balance first is like trying to build a sturdy, stable house around crooked framing.

Finding out for yourself . . .

Stand with both feet firmly on the floor and observe the following by becoming aware of the sensations in your body:

1. Where is my center of gravity?
2. Does my body feel heavy or light? (This has nothing to do with how much you weigh.)
3. Is my weight equally distributed between both feet?
4. What happens to my body when I want to rise on my toes?
5. Can I feel my whole foot on the floor?
6. Do my shoulders feel level?
7. Do my hips feel level?
8. Is there pressure anywhere along my spine?
9. Where is my breathing centered?

Experiment by rocking back and forth and then side to side until the body finds a new feeling of balance. Learn to feel your balance first and then check in the mirror for confirmation.

Remember: How you think you look and how you actually look are usually different.

A healthy human being is capable of maintaining balance against gravity with minimal effort, or with varying degrees of difficulty. As a child of two or three you probably had perfect alignment and balance with the head poised beautifully over the shoulders and hips. Notice young children around you; they normally exhibit this balance. They use few muscles and little energy to maintain this stance. Later, as children begin to develop various inefficient postural habits from sitting in chairs for long periods of time to imitating various role models from family or peers, they call into play more muscular energy and brain function. This creates an energy-draining situation in which many unnecessary muscles are needed to maintain balance. Such posture is known as collapse, not relaxation.

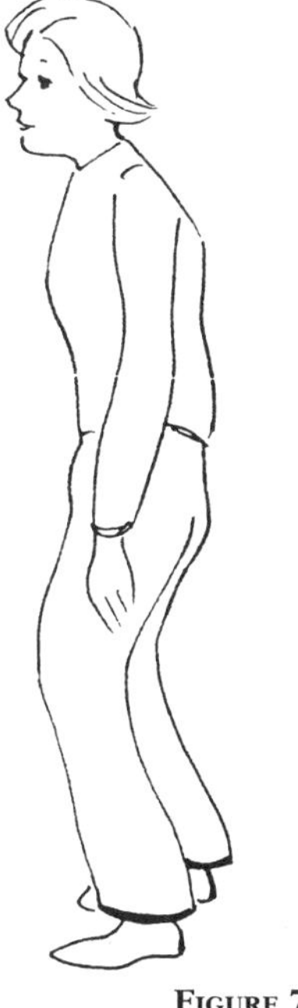

Figure 7.1
Poor posture

One postural habit that drains energy is pushing the head forward rather than aligning it over the shoulders (see Figure 7.1). This can happen when you spend long hours in front of a computer or over a desk with a slumped back or carry a heavy book pack on your back. When the head hangs forward, a huge strain is put on the muscles that run from the skull to the shoulders. These muscles contract strongly just to keep your head from falling off, so to speak. As a result of this constant contraction, the spine is pulled out of place at the top of the back, the shoulders ache, and the head hurts from the tug of the muscles on their insertion points on the back of the skull. Making it worse, to counterbalance the head as it pushes forward, the bottom goes backward. This is the way poor postural habits contribute to pain and potential injury.

Experts in physical function, including those who study biomechanics and other techniques such as Alexander, have agreed on the following description of good posture. When a plumb line is dropped beside you, it falls through the ear, the point of the shoulder, the highest part of the hip-bone, just behind the knee cap and barely in front of the ankle (see Figure 7.2). How well do you fit this description?

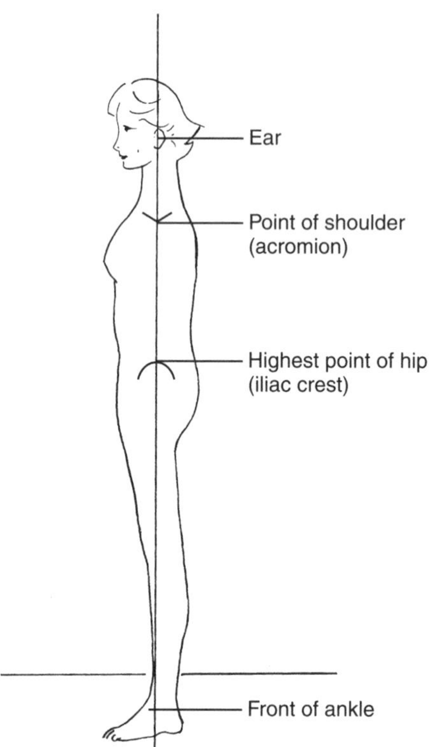

FIGURE 7.2
Efficient alignment

Guidelines for Good Physical Balance

Here are some generally accepted guidelines for establishing good physical balance. Some of these are repeated from Part One with added detail.

- Feel as if the soles of your feet are superglued to the floor.
- Feel your neck lengthen by allowing the crown (cowlick area at the top-back) of the head to move upward without disturbing the tilt of the chin. It is important to begin with the head rather than some other part of the body. The whole spine has a chance to lengthen when you begin at the top. You can also imagine that your head is being supported and pushed upward by an invisible hand placed between your shoulder blades.
- Make sure your knees are gently loose. Locked knees tend to contribute to an overly arched back. Loose knees will give the tail a chance to drop down and lengthen the back.

- Feel the ribs of the lower back move backward over the hips. (When the back is locked you will not be able to feel this.) You can encourage lower rib movement by placing the backs of your hands on them and inhaling into the hands and pushing the lower ribs backward with the breath (see Figure 7.3).
- If you still have problems feeling the lower back ribs move, lie down in a semi-fetal position and allow the breath to fill your back. Take about ten breaths this way until you are sure those ribs move with the breath.
- Balance in the centers of your feet. Check your balance by rising on your toes without disturbing the rest of your body.

Figure 7.3
Placing hands on the lower ribs

More ways to improve your posture:

1. Leave sticky note reminders to yourself by the telephone, on your mirror, on your music, on the piano, or any place your eyes fall during the day. When you are preoccupied with lots of other things, you need visible reminders. Do this for a few weeks and your body will begin to tell you when to adjust your posture. It will no longer care for the old one.
2. Feel as if there are two triangles that form your back: one with its apex on the spine just below the ribs and its base along the base of the spine and hip joints (see Figure 7.4) and the second with its apex on the spine just below the ribs and its base across the top of the shoulders. As you sit or walk, imagine that you get taller by expanding both triangles in opposite directions.
3. Lie on the floor with knees bent and your head on a book. (Make sure that your chin is not tipped toward the ceiling or pulled down onto your neck.) Gravity will help pull your back down. Breathe into the arched part of the back so that it reaches the floor. This is a good way to relax after a strenuous day of practice and study.
4. Get help from outside sources such as Alexander technique, yoga, martial arts courses, Feldenkrais work, Body Mapping, or Pilates.
5. Visualize how you want your body to look and feel.

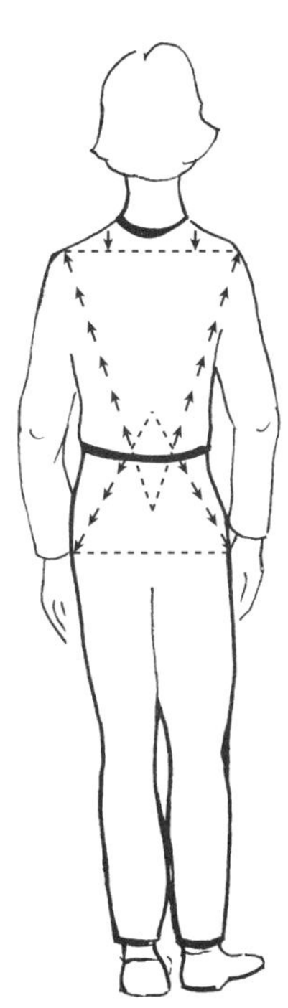

Figure 7.4
Triangles of the back with imaginary lines of direction
(Suggested by G. MacDonald)

CHAPTER EIGHT *Breathing*

Breath is the essence of life and sound, and normally breathing is a subconscious process. The regulation of the body's chemical balance depends on breathing. Also, air is the medium of transport for sound.

During low-energy activity, like sitting and reading or watching television, we need little air. For activities that require more energy, like singing and dramatic speech, we generally use more muscular effort and therefore need more air. However, you may need less air than you think for singing, particularly when your alignment and the balance of muscle use and airflow are maintained.

Airflow is a matter of balance between the pressures of the air outside and inside the chest. When we breathe out, a negative pressure is created inside the chest, leaving a space for the breath to then re-enter and equalize the pressure. This is an ongoing pattern that exists until we die. The air comes in without effort when the mouth is slightly open and the neck and larynx are free of muscular tension.

For now, remember the two most important things: (1) use the most physically and vocally efficient way of breathing, and (2) keep the air moving rather than attempting to hold it back. There are many theories regarding breathing for singing—some bordering on the strange and exotic. However, efficiency of breath is the ultimate factor in vocal health and quality of sound.

Subconsciously, we take about 24,400 breaths a day. If you had to take each breath consciously, you would have time for nothing else. When people walk or march while singing, they take air in without thinking about how they do it, and it seems to work with no problem. The breathing process happens below the level of consciousness without our interference. However, when we become conscious of the need to take in air while singing, we can develop many misconceptions and worries.

The perceived need to control air, the fear of running out of breath, and a sense of near panic or nervousness have caused the greatest breathing problems for singers. These fears are tantamount to self-sabotage and have led to general misuse of the breath and a misunderstanding about the physical process of breathing. The body and brain are capable of regulating the breath when the analytical-critical mind does not interfere with the automatic processes of the body and the vocal mechanism. The body behaves in a logical way, and this applies to breathing.

Note: There are good singers who breathe badly. They sing well in spite of themselves and might sound even more wonderful with a better technique. Most of us are not so fortunate, so pay attention and develop good habits from the beginning. Efficient breathing is not just for "classical" singing; pop singers could improve immensely from work on their breathing as well. You might be surprised to know how many noisy breath sounds have to be removed in the editing and processing of their recordings.

Let's begin with some simple concepts first. In normal, quiet, or passive breathing, the chest must expand to let air in and diminish in size to let it out. This is accomplished subconsciously with minimal physical effort. People breathe in many ways according to their postural habits and physical health. However, for singing, there are only efficient and inefficient ways of breathing. The efficient way was discussed briefly at the beginning of this book. We will now look at it in more detail so you can understand what is happening.

Efficient Breathing

1. The body is physically balanced and poised for action.
2. The intake of air is silent—no gasps!
3. There is no visible muscle tension—especially not in the face, mouth, neck, shoulders, or chest.
4. The feeling of breath begins deep in the lower part of the body.
5. The focus is on sensing the action of the lowest ribs in the back and the lower part of the abdomen in the front.
6. The abdomen and ribs are flexible and available to respond to the demands of singing.
7. The muscles of the abdomen are able to work with reasonable effort to help the air flow out without interference by the chest or neck.

INHALATION

When you look at a skeleton, you will see that the largest open space of the chest is at the bottom of the rib cage (see Figure 8.1). So it makes sense that when we want to create more space for air we need to expand in that area. This is precisely what happens in natural and efficient breathing.

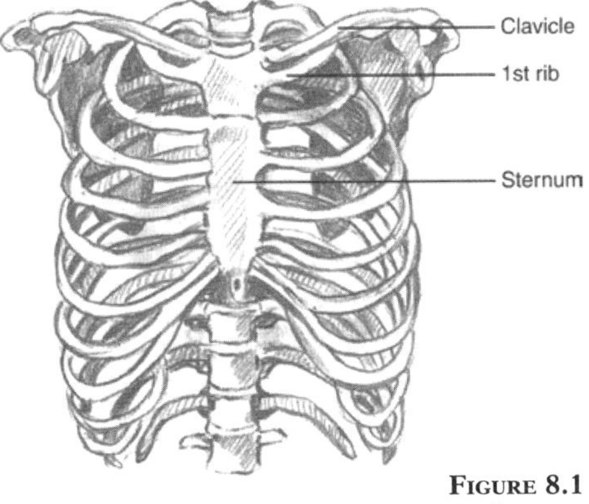

Figure 8.1
Rib cage

PART THREE

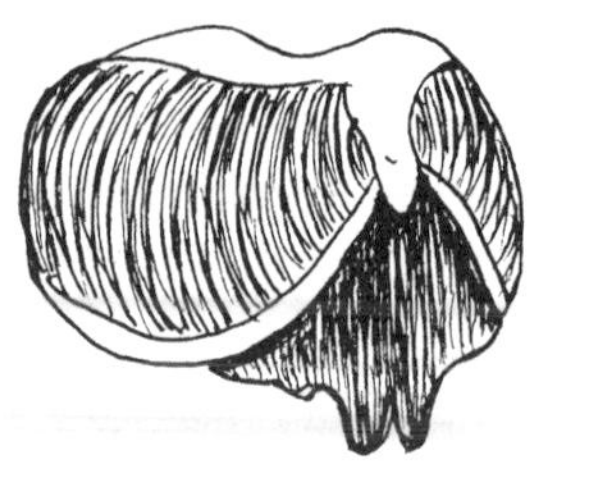

FIGURE 8.2A
Diaphragm as a "hat"

A very large dome-shaped muscle called the diaphragm occupies the lower part of the rib cage (see Figure 8.2a). The diaphragm is so "fabled" in singing lore and so unfamiliar in appearance to most people that they are amazed when they finally see the real thing in a science lab. It is the most important muscle of inhalation (inspiration) and acts as a partition between the chest and abdomen. Picture it this way: Imagine inserting into an empty skeleton a large, strangely shaped muscular hat that has its lower brim stuck around the bottom edges of the rib cage and the spine at the level of the last rib (see Figure 8.2b). The top part of the dome is tendonous and located centrally just below the heart; it does not have the capability to move very much. (Your heart has enough work to do without jumping up and down every time you breathe.)

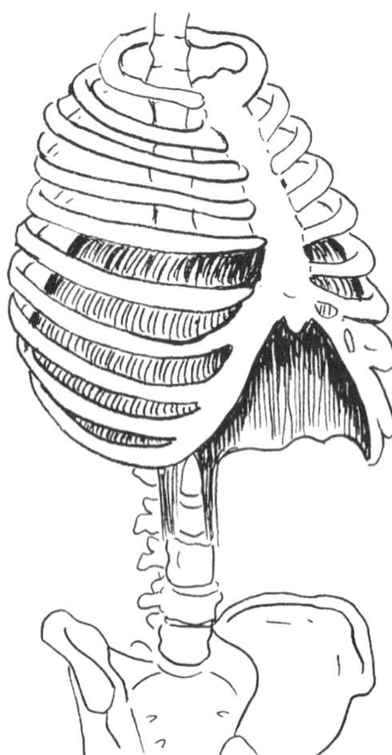

FIGURE 8.2B
Diaphragm placed in rib cage

The edges and main body of the diaphragm are formed of thin muscle and the center is a thin, flat tendon. When the diaphragm contracts, it moves downward, displacing the lower ribs and the organs and soft structures below it. It is not capable of moving below the ribs, including those in front. It does not invert. The action of the diaphragm causes the abdomen to expand and the lower ribs to move outward. This abdominal expansion is caused by organs being displaced and has often caused people to mistake it for the diaphragm itself. When the body is in good alignment, this action will happen easily without specific attention paid to the diaphragm. Without such alignment, efficient breathing becomes difficult to master.

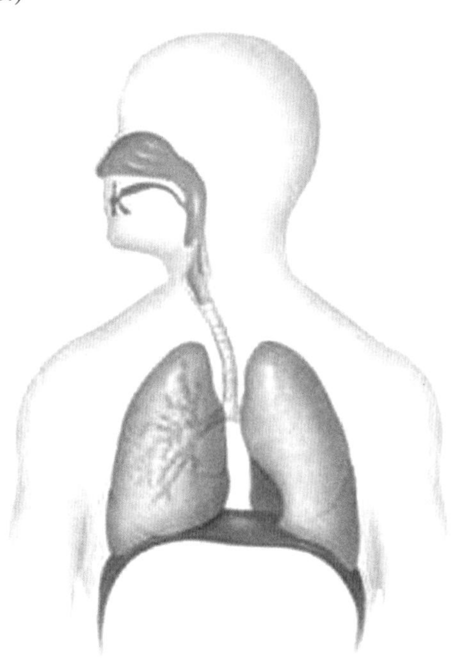

Carlyn Iverson
Photo Researchers, Inc.

FIGURE 8.2C
Position of lungs in relation to diaphragm

Twelve pairs of small muscles elevate the ribs from behind and help the diaphragm. Each of these muscles runs from projections on the sides of the vertebrae (transverse processes of the spine) down to the angle of the rib below (see Figure 8.3). They make up what are called the *levator costarum.* This puts them in a good position to raise the ribs slightly and swing them outward. The effectiveness of this movement relies on the freedom and flexibility of the back. A rigid back will hinder these muscles from doing their job.

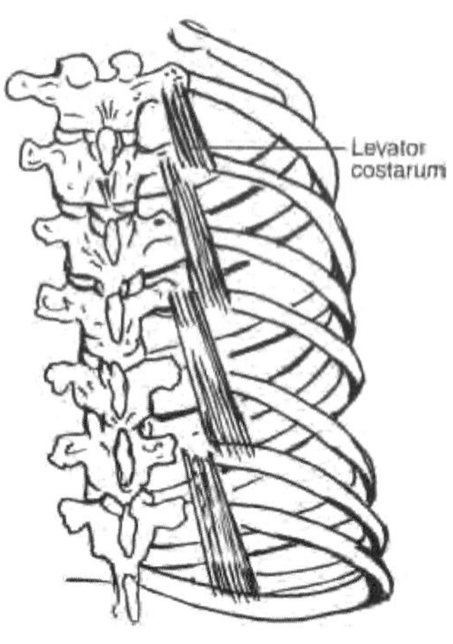

FIGURE 8.3
Levator costarum muscles (posterior view)

Numerous other muscles attached to the neck, rib cage, and back also work to maintain stability during the breathing process. The muscles between the ribs (intercostals) are often mentioned as contributing to inhalation and exhalation. However, they are most effective as stabilizers of the ribs. All these muscles seem to work very well when we stand properly. Only the primary muscles have been included in this discussion in order to leave your mind relatively uncluttered. More detailed knowledge can be obtained through reading some of the texts mentioned in the "Further Reading" section at the end of the book.

Finding out for yourself . . .

With a partner, experiment with some common but inefficient inhalation patterns.

What happens to the body when you take breaths in the following ways and then sing? What happens to the quality of the sound? Into what physical patterns does each exercise force the action of breathing? Carefully watch the chest and abdomen during these experiments.

1. **Take a breath with the tummy held in tightly.**
2. **Take a breath with the back held rigidly.**
3. **Take a breath with the back overly arched (but not exaggerated).**
4. **Take a breath while slouched in a chair.**

Why are these patterns less useful for good singing?

Now feel the difference in the vocal tract and chest when you inhale low in the body with good alignment and a released head and neck. Describe the difference in how you feel and look. Ask your partner to describe the difference in the vocal quality.

EXHALATION

Because most people assume you have to take air in to get it out, inhalation is usually discussed first. Ideally, singers think first of exhaling, and then of allowing the inhalation to be a reflex action. It is just as easy to think of breathing out to breathe in. After all, the body is just creating a cyclic balance. Exhaling during the introduction of a song and then allowing a reflex breath a beat or two just before you sing is a more secure approach. Most people panic during an introduction, and go through a pattern of breathing in and out, and somehow are never ready when it is time to sing, hence the last-minute gasp.

Exhalation during minimal physical activity is a simple matter of releasing the muscles of inspiration (such as the diaphragm) and letting the elastic recoil of the lungs and gravity do the rest. This is done for us by the subconscious. For singing, we need to use more muscular effort, and it is best accomplished by the muscles of the abdomen.

The abdominal muscles form a kind of girdle around the abdomen and are located in the best place to facilitate breathing without interfering with the vocal tract. There are three paired muscles (*transversus abdominis* and the *internal* and *external obliques*) that form this girdle and a fourth set, the "six-pack" (*rectus abdominis*) that goes up and down the mid-line of the abdomen from the ribs to the pubic bone. The muscles that form the abdominal girdle tend to work as a unit for breathing. They contract and cause the abdominal contents to move toward the back and the diaphragm, thus helping the diaphragm to return to its original position and to send air out of the lungs (see Figure 8.4). Normally, the action of the rectus muscle is to bring the rib cage and pelvis closer together, as in curling forward. However, some singers use it sparingly and gently to add a little top-up breath pressure or emphasis to a phrase or note.

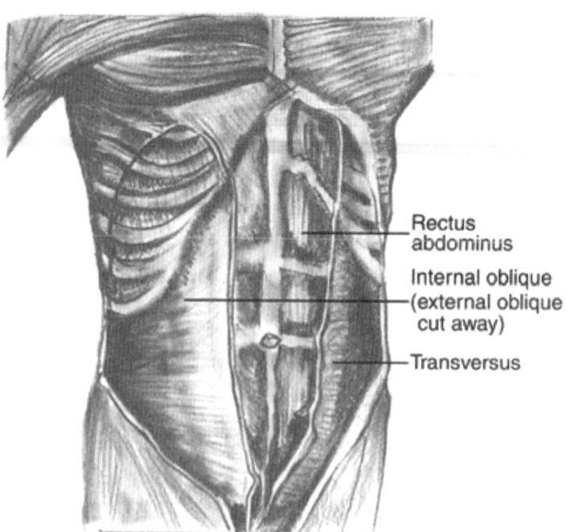

Figure 8.4
Abdominal muscles: obliques and rectus abdominus

If you have done "abs" workouts in a gym, you will know that you can contract your abdominal muscles in different areas. Various kinds of sit-ups help to develop the upper or lower abs. *Where* the singer chooses to activate the abs is very important. The most efficient area is the lowest one near the pelvis. Contracting the muscles in this area sends pressure toward the diaphragm and lower back ribs from below. Using the middle or the top abs tends to cut the

Finding out for yourself . . .

Playing with balloons

Imagine that a blown-up balloon represents your whole abdominal area. Draw the rough outline of the pelvis, sacrum (fused bones that form the lowest part of the spine), and lower ribs on it. The top of the balloon represents the diaphragm and the lowest part the pelvic floor muscles (sometimes called the pelvic diaphragm).

Note what happens when you push on the top of the balloon —remembering that in reality, the bony parts will not move.

What happens when you hold the front tightly and try to push the top down? This is the equivalent of holding in the abdomen and trying to take a good breath. In this situation, the diaphragm cannot really descend in this situation and the chest is forced upward.

What happens when you squeeze the top of the balloon?

What happens when you squeeze the lower part of the front of the balloon? Notice particularly what happens to the top. It tends to enlarge and spread. This is similar to what happens to the diaphragm and lower ribs when you use the lower part of the abdomen to help send the air back out.

singer in the middle and send energy up and down at the same time. Inefficient use of the muscles of exhalation can cause unwanted tensions to transfer to the neck, throat, and jaw. The better you maintain your good posture, the easier it will be to use the more effective lower part of the abdomen for exhaling. Collapsing the body will cause the air to release too quickly and you will pay the price by running out of breath.

Balancing Breath and Music

There are days when singing seems easy and effortless; on other days it seems like hard work. The easy days probably occur when the body, breath, and voice are working as a unit rather than fighting each other. The first months of learning to sing can seem like a battle between old and new habits. However, it will all prove worthwhile when you finally achieve good coordination; it is easy to sing and the resulting "high" or being in the singing "zone" is satisfying. That is when singing can become addictive.

A number of things are happening when the coordination is good: There is a balance of pressures in the abdomen, chest, at the level of the vocal folds (vocal cords), and in the mouth that help the singer maintain steady airflow appropriate to the music and phrasing of the text.

These pressures include (1) the lower abdomen contracting up toward the lower ribs at the back, slowing the return of the diaphragm and ribs; (2) the flow of air meeting resistance of the vocal folds as they close for phonation (see Chapter Nine), keeping a certain amount of pressure in the chest and resistance to the diaphragm (see Figure 8.5); and (3) the exhaled air hitting the palate, teeth or even lips and moving back toward the vocal folds creating

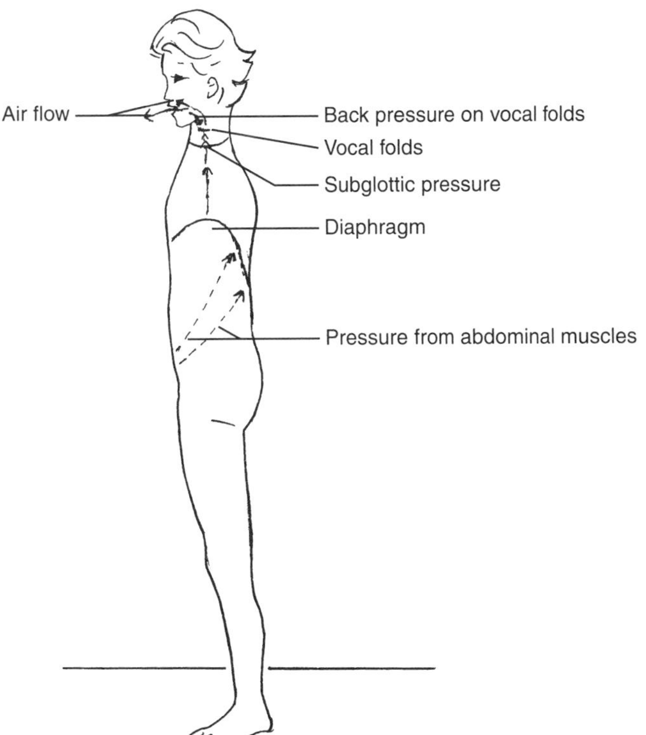

Figure 8.5
Balance of pressures while singing

back pressure in the mouth. These pressures are the product of coordinated muscle action and breath. They are not goals in and of themselves. When any one of these areas is out of sync, you can have difficulty with airflow and phrasing. In the *Finding out for yourself* box above you were playing with balloons. Go back and look at this again. It can give you a sense of the physical buoyancy that happens when you sing well.

Poor Breathing Habits

After reading (or singing) all this information, it would be ideal if you had no poor habits. As that is rarely the case, poor habits must be addressed. Watch the breathing of singers in concert and on TV and video. You will see examples of some of the most common faults, discussed next.

COLLAPSING PHYSICALLY WHEN BEGINNING TO SING

Look in the mirror at your upper chest. Sometimes the downward movement that happens at the beginning of a phrase is quite obvious and at other times it is very subtle. Such a movement is very inefficient for breath control and sound quality.

GASPING

This is simply counterproductive. It locks your body and larynx and makes a dreadful noise. Too many singers have been told that they need large amounts of air. This causes them to end a musical phrase by gulping air in immediately. This gasp at the end of exhalation is a common habit causing the vocal folds to clamp shut and create excess pressure in the chest. Singers are then unable to recover in time for the next phrase.

Remember your wide breathing pipe discussed earlier. It cannot be squeezed at the level of the larynx. Let your air flow easily as you sing and allow it to cease moving by stopping the abdominal pressure. Leave yourself reminders everywhere so that good breathing becomes

Figure 8.6 *Imaginary breathing pipeline*

Exercise to eliminate gasping . . .

Choose a song you know and patiently sing each phrase separately so you can make sure your breaths have no associated gasps:

Using your hands (at the level of your neck and upper chest), indicate the stable width of your breath channel (see Figure 8.6).

Breathe out before you begin. When you inhale to sing the first phrase, imagine that it is through that very wide channel.

At the end of each phrase you sing, allow the breath to go out through the wide channel. It does not matter how long it takes. The rhythm and timing of the breaths will be distorted in this exercise. Do this for every breath that you take in the song.

After you have done this with no physical and breath tension, sing several phrases together in their correct rhythm. When there are no gasps, continue singing the song the same way.

a habit. This is also important for centering and creating peace in yourself. Breathing techniques are used in many types of meditation.

Be careful in your conversations with friends. You do not have to gasp and heave your chest when you are enthusiastic and excited. Excitement without a gasp is the key thought.

TAKING IN MORE AIR THAN YOU NEED

Five short notes of music do not need twenty-five notes' worth of air. You cannot save it. Take what you need and use all of it. Otherwise you will tank up, close the vocal folds to hold it in, create a tremendous pressure in your chest, and feel as if you do not have enough air. No one wants to sing feeling like that!

Chapter Nine *Making Sound*

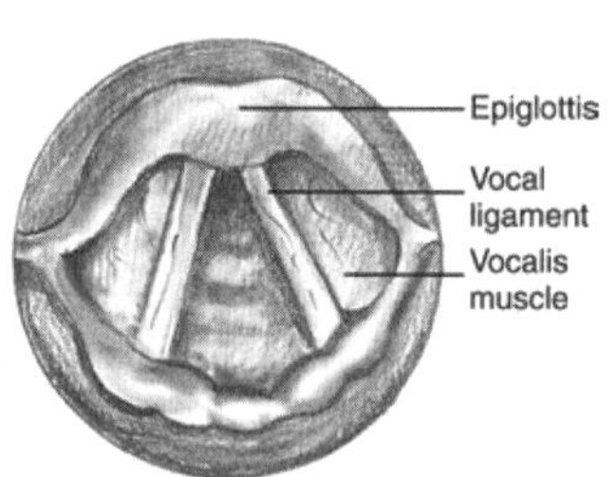

Figure 9.1
Vocal folds viewed from above

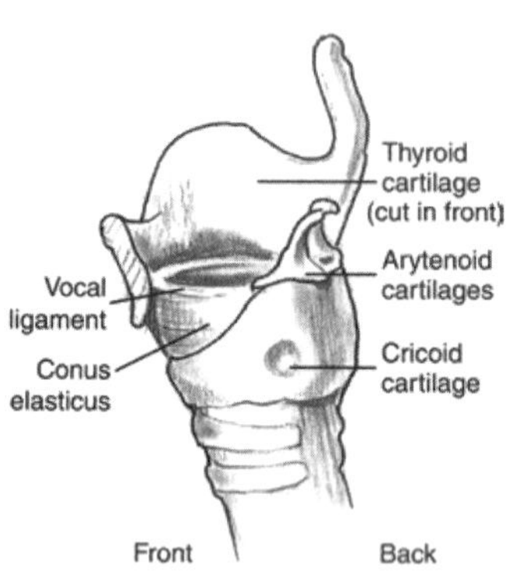

Figure 9.2
Cartilages of the larynx

Sound is made and amplified in the vocal tract, which consists of the voice box (larynx) and throat area all the way up to the soft palate (and the nose, for nasal sounds). The initiation of the voiced sounds we make comes from the vibration of two folds of muscle, housed in the larynx (Adam's apple) that sits on top of the windpipe (*trachea*) (see Figure 9.1). These folds are commonly (and incorrectly) known as the "vocal cords." When relaxed, they are about the size of your thumbnail and a little longer than that when stretched for higher pitches. If you have ever blown up a balloon, pulled the opening wide to release the air, and listened to the resulting squeal, you will have a good idea of how the vocal folds work.

The larynx consists of several cartilages and is a housing for the vocal folds that are activated by airflow from the lungs (see Figure 9.2). The sound is then modified and amplified by resonating in the "vocal tract" (the *pharynx* or throat and mouth). Alterations in the position of the larynx will affect the shape of the vocal tract, change the voice quality, and possibly affect the efficiency of the vibration of the vocal folds. When air is sent through these folds with the intention of making sound, they vibrate, creating the sound and the pitches we use for speech and singing. The cleaner and more efficiently these folds vibrate, the clearer and healthier the sound. The number of times the vocal folds vibrate per second determines the pitch. For example, for A 440 (the A immediately above Middle C), the folds vibrate 440 times per second.

The larynx is suspended and supported in the neck from in front, behind, above, and below by groups of paired muscles (see Figure 9.3). It is not stuck in the neck but is able to move freely when we swallow and speak. You can put your finger on your larynx and feel its movement when you swallow. While the larynx can be looked at as a separate unit, it never functions in that manner; the connections are too complicated. It has a complex relationship with the throat (pharynx), soft palate, tongue, jaw, neck, and chest. The position of the neck and chest, movement and tension of the tongue and jaw, and flexibility or constriction of the muscles of the pharynx all contribute to laryngeal efficiency and affect tone quality.

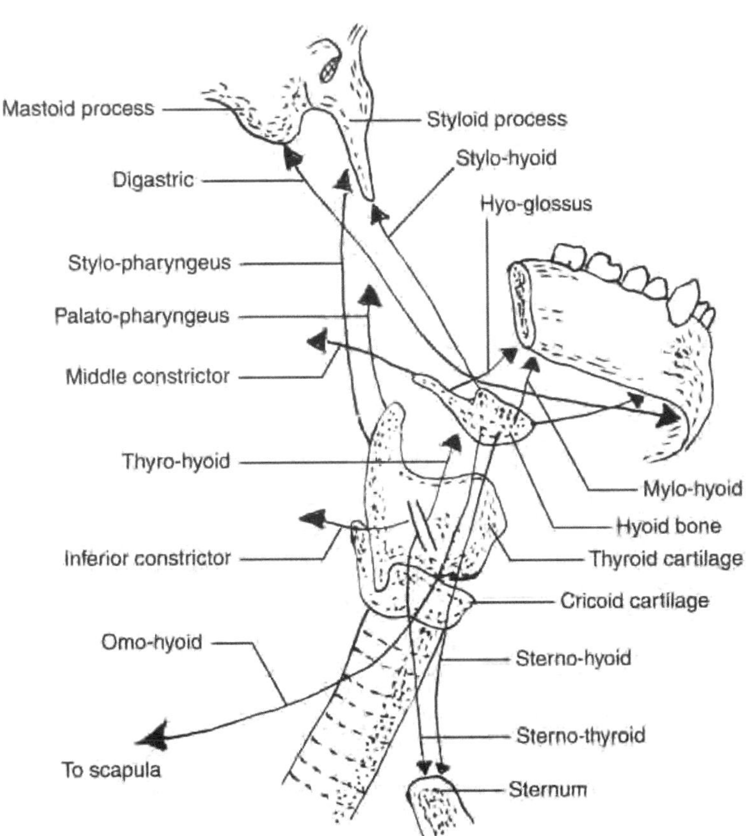

Figure 9.3
Diagram of muscles suspending the larynx

The vocal folds act as a sensitive valve and guardian for preventing foreign material from entering the lungs. They close tightly when we swallow or cause us to cough when anything other than the smallest imaginable particle tries to enter. You have probably experienced the powerful coughing reflex that occurs when something goes down the wrong way. Swallowing raises the larynx, shortens and narrows the throat, and causes the vocal folds to react by closing tightly to prevent food from going down into the lungs. Singing demands the opposite physical situation from swallowing—a wide-open air passageway with no constriction or hindrance to the balance of the larynx in the neck or its ability to vibrate freely.

Structure of the Larynx

Knowledge of the basic anatomy of the laryngeal mechanism is useful for dispelling some of the mystery of that "box" inside us that enables us to speak and sing. Like the rest of the body, its skeletal structure supports the movements of the muscles needed for us to make sound. The main structure of the larynx consists of four cartilages and a bone (see Figure 9.4):

- The cricoid looks like a signet ring with the highest part at the back. It sits on top of the trachea and forms a stable base for a pair of small arytenoid cartilages. On both sides of the cricoid there is a small joint formed with the lower horns of thyroid cartilage.
- The two arytenoids look like two small pointed hats and sit atop the back of the cricoid. Attached to them are the vocal

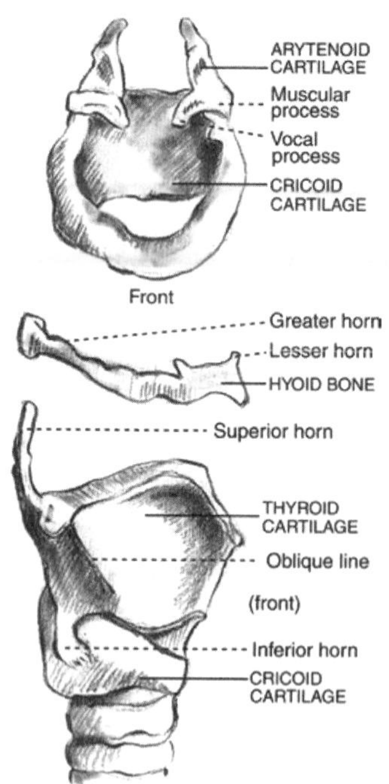

FIGURE 9.4
Skeleton of the larynx

folds, the muscles that move the vocal folds together and apart, and the vocal ligament.

- The thyroid cartilage is shaped somewhat like a shield, is open at the back, and has upper and lower horns. It serves as an anchor for the vocal folds and forms a joint with the cricoid on each side. There are muscle attachments to the hyoid bone, the sternum, the pharynx, underneath the skull, and the palate. This complicated set of attachments forms part of the sling in which the larynx hangs.

  Note: Most of the muscles attaching to the thyroid come from above.
- The hyoid bone is shaped like a horseshoe (sitting horizontally), is located between the jaw and thyroid cartilage, and is considered part of the laryngeal structure. It has complicated attachments and is suspended in the neck by muscles and membranes that attach to the thyroid cartilage, sternum, scapula, jaw, tongue, pharynx, and skull (see Figure 9.4).

Finding out for yourself . . .

One of the best ways to understand the larynx is to make a three-dimensional clay model of the cartilages. It is not the artwork that is important; it is the process. By going through the process of making this model, you will gain a very different understanding and appreciation of the structure. This will then give you the basis for understanding how the muscles work.

1. **Build the cricoid cartilage as a base. Look carefully at its shape before you begin. Note that the back rises at a steep angle from the front. (Some people like to build a solid trachea for it to sit on, but this is not necessary.)**
2. **Now look very carefully at the shape of the arytenoid cartilages and create them. Note their relative proportion to the cricoid and thyroid. It is worth measuring your picture or diagram to determine the ratio. Now set them on the back of the cricoid cartilage.**
3. **Next build the thyroid cartilage. Again, look carefully at its features and dimensions. Exactly where is the joint of the thyroid and cricoid on each of these cartilages?**
4. **You may wish to add the vocal folds that attach to the vocal process of the arytenoids and the inside front of the thyroid.**
5. **The epiglottis can be attached to the inside front of the thyroid cartilage just above the attachment of the vocal folds.**
6. **The hyoid bone can now be made. You will probably need some toothpicks to hold it in place.**

You now have a structure to work with. As you learn more about the muscles, you can take something like small ribbons and cut them in the shape of the muscles and stick them on with pins.

Important Muscles of Phonation

To make sound, the vocal folds need to come together. To breathe, they need to open. To create higher pitches, the vocal folds must be able to stretch. To accomplish all this some small muscles do a lot of work without our having to think much about it. They are placed in very logical positions to execute these skilled movements.

First, let's define a vocal fold more precisely. A vocal fold consists of a muscle (the *vocalis* or *thyro-arytenoid*) that runs from the front of the arytenoid cartilages (vocal process) to the inside of the back of the thyroid cartilage. The muscle is covered with mucous membrane and there is a ligament on the inside edge of each fold known as the vocal ligament. This ligament is the loose end of a structure called the *conus elasticus* (Figure 9.2), a tough ligament-like structure that looks a little like a tent. It arises from the top of the sides of the cricoid cartilage and forms a support for the vocal folds, with the upper free edge becoming the vocal ligament. When your voice is healthy, this ligament looks pearly white. Generally speaking, the vocal folds are thick and loose when relaxed or singing on low notes; they are stretched as you move higher in pitch.

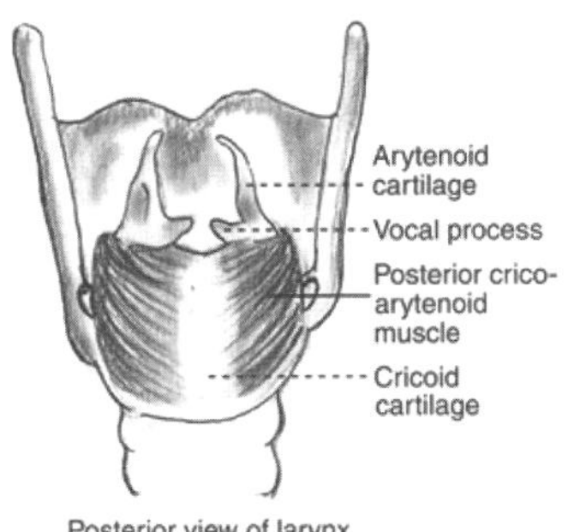

FIGURE 9.5 *Posterior crico-arytenoid muscles*

MUSCLES THAT MOVE THE VOCAL FOLDS APART

On the back of the cricoid cartilage are two muscles that move the vocal folds apart (abduct them) for breathing. These muscles run from the base of the cricoid up and outward to insert on the outside (lateral side, muscular process) of the bases of the arytenoid cartilages. They are logically called the *posterior crico-arytenoids*. When these muscles contract, they swing the arytenoids wide taking the vocal folds with them (see Figure 9.5).

MUSCLES THAT BRING THE VOCAL FOLDS TOGETHER

It takes two sets of muscles to fully close (adduct) the vocal folds for phonation. Running from the upper edge of either side of the cricoid cartilage are muscles that attach to the sides (muscular processes) of the arytenoids. These muscles are called the lateral crico-arytenoids. When they contract they swing the front of the arytenoids (vocal processes) together causing the vocal folds to meet in the center (see Figure 9.6). However, the meeting is not complete; this leaves a small chink between the arytenoid cartilages where air can escape. To complete the process and ensure a clear, clean sound, the arytenoids must slide toward each other and close the gap. The muscles that contract to do this are a group called the interarytenoids—all very logical.

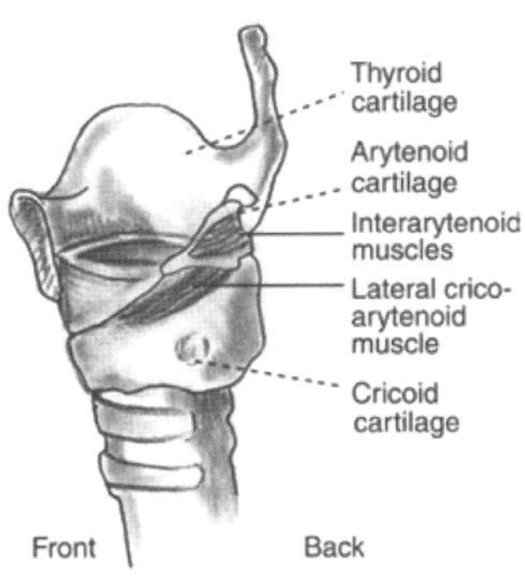

FIGURE 9.6 *Interarytenoid muscles and lateral crico-arytenoid muscles*

MUSCLES RESPONSIBLE FOR PITCH CHANGES

The vocal folds are relaxed for the lowest pitches and are lengthened to create higher pitches. Common sense tells us that there need to be muscles in place to cause the thyroid and cricoid cartilages to move apart and create the stretch. The pair of muscles that performs this task are the cricothyroids, running from the front of the cricoid to

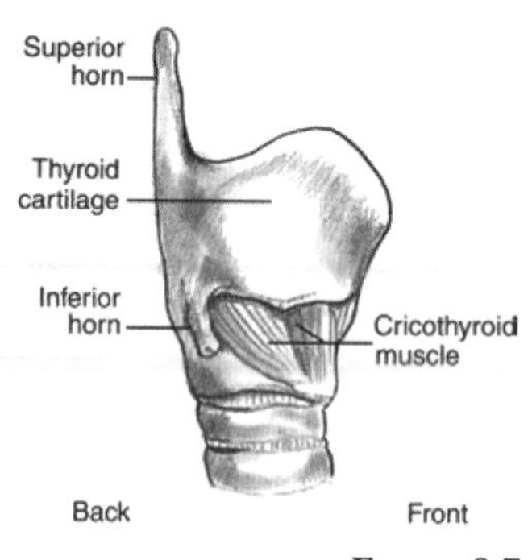

FIGURE 9.7
Cricothyroid muscle

the lower front edge and horns of the thyroid. When they contract they tilt the thyroid cartilage forward and the cricoid backward a little, creating a pull on the vocal folds (see Figure 9.7). When the lengthening of the folds is done smoothly and evenly with no extra tension in the throat and larynx, the pitch change happens easily. At the highest pitches, the vocal folds are fully stretched and the vocal ligament vibrates. When the vocal folds are not stretched, they are thick. This configuration produces the low, heavier sounds (sometimes called "chest" voice). When the folds are stretched, the sounds are higher and lighter. It is when you sing the high notes with a very heavy sound that "muscular arguments" (antagonism) can occur and create uneven changes in the sound.

A NOTE ABOUT PITCH

While the vocal folds are responsible for initiating the pitch, they are not the only determining factor for singing on *pitch*. Poor vocal technique can cause a singer to go out of tune by going flat (too far below the pitch) or sharp (too far above the pitch). Extraneous tension of the tongue, jaw, and neck can pull your larynx out of line and hinder the efficiency of the vocal folds. This can cause the vocal folds to vibrate awkwardly so that the voice is "out of tune" with itself. Some singers have been accused of having poor musical ears when that is not the case at all.

The vocal folds themselves tend to be passive in that they have other muscles moving them most of the time, either stretching them or moving them toward or away from each other. When they (the vocalis muscles) contract, they become bulkier and shorten the distance between the thyroid and arytenoid cartilages. This can cause them to act as antagonists to the muscles working to open and close them, and make the voice heavy sounding.

Note: If you had to think about all the muscles we have discussed, you would not be able to function as a singer. It would be like analyzing all the muscles in your arm before you swung at a ball. The ball would be long gone by the time you swung the bat. Fortunately, the body is more clever than we are and manages to regulate all of this by the intention to sing, by imagination, and by good physical alignment. It is when we have a problem that we need to address something specific. The larynx has been researched more than any other area of voice because scientists and doctors can see and analyze this area best. However, remember that the larynx is mainly the initiator of the voice that begins the sound and furnishes the pitches.

Sounds Made by the Vocal Folds

THE INITIATION OF SOUND

The initiation of vocal sound is called the onset or attack. For a clear sound, the vocal folds need to touch each other cleanly and gently. This happens when the muscles of breathing, the airflow, and the onset of sound are well coordinated. When the folds close with a lot of pressure, they can beat on each other and create little explosions of sound (glottal attacks). The sound this makes is usually tight and irritating to the ears. Continual abuse like this can cause growths on the folds called nodules.

Inefficient coordination can also cause the sound to be too breathy. This happens when the folds do not close well and air leaks out. It is all right to make a deliberately breathy sound for some popular styles, but a consistently breathy sound is indicative of poor vocal balance. And do not confuse breathiness and hoarseness. Hoarseness is discussed in the chapter on vocal health.

QUALITY WITHIN THE VOCAL RANGE

Sometimes in inexperienced singers, the lower voice will seem rich and strong and the upper voice will sound small and thin. In these singers the change in quality can be obvious. This happens when the highest and lowest areas of the vocal range are not connected by smooth coordination of the vocal mechanism. Generally it is desirable to have an even sound in classical music, but consistency is less important to nonclassical singers who happily use much more variety of vocal sounds in their singing. Pop singing, jazz, and many other styles are more adventurous with sound and may not be so concerned about equal quality throughout the range.

In vocal literature you will find these differences in sound referred to as vocal registers. A balanced voice produces a sound that is even from the bottom to the top of the singer's vocal range. Many of the nonclassical styles emphasize a sound that is closer to normal speech quality, and they use extremes of range for effect. This is true of most female and some male singing. However, it is the current fashion for male soloists and groups to use a lot of light high sound that mainly involves the vibration of the vocal ligaments and edges of the vocal folds.

It is important to understand that most people have a speaking voice that is close to the lowest pitches of the voice. Because this is the sound we hear most of the time, we become accustomed to that quality. This can make the higher qualities sound high and thin, or even like yelling, to the ears of singers when they first begin to sing healthily. The more you practice and the more you use audio and video feedback, the faster you will rid yourself of that concept. Trust the process.

Faulty perceptions of the singer can cause imbalance as well. An example of this might be the alto who is trying to sound like her perception of an alto, and therefore putting a lot of pressure on the voice by singing heavily. This can happen also to nonclassical singers who try to sing in a heavy, throaty voice throughout their range. When this occurs, it puts quite a strain on the vocal folds and can cause a break in the voice and even physical damage.

Note: It is easy to get hung up on creating an even sound *inside your head.* This is one of the jokes played on you by the acoustics of the voice. When you allow your inner hearing or analytical-critical brain to dominate control of the sound, the joke is on you because it does not come out that way to the audience. Singers who do this find it hard to believe that they are being fooled—but fooled they are. For the singer, the motor is inside the body and all the mechanics can be heard. Good singing can be very noisy internally and will sound and feel very uneven and buzzy to you. This is why it is imperative to have a teacher with good eyes and ears, or audio, and preferably, video feedback.

VIBRATO

As beginning singers develop an easily produced sound, they often feel and hear their voices become pulsating and "wavy." The common response is, "Does that make me sound like an opera singer?" There is a fear that the voice is becoming too stylized, and the reference in this case is negative. However, you need to know that the voice has a natural vibrato that contributes to the pleasantness of the sound. It is a factor that successful pop singers use frequently.

The vibrato is an acoustic phenomenon that occurs in most voices. It was so valued by instrumentalists that they have mimicked it in their playing. It is like waves or ripples of sound. These waves can be fast or slow (frequency), deep or shallow (amplitude), and narrow and wide (variance)—much like the ripples in water. They add beauty to the sound and are acceptable to the ear as long as they vary no more than a quarter of a tone on either side of the pitch. An amplitude that is too wide will produce a sound that varies too much around the pitch and is unpleasant to the listener.

When these waves of sound are too fast and too close together, they are like a bleat—usually caused by pushing the voice too much from the throat. This bleat can occur when you try to restrict airflow at the level of the larynx rather than use the breathing muscles appropriately. When the frequency of the vibrato is too slow and wide, a wobble is heard. This can be caused by a number of factors from poor breath management to muscle fatigue. Comics like to mimic opera singers by producing a big fat sound with a wobble. It does not have to be that way. Note that it is not useful for the singer to think of controlling the vibrato. The keys to even sound are good alignment, efficient muscle use, deep breathing, and consistent airflow.

The ideal vibrato has consistent, even acoustic waves. They are not perfect like a computer, which can generate perfect waves but not beautiful vocal sounds. The ear prefers a vibrato that occurs from five to eight times per second and varies a semitone around the pitch. Any voice or acoustics lab can show you exactly how all the variants of the vibrato look spectrographically.

STRAIGHT SOUND

Some types of music demand less vibrato and more speech-like sound. Certainly speech quality is used in a variety of styles such as pop, jazz, rap, rock, and some world music. An acoustic reading will demonstrate that this sound irons out the peaks and troughs of the vibrato. There is nothing wrong with a straight sound as long as it is not blatant, strained, or tight. Every singer needs variety of sound and expression. When you use your imagination, you will be surprised at the spontaneous response of your voice in color and quality.

When you sing in a choir, you may hear the conductor ask the singers to produce a straight tone with less vibrato. Conductors find it difficult to get a balanced matched sound when there are so many diverse vocal techniques in the choir. It is the conscientious singers who follow the directions and the not-so-concientious ones who keep their vibrato; invariably the straight tones get straighter and the vibratos increase, thus defeating the purpose. Your training in the basic principles of good singing with work on posture and breath will cause many of the issues of vocal imbalance to go away.

Finding out for yourself . . .

Many schools have voice or acoustics labs with spectrographs or oscilloscopes. Experimenting on these machines while making various tones can be very enlightening for the singer. You may even have a software program on your computer that will do this for you. Visit the acoustics or language lab in your school or some place nearby and experiment with well-coordinated vocal attacks, breathy sounds, deliberate vibrato, and straight tones.

Chapter Ten

Voice Quality and Resonance

Each person has his or her own unique vocal signature or vocal quality. This is why you can recognize people simply by hearing their voices. As children learn to speak, they mimic the muscular speech patterns of close relatives, peers, and the local community. Regional speech patterns are referred to as dialects or "accents." Your accent is a result of the infinite variety of shapes formed in the throat or the pharynx and the movement patterns of the tongue and jaw.

While the sound is initiated in the larynx, the quality of sound depends on the shape of the pharynx. The pharynx (throat) is highly flexible and capable of forming many different shapes. Each variation in shape will cause your voice to produce a different voice quality.

Finding out for yourself . . .

Find a way to watch or listen to three or four singers with different styles—country-western, jazz, gospel, pop. Note particularly what they do with the vowel sounds, and their lips and jaws. See if you can discover what makes them different.

Imitate several of these styles. What do you have to do to sing that way? What changes do you feel in your throat when you do it?

The pharynx serves a dual purpose by acting as an air and a food passageway. For breathing it needs to be relaxed and spacious; for swallowing it closes around the food and squeezes it down into the esophagus. When you swallow, the whole pharynx is pulled up and narrowed to squeeze the food down. This brings the larynx up with it. Therefore the whole throat becomes short and narrow—not a good space for singing. When the muscles of the pharynx relax, the space is wide and long—the optimum for the most resonance and a freely produced sound. People sing in many gradations between the closed and open throat.

> **Finding out for yourself . . .**
>
> **Put your finger on your larynx and swallow. Note what happens. Now sing something in the position of the "swallow." What does it sound like?**
>
> **With your finger still on your larynx take a nice breath with your mouth open. What happens now? Sing something with that feeling of space.**

Structure of the Pharynx

The pharynx is a muscular sleeve-like structure that hangs from the base of the skull and attaches itself to various bones and cartilages along the way. It has openings into the nose, the mouth, and the larynx, and then it becomes completely circular and continues as the esophagus.

DIVISIONS OF THE PHARYNX

Anatomists and acousticians usually divide the pharynx into three main sections: the nasal pharynx, the oral pharynx, and the laryngeal pharynx (see Figure 10.1). The nasal pharynx is located between the base of the skull and the soft palate. The soft palate (the soft part located at the end of your hard palate) can move up and close off the nose as in making non-nasal sounds or swallowing, and it can be lowered for nasal sounds or breathing (you will have a chance to experiment with this later).

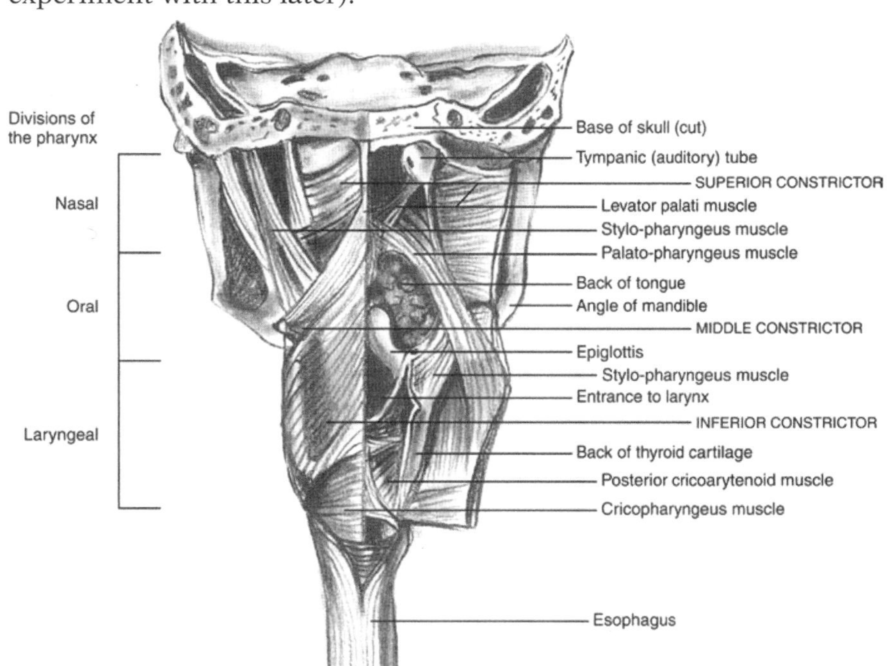

Figure 10.1
Pharynx (from behind)

> **Finding out for yourself . . .**
>
> **You can find your soft palate by running your tongue along your hard palate until you reach the soft flexible part at the back.**
>
> **You can feel the soft palate lower when you sniff or sneeze. You can feel it rise when you yawn or try to blow through closed lips.**

The oral pharynx begins at the level of the soft palate and continues to the level of the middle of the epiglottis near the back of the tongue. This area is the most flexible and subject to many different shapes. Because the soft palate can move up and down and your tongue and larynx can move as well, the oral pharynx can get taller, wider, narrower, shorter, and so on. It is the place where most of your vocal resonance occurs.

The laryngeal pharynx is the area from the middle of the epiglottis to the lower border of the cricoid cartilage. This area is credited with contributing to the acoustic part of the voice responsible for its carrying power. In pedagogy books it is referred to as the "ring" of the voice.

These three areas are continuous but are usually described separately to help explain the structures better. Now we can look at more details.

BONES AND CARTILAGES TO WHICH MUSCLES OF THE PHARYNX ATTACH

The key to understanding the pharynx is to look at the bony structure to which the muscles attach (see Figure 10.2). In the illustration there are arrows pointing to the base of the skull, the pointed

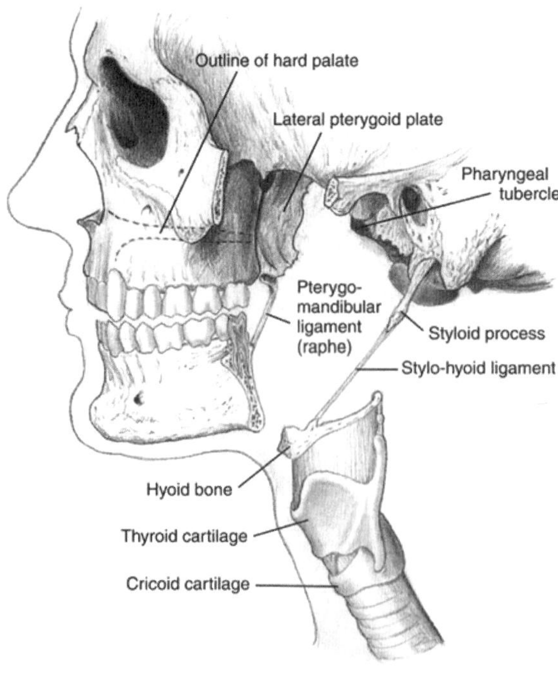

FIGURE 10.2 *Bony structure of the pharynx*
(With permission of Springer-Verlag and M. Bunch. From *Dynamics of the Singing Voice*, M. Bunch.)

process that hangs from the skull (styloid process), the ligament from the styloid to the hyoid bone (stylo-hyoid ligament), the hyoid bone, and the thyroid and cricoid cartilages. Seeing these will help you understand the complex relationship between the muscles of the pharynx and the other structures of phonation.

IMPORTANT MUSCLES THAT FORM THE PHARYNX

Let's look again at the actions of the pharynx from a logical standpoint. We know that to swallow something the muscles need to contract and narrow the back of the throat in order to squeeze the food down. We also know that the larynx comes up under the tongue as part of the same action. What muscles are contracting to cause these actions to happen?

The pharynx is considered to have two layers of muscles: an outer circular layer and an inner longitudinal layer. The outer layer squeezes the food down in swallowing and the inner layer pulls the pharynx and larynx up. The outer circular layer consists of three paired constrictor muscles (inferior, middle, and superior). The lowest part of the inferior constrictor, called the crico-pharyngeus, forms the beginning of the esophagus. The constrictors arise from bones, ligaments, and cartilages at the sides and meet in the center at the back. The crico-pharyngeus simply begins on one side of the cricoid cartilage and continues to the other side forming a sphincter-like opening (see Figure 10.3). When the constrictors contract, they exert a pull on the least stable area—in this case, the back of the throat—and cause a narrowing of the throat.

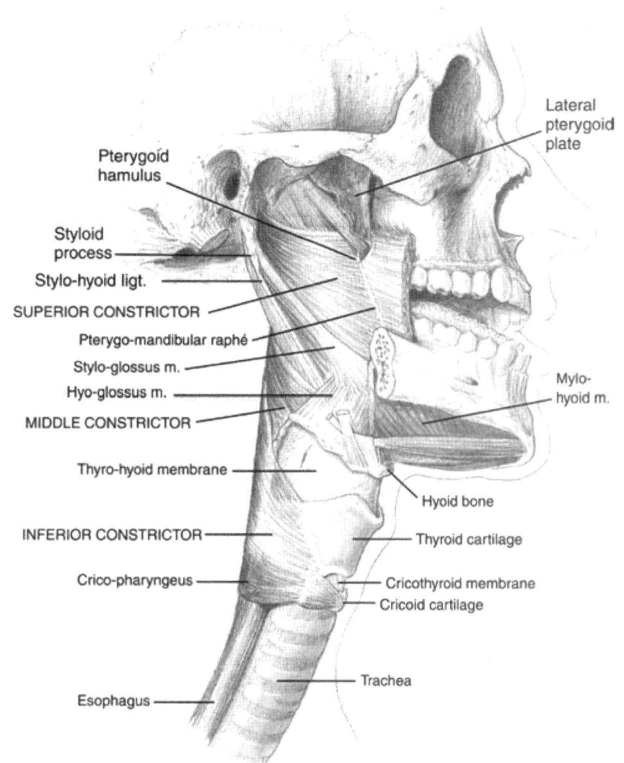

FIGURE 10.3
Muscles of the pharynx
(With permission of Springer-Verlag and M. Bunch. From *Dynamics of the Singing Voice*, M. Bunch.)

The second layer of muscles runs up and down and forms the longitudinal layer. These muscles run from the skull (styloid process—stylo-pharyngeus) and the palate (palato-pharyngeus) to the back of the pharynx and thyroid cartilage (see Figure 10.1). When they contract they shorten the space by pulling up the back of the throat and the larynx.

Notice that we have been discussing the muscles that make the pharynx narrow and short. This is not an ideal configuration for singing or speaking. Are you becoming aware that in order to have a wide, long pharynx you must release or relax these muscles?

Soft Palate

The palate has been mentioned above. It is not considered part of the pharynx, but through shared muscles the two are linked intricately. The soft palate is very flexible and is capable of moving up and down. It closes off the back of the nose during swallowing to prevent food from entering the nasal passages. In efficient vocal production, the palate does the same thing to prevent air from going into the nose and causing an unwanted nasal resonance. The raising of the soft palate also creates more resonance space in the throat. The palate will be lowered during intentional use of nasal consonants or sounds.

Note: Good singing can feel "nosy" without being nasal. If you wish to check whether your sound is nasal, hold your nose while singing non-nasal consonants. For example, sing something like "all is light." There are no nasal sounds and the voice will be clear if the palate is up. However, if air is escaping through the nose you will get an exaggeration of the nasality.

Finding out for yourself . . .

Stand in front of a mirror and look at your soft palate while saying [a] and a nasal [ã]. You will see the palate move up and down as you say each one alternately.

Sing a phrase of a song while holding your nose. When the palate is up, the sound will be clear. However, when the palate drops for the nasal consonants you will sound like you have a very bad cold and blocked nasal passages.

MUSCLES OF THE SOFT PALATE

Four main muscles form the soft palate: two that are above it and two below it. There is a pair of muscles that lifts the palate (levator palati) and a pair that widens it (tensor palati) (see Figure 10.4). The levator muscles come from the skull and pull the palate up. The tensor muscles are a little more complex. They have an attachment to the Eustachian tube and are thought to help adjust pressure in the inner ear.

Two muscles go down from the palate to the sides of the tongue at the back. They are named, logically, palato glossus (glossus means

Base of the skull
Auditory tube
Tensor palati muscle
Levator palati muscle
Pterygoid plate
Back of the nose
Hamulus
Palato-pharyngeus muscle
Uvula
Posterior

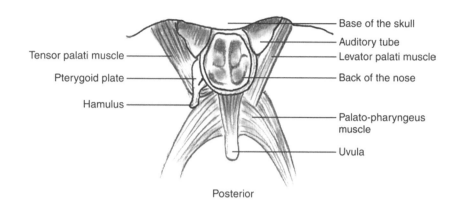

FIGURE 10.4
Muscles of the soft palate (posterior view)

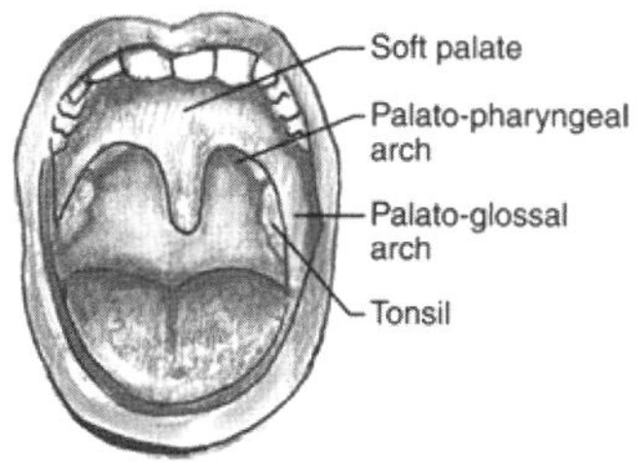

FIGURE 10.5
Inside the mouth

tongue). You can see these muscles when you open your mouth and look in a mirror. On each the side of your tongue is a fold that forms an arch with the uvula hanging down in the middle (see Figure 10.5). That fold is the palato glossus muscle. Behind that fold is another one that is formed by the other two palatal muscles that go from the palate down to the back of the pharynx and the superior horns of the thyroid cartilage.

You can begin to see some of the complex relationships that exist in the head and neck (see Figure 10.6). The tongue and palatal relationship is a particularly important one. When a singer has the habit of tensing the tongue or pulling it down in the back to make sound, the soft palate can be prevented from going up because the palato glossus is acting as an antagonist to the levator palati. The sound that results is a bit garbled and not too pleasant.

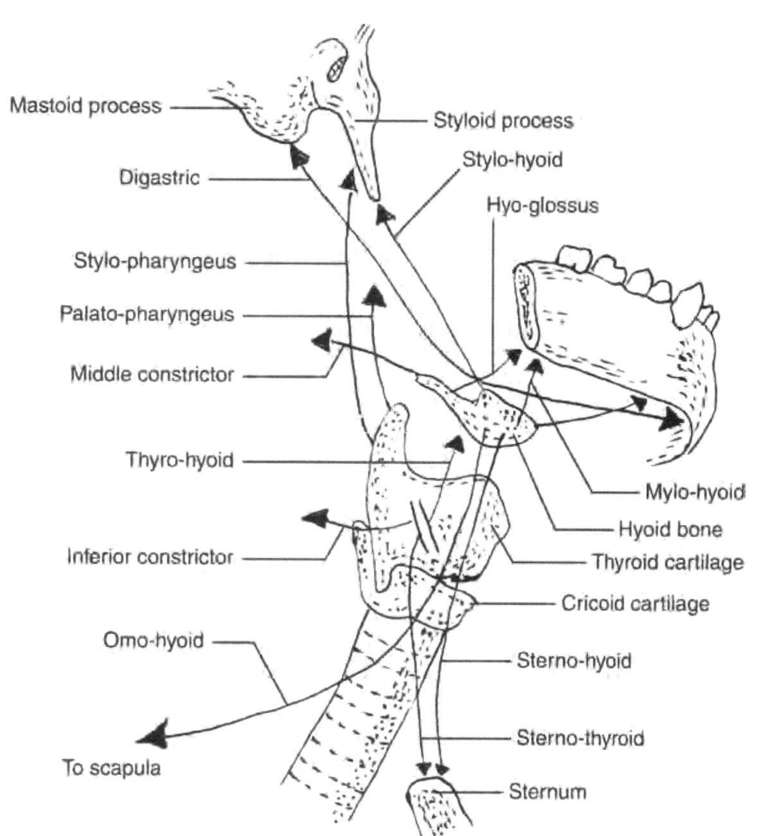

FIGURE 10.6
Directions of muscle pull on larynx and hyoid bone

Finding out for yourself . . .

Stand in front of a mirror and observe your soft palate. When you take a surprise breath, the palate will probably go up. However, when you deliberately pull your tongue down, notice what happens to the soft palate.

Relationship between Pharynx and Larynx

The first illustration in this chapter demonstrated the relationship of the skull, jaw, hyoid bone, and larynx. When these structures are in alignment, the muscles of the pharynx and the position of the larynx is freely suspended in the neck. They are in position to respond easily to what is asked of them. When the head or jaw pushes forward, this alignment is distorted and the pharynx and larynx are put at a disadvantage. The roles of the tongue and jaw are explained in Chapter Eleven, which discusses articulation. Your posture is the key to allowing the muscles of the throat to respond to the sound you wish to make.

Acoustic Deception

It is worth repeating that how you think you sound and how you actually sound can be very different. The reason is that you have so much feedback inside your head. Your bones act as conductors of vibration. Your larynx buzzes, and sound bouncing around your throat can be noisy and deceptive. Interestingly, your audience does not hear all of this.

Your acute sensitivity to the mechanical workings of your instrument can cause you to have a very unbalanced idea of your own sound. Do you remember the first time a recording of your voice was played back to you? Most people respond to this by saying, "I don't sound like that, do I?" And the answer is, "Yes, to the rest of the world you do." This is why a teacher or video feedback is so important—particularly at the beginning of your study. In time you will learn your own voice well enough to have a better idea of your external sound. However, as long as you sing, outside feedback will be very important to you.

Even Tone

Many singers, especially classical ones, aspire to create a beautiful, even sound throughout their ranges, but trying to do this by exerting excessive control over everything in the throat and mouth results in an even sound inside the head and an uneven or tight one to the listener. With freedom and pure vowel sounds, your voice will be consistent throughout.

Creating Vocal Variety

It is not necessary for you to consciously manipulate the muscles in your throat to color sound. This will only create tension and an undesired vocal quality. Your expression and vocal color will respond to your understanding of the text and to your imagination and energy. Focusing on and deeply understanding your message will go a long way toward creating the vocal effects you want—whether they are dark, bright, light, or heavy. You can sing any song in a variety of characters—old, young, king, queen, witch, or any other you desire.

What Is a Resonator?

A resonator needs to be hollow and have an opening for the sound to escape. In singing, your throat acts as the primary resonator with help from the nose (nasal sounds) and mouth. There are many anecdotes regarding resonators of the voice—including the great line from the comedienne, Anna Russell, who said, "Singers have resonance where their brains ought to be." The sinuses are often credited with adding resonance. You may feel their vibration but it is inaudible to the audience. And the tiny openings of the sinuses are not large enough to qualify for a resonator. Even when your sinuses are blocked with an infection or cold, you can sing without a sinus sound. While this honky sound can be heard when you speak, it rarely comes through when you sing because singers are more conscientious than speakers about raising the soft palate.

Vocal Problems and the Pharynx

Tension is the main problem associated with the pharynx. Tension will narrow the space of the throat and cause the larynx to rise under the tongue. The quality of the sound is then compromised. Because we swallow many times during a day, it is easy to get caught somewhere between the full swallow and full relaxation of the throat. Don't get caught in a tense swallowing position when you need to be relaxed for singing.

Misalignment of the head and shoulders is another major contributor to poor tone quality and to potential vocal damage. Pushing the head forward toward the microphone or audience is extremely common and exaggerated in the pop singing world where singers manage to copy the bad habits of famous singers rather than the good ones. All singers need to keep their heads over their shoulders!

Your Speaking Voice

How many times have you heard someone sing well and then speak poorly? Some singers work very hard to create optimum quality in singing and then become completely slovenly when speaking. Your speaking voice needs the same careful attention that you give to your singing. The same principles and habits of good singing discussed in this book apply to speaking. Bear this in mind.

Using good speaking habits may feel artificial to you at first, but keep working at it. The change will not be drastic; you will probably sound clearer and articulate your words better. Using good speech habits will make it much easier for you to sing.

Chapter Eleven *Articulation and Expression*

Music alone can convey many emotions, but it is words that enhance and underline the emotions in vocal music. In the first section of this book, you were asked to learn the text of your song before learning the tune. It was one indication of how important words are to the music. Typically, composers begin with a text and then set it to music. With some of the more improvised forms of music, such as jazz, rap, and pop, music and words are often created concurrently.

Words are meant to be heard and understood. This sets the singer apart from instrumentalists. Therefore, it is vital that the text of the music be clear, efficiently produced, and expressive. Physically, this means that the structures of articulation—the soft palate, jaw, tongue, and lips—have to be loose and available to respond to the text. Tension in any of these areas restricts their movement and makes it difficult to articulate quickly and easily. This is where speech habits can help or hinder your ease of singing. Poor speech habits will become exaggerated when you begin to sing. This does not mean you need to create an entirely different voice—simply that you correct any poor habits.

Finding out for yourself . . .

You can feel the various actions of the jaw by doing the following:

Put a finger in or just in front of your ear and gently and slowly move your jaw forward, backward, downward, upward, and sideways. Make sure that you are not moving your lips instead. Many people with a tight jaw will compensate by doing strange things with their lips. Next, with a partner, deliberately sing with your jaw in these positions:

- Forward
- Backward
- Clenched
- Deviated to one side
- Loose and hanging freely

What is the difference in sound in each position?

When someone complains about not being able to understand the words, the singer usually responds with increased muscular effort with the jaw and lips. It is common for singers to think that they need to exaggerate the movement of the lips and jaw to make the sound clearer. Nothing could be further from the truth. Over-exaggeration of consonants and vowels causes unwanted changes in the shape of the throat, distortion of the words, and singing that is off pitch. Rap and patter songs—fast, wordy, theater songs such as those by Stephen Sondheim or Gilbert and Sullivan—demand rapid, almost shotgun speed of articulation. For this you need loose lips and jaw, and a flexible tongue. It would be extremely difficult to sing fast music with lots of words with a tense jaw or lips.

Structures of Articulation

Let's take a closer look at the structures that help us to articulate. As in the case of the pharynx, these structures are heavily involved with the process of eating, particularly chewing. The muscles involved are very powerful because they are used so much.

THE JAW

The jaw bone, or mandible, is shaped a bit like a horseshoe with long upward portions at the ends, and it hangs from the skull by means of ligaments and muscles. Those upward portions form a joint with the skull on each side just in front of the ears (see Figure 11.1). Most of the muscles of the jaw are used for chewing (muscles of mastication) and are responsible for moving it up and down, forward or backward, or side to side. Since you spend the majority of your time with your mouth closed (unless you breathe through your mouth or talk incessantly), the muscles that elevate the jaw are active continually. Therefore, to allow them to relax and let the jaw hang freely during singing or speech require concentration and willpower on your part.

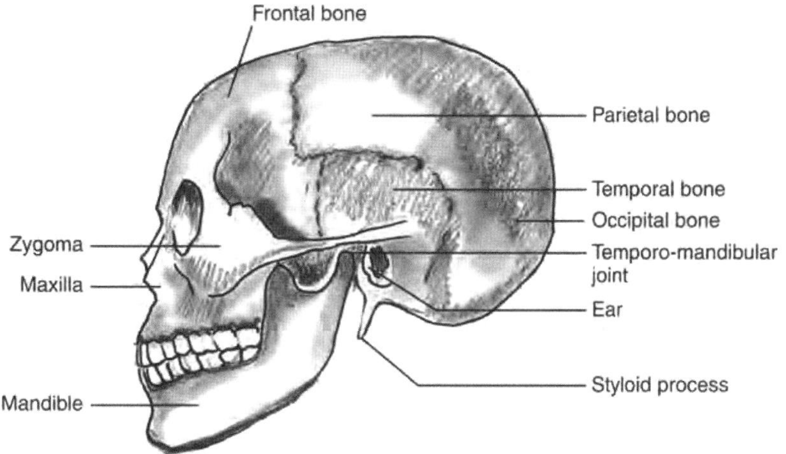

Figure 11.1
Skull, jaw, and temporo-mandibular joint

MUSCLES THAT MOVE THE JAW

Two powerful muscles elevate the jaw. The first (*temporalis*) is located in the area of your temple and above and behind the ear. You can feel the action of this muscle by spreading your fingers just above and behind your ear and slowly moving your jaw up and down. As you move your jaw up and down, you can feel the temporalis contract and become bulky under your fingers. It occupies most of the area above your ears and attaches very strongly to the jaw (see Figure 11.2).

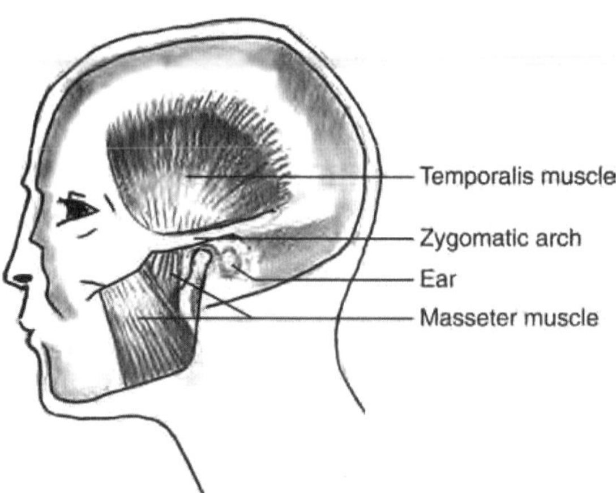

Figure 11.2 *Temporalis and masseter muscles (schematic drawing)*

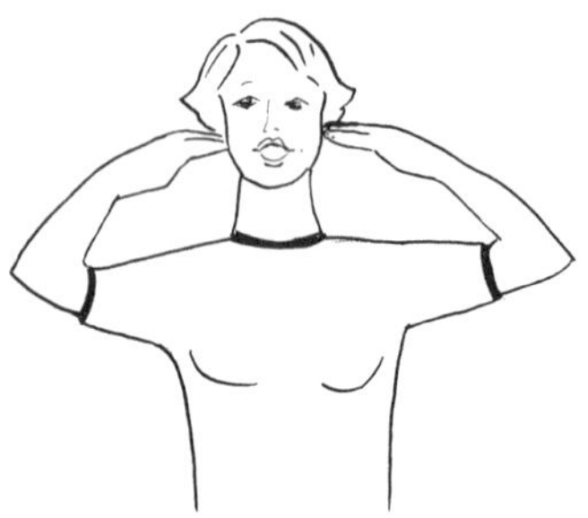

Figure 11.3 *Feeling the actions of the jaw*

Note the directions of its fibers: Some are straight up and down while others slant backward. This tells you that the muscle is capable of both elevating and retracting the jaw.

The second set of muscles that elevate the jaw is located between the cheekbone and the angle of the jaw (*masseter*) (see Figure 11.2). It becomes bulky when you grind your teeth. You can feel its action by placing your fingers along the side of your face and grinding your back teeth—gently (see Figure 11.3).

Muscles on either side of the skull that attach to the joint area of the jaw (*lateral pterygoids*) cause side to side movements (see Figure 11.4). They coordinate with one another, that is, one is active and the other is passive depending upon which side of the jaw is moving. When they act together, they help protrude the jaw or bring it forward. There is another set of pterygoid muscles (*medial pterygoids*) that elevates the jaw or can work with the lateral pterygoids to protrude it.

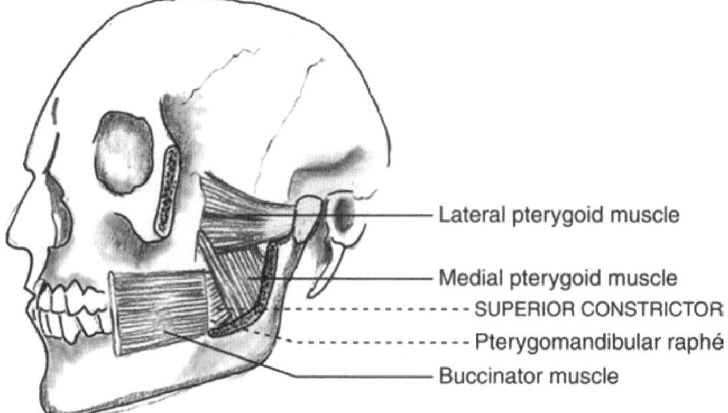

Figure 11.4 *Pterygoid muscles*

PROBLEMS RELATING TO THE JAW

The jaw has many complex relationships with the skull, the pharynx, tongue, and larynx. Therefore, when the jaw is displaced forward or jammed open, the whole vocal tract is affected. A number of regional (southern and other) speech patterns include slightly moving the jaw forward for consonants—particularly the ch and j consonants. (If you watch very closely, many people pronounce these consonants with a slight forward movement of the jaw.) The jutting jaw is unnecessary and it causes vocal havoc. It pulls the back of the throat forward, tends to raise the larynx, and makes it difficult to use the tongue efficiently.

A number of things can cause the jaw to deviate to one side as it opens. Chewing mainly on one side will strengthen the muscles on that side and tend to pull it in that direction. Also, people who have poor hearing in one ear will tend to open the mouth in the direction of the good ear. They can hear themselves better that way.

One enormous problem relating to the jaw is that of over-opening it. When the mouth is open too wide, the back of the throat tends to close. It becomes physically impossible for the tongue to reach the palate so the consonants and vowels become distorted. Ideally the jaw just hangs—freely available. The energy yawn exercise in Part One is good for releasing the jaw.

MUSCLES OF THE TONGUE

While the jaw and hard palate provide the stable structures for articulation, the tongue, lips, and soft palate do most of the work. The tongue, in particular, carries a large part of the responsibility for the production of vowels and consonants. It is composed of several groups of muscles (see Figure 11.5) that come from the skull, soft palate, mandible, hyoid bone, and some intrinsic ones that have no bony attachments.

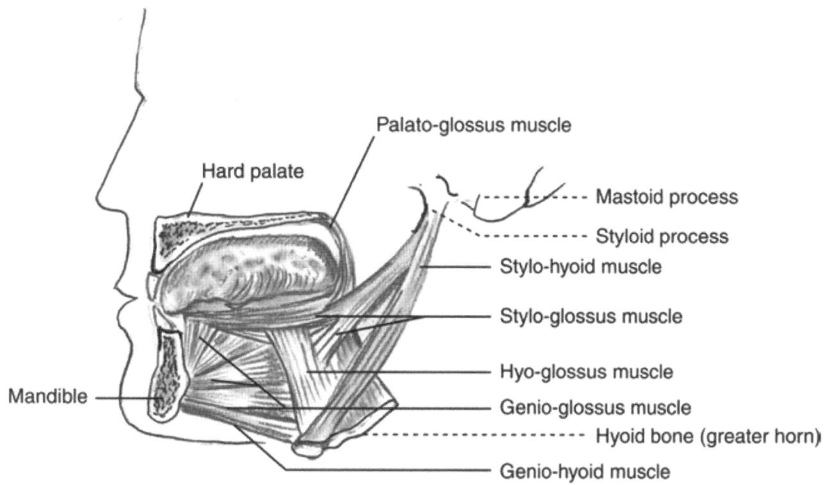

FIGURE 11.5
Muscles of the tongue

The muscles that attach to the skull pull the tongue back and up (*stylo-glosssus*); those attaching to the hyoid bone (*hyo-glossus*) pull it down at the sides at the back (a common American speech pattern that is not helpful for singing); and those attaching to the soft palate (*palato-glossus*) can either pull the back of the tongue up or act antagonistically to the elevators of the soft palate. Tension in any of these muscles is not helpful at all.

A muscle having several bundles (*genio-glossus*) makes up the bulk of the tongue. These bundles act together to protrude your tongue. When acting separately they can draw parts of the tongue downward.

Other acrobatic movements such as grooving the tongue or turning it over are attributed to the small intrinsic muscles that are located between the other muscles. Some of these movements may be hereditary.

Finding out for yourself . . .

With a partner sing a few phrases in the following ways:

- **With your normal singing pattern**
- **With the tongue pulled down as if trying to flatten it**
- **With the tongue tip returning to the edge of the lower teeth each time**
- **Flicking the tongue in and out of your mouth as you sing**

How do you compare the various voice qualities produced in this exercise? What have you learned about your own habits?

PROBLEMS ASSOCIATED WITH THE TONGUE

In this age of close-up television, it is easy to see what a singer does with the mouth and tongue. Many good singers show a flat tongue that is a natural characteristic for them. However, this is not the same as deliberately pulling the tongue down. When done purposely, there is excess tension, the soft palate is pulled down, the pitch is poor, and the tone is garbled. You can experiment with this by putting your thumb in the soft area under your jaw (under the tongue) and checking for tension. If there is no tongue tension it will be loose and your thumb will not encounter resistance; with tension there will be a lump. You can feel this when you pull down the back of the tongue.

SPEECH PATTERNS THAT CONTRIBUTE TO TONGUE TENSION

Two of the most obvious characteristics of the American dialect or accent are the backed [a] (made by pulling the back of the tongue down) and the tense [r]. Pulling down the back of the tongue creates a garbled, strangled [a] that interferes with easy vocal production. Singers who want to learn to sing any of the European languages often despair at learning a correct, vocally pure [a] sound.

The American [r] is famous—or infamous—and imitated by anyone wanting to sound American. It is a problem because the tip of the tongue curls backward and completely changes the vocal quality —for the worse. While country-western, folk, and pop singers may love it, it is not useful for other styles and creates many vocal problems. We sustain sound on vowels and when the tongue slowly curls while you are singing a vowel, the distortion becomes obvious. You can try this out with a friend by singing and exaggerating the "rrr."

Some performers have too much tension in the tongue when they sing. When this is so, the inner sound can be perceived as loud and feel gratifying to the performer. However, the audience is getting a very different perception. This is another area in which there can be poor acoustic perception. A good tape recorder will let you know whether the audience would perceive your sound in the same way.

THE SOFT PALATE

The soft palate was mentioned in the chapter on vocal quality. Because the soft palate is interlinked muscularly with the tongue and pharynx, movements of the jaw and tongue can cause its ideal function to be compromised. The whole area around the soft palate, tongue, and jaw can create a lingering problem because it is difficult to know where to put the blame when something is not quite right. Create a checklist for yourself when you cannot find out what is causing you difficulty. Always begin with posture and breathing, then check the mirror for any deviations of the jaw, tongue, and lips. Become a vocal sleuth.

THE LIPS

One of the first things you learned to do as a child was to enjoy games with adults by making funny faces. Playing with different lip configurations and making sounds like "raspberries" was all part of the fun. We would lose much of our expression if we had little or no possibility of movement of our lips. The feel-good effect that a smile has on your own body and on others is well known. We prove it every day.

The lips are part of a large group of muscles that belong to facial expression. The muscles that form the lips come from the cheekbones, the face next to the nose, and the area near the upper teeth and the jaw; they form a muscle that encircles the mouth (sphincter). These muscles are in position to move the lips to create expressions such as smiling, frowning, puckering, sneering, pouting, and many other variants (see Figure 11.6). Their names usually reflect

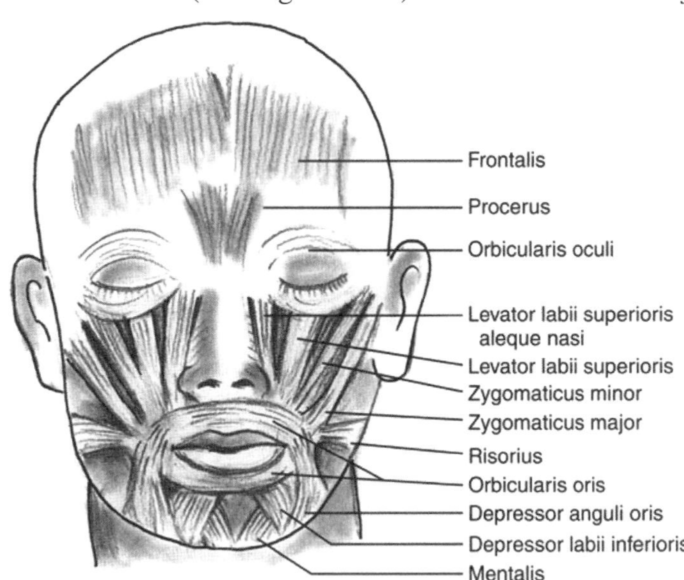

FIGURE 11.6
Muscles of facial expression

PART THREE

their actions (for example, the *levator anguli oris* means the elevator of the angle of the mouth).

The lips, together with the tongue, are responsible for most of the consonants we use. Therefore, like the rest of the vocal mechanism, they need to be flexible and free. Try singing a very fast song with tense lips. You will soon find that the rhythm and phrasing get slower and slower. Your jaw will begin to ache because tense lips will inhibit its movement.

Muscles of Facial Expression

The muscles of facial expression are a very magical group of thin muscles that have few or no bony attachments. They lie just under the skin of the face and enable us to express our feelings and emotions. These muscles are in the scalp (for those of you who can wrinkle your scalp), the forehead (we see these when people look worried or intense), radiating from the ears (some people can wiggle their ears), and around the eyes, the lips, and the chin.

You probably know people who say everything with the same facial expression. What effect does that have on the sound and your gut reaction to what they are saying? The exercise below demonstrates what happens when the facial expression and words are not matched.

Finding out for yourself . . .

This is an exercise to be done in pairs.

Choose one or two lines of a song that you can sing over and over (each person is to chose a different song). Get your partner to fill in the form as you sing the same lines each time in the following ways:

	How does it look?	How does it sound?	What's your gut reaction?
1. with furrowed brows			
2. with staring eyes			
3. with alive, seeing eyes			
4. with lips protruded			
5. with lips tense			
6. with an overly broad smile			
7. with a frown (a downturned mouth)			
8. with the jaw jutting forward			
9. with the jaw jammed downward each time you open to sing			
10. with the jaw hanging freely			

The exercise described above is good for indicating what happens when we have speech or singing habits that are fixed for everything we sing. Both the tone and the intended message are affected. It can be very funny, yet give a seriously flawed message when you have any of those habits.

Vowels and Consonants

The building blocks of languages are vowels and consonants. Without vowels there would be no way of sustaining sound—unless you want to spend your life humming. Consonants enable us to define the sound and communicate meaning and language. We have discussed the main physical structures of articulation and how they work individually. Now let's look at how they combine to produce vowels and consonants.

VOWELS

The position of the tongue, with some help from the lips, is mainly responsible for shaping the vocal tract and creating the resonances that are recognized as vowels. Fine movements of the tongue and its position in the mouth make all of the vowels and their various hybrids. The role of the tongue may come as a surprise to you if you have learned exaggerated movements of your lips and jaw as part of your speech patterns and regional dialects. Regional speech dialects can include some strange vowel shapes and sounds. For example, some dialects can include several vowel sounds together when only one is needed for singing. (Two vowel sounds used together make up a *diphthong;* three vowel sounds are a *triphthong*.) And they can make sounds that were intended to be diphthongs into one sound. For example, the vowel sound in the word "fine" is a double vowel, [ai], but often pronounced [a].* This happens on many occasions in speech and must be corrected in singing. The full sound of each word is important in classical singing. Other styles incorporate more everyday use of language sounds. However, it is still important for the words to be understood.

Singers who adjust their vowel sounds for optimum singing are often said to sing "without an accent." American singers often comment that British singers (such as the Beatles) lose their British accent when they sing. In fact, the prevailing pop song accent at the moment is American.

Singers can create very uneven vowel sounds by exaggerating mouth and lip positions. (This distorts the vocal tract.) There is a common misconception that the vowels are made by the lips. Notice what happens to the quality when you sing an [i] sound with wide smiling lips. It will become very bright compared to the vowels that are made mainly by the position of the tongue. The pictures below indicate the tongue positions for the main vowels: [i], [a], [o], and [u] (see Figure 11.7). Any changes in the tongue position while you are singing a vowel will begin to distort it or change it, and may confuse the audience about what you are singing.

*For a guide to the International Phonetic Alphabet, see Appendix C.

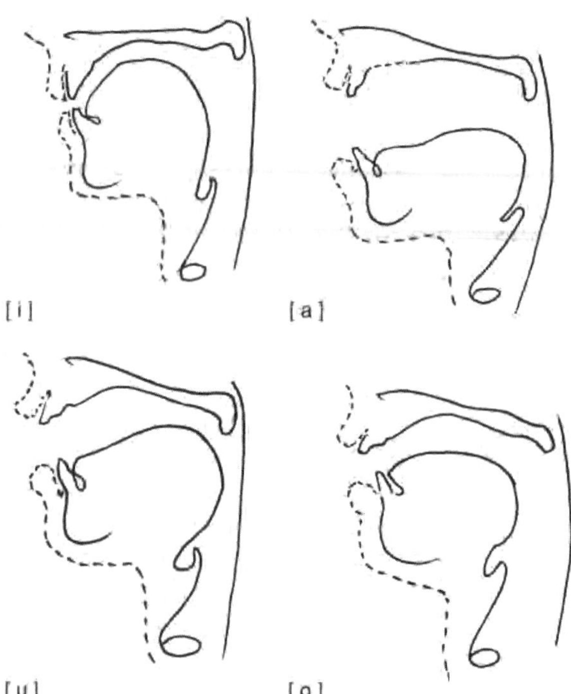

FIGURE 11.7
Tongue positions for [i] (beet), [a] (father), [u] (boot), [o] (boat)

> **Finding out for yourself . . .**
>
> **With a partner or a mirror, sing the vowels on one pitch with:**
>
> - **exaggerated mouth and lips for each one**
> - **different jaw positions for each vowel**
> - **a finger between the teeth with no jaw or extra lip movement**
>
> **Try to sing an [i] with a flat tongue. What happens to the sound?**

CONSONANTS

Clear words are the result of efficient pronunciation of consonants. Slovenly consonants and speech habits can be the downfall of good vocal communication—even in nonclassical styles. Good articulation of consonants requires an efficient, coordinated movement of lips and tongue, with little or no action from the jaw. (*Note:* the jaw needs to close only for sounds such as [sh], [j], [ch], [s], and [v].) All movements are articulated centrally, along the middle of the face. When any of the consonants are produced physically off-center the sound becomes distorted. This is called "chewing" the sound.

Consonants are classified according to how they are physically made, and whether they are voiced or unvoiced (see chart below). You can experiment with these by pronouncing [p] and [b], [v] and [f], [d] and [t]. These are all pairs that are physically alike, yet one is made with vocal sound and one without.

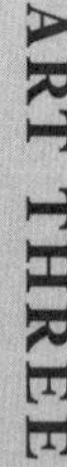

CLASSIFICATION OF CONSONANT SOUNDS

Physical action	*Examples*	
	Voiced	*Voiceless*
Upper and lower lips	b. m*	p
Upper teeth and lower lip	v	f
Upper teeth and tongue	th (thing)	th (this)
Alveolar ridge (just behind teeth) and tongue tip	d, n*, l, z**,	t, s**
Alveolar ridge — palate boundary and tongue blade	z (seizure)	s (she)
Hard palate and tongue blade	j	
Soft palate and back of the tongue	g	c, k, q
Glottis (opening between vocal folds)	h	

*Nasals   **Fricatives (noisy, escaping breath)

Some consonants are more like vowels. These include the w and y. The r has been discussed earlier in connection with the tongue.

Note: When the tip of the tongue deviates to the side of the teeth to make an s, air escapes out the other side of the mouth and gives you a lisp. This is not useful for singing. In fact, any deviation from the center of your mouth by the tongue or lips will distort the consonants or vowels. You can correct this with some patient work in front of a mirror by making sure the tip of your tongue stays in the middle when you are pronouncing your words.

Attention to articulation can pay huge dividends in singing. It can help your vocal technique and enable your audience to take part in the song. While the discussion above has been quite technical, it will serve as a guide and reference for you if you have any problems.

Finding out for yourself . . .

You can find out just how clear your consonants are by doing the following:

- First, sing a song your usual way.
- Next, place the tip of a finger centrally between your upper and lower teeth and gently close the teeth on your finger. Do not change this to do the exercise below.
- Sing the song again with finger inserted.
- Did you find that you were trying to chew your finger?

Rest assured, you are able to pronounce your words this way. There may be some minor distortion of the consonants that require the lips to touch in the front. However, they will be making contact with your finger for that sound, and it is usually clear enough for the purposes of this exercise.

Another important thing to learn from this exercise is that you can sing most of your song without the need of excessive jaw movements. Crucially, the back of your throat and soft palate will begin to respond appropriately because you have not dragged them out of place by over-opening your mouth. Over-opening the mouth can cause the back of the throat to narrow rather than widen.

Expression and Words

Expression of your message comes from your imagination, understanding of the text, and motivation. Mindless manipulation of text and concentration on the forming of words will not help you communicate with your audience. Your listeners need meaning if they are to be moved by your singing.

If you do not know this word, spend some time thinking about it: *onomatopoeia*. It relates to how the sounds of words mimic their meaning. The words *buzz* and *hiss* are good examples. The sounds of all words are important. Pictures, symbols, and sounds came before the actual words. It is important to remember this when you rehearse your music. In Part One, Chapter Four, a lot of space was given to the importance of the text and how to approach it. It is worth going back and rereading that section. Revisit the exercise of miming the words with your hands. The clarity of diction, meaning, and motivation will begin to happen for you.

CHAPTER TWELVE

Maintaining a Healthy Voice

If someone gave you a car when you first learned to drive and told you that it had to last your whole life, how would you treat it? Your body was given to you at birth and it lasts for your lifetime. How are you treating it? Your voice is directly affected by how you treat your body. Your general health and sense of well-being will always have an effect on your voice, so treat your body well.

A singer is a "vocal athlete"; you will sing better if you are in shape. Being in shape comes from appropriate physical exercise, mental focus, good nutrition, and a reasonable amount of sleep. Being an athlete or a singer requires responsibility and wisdom in the way you take care of yourself.

Important Health Habits

A POSITIVE ATTITUDE

Many research studies have shown the effects of positive thinking on the immune system. It is true that we create our own reality. A positive attitude about your goals, your abilities, your body, and your singing is step one toward vocal health. Striving for perfection is laudable; kicking yourself for not being perfect is the best way to achieve little and destroy your chances of reaching your goal. Find a way to be positive.

Visualization was discussed in Part One. This is an indispensable tool for achieving what you want. It takes no time—only a second to see yourself being able to do what you want to do technically, physically, and for your life.

Another tool is meditation. It is a fine way to still a hyperactive mind. There are many forms of meditation, from total silence to the chanting of mantras (repeated words or sounds). A group silence is very powerful and can refresh you as much as a short nap. Learn to practice mental "traffic control" by simply stopping what you are doing at several points during the day and experience silence for one or two minutes. Such a discipline can make a huge difference to your study and practice. Meditation is known to focus the mind, to still the body, and even to lower blood pressure. Many people are practicing meditation to alleviate their stress. The "being still" exercise in Part One is a quick way to get into a meditative state.

SLEEP

The body needs sleep for healing itself and regrouping. You can lose sleep for just so long before the body and mind become sluggish and the mind is unable to think clearly. That's why sleep deprivation is used as a form of torture. Sitting in front of a computer all day and night is a recipe for developing poor sleeping patterns. While different people need varying amounts of sleep, the important thing is to get sound, restful sleep most nights. Some things that contribute to healthy sleep patterns are moderate exercise during the day, relaxation and quiet time before going to bed, maintenance of regular hours, and no heavy meals, caffeine, or alcohol just before bed.

NUTRITION

To return to the analogy of a car, what would happen if you mixed the oil and gas in your car with a bit of dirt and water? The car would work for a short time, but after a while would stop. Your body is more tolerant of what you put into it for a while. Eventually, however, it will complain and threaten to stop working well. Your body works hard to keep itself balanced chemically, and everything you take in either sustains or alters that balance.

The first thing your body needs is plenty of water. More than 70 percent of your body is water and what is lost on a daily basis needs to be replenished. Pure water is needed, not just any form of fluid. (Other fluids tend to be regarded as food by the body and treated differently from water.) For singers, the lubrication of the throat and vocal folds is important. So keep your water bottle handy whenever possible.

Like everything else, however, having to drink water can become a kind of obsession. So make sure you are well hydrated *before* important events like concerts. Seeing a singer drinking water on stage can be very off-putting and distracting for the singer and the audience. Drink your water offstage during the intermission or during breaks. Carry it onstage only if you are having some kind of vocal problem or sore throat.

Foods that contain high water content are considered very healthy. This includes most fruits and vegetables, but a diet of only fruit and vegetables does not give us enough muscle-building protein. Protein comes in many forms, so you are able to choose freely from meat, cheese, yogurt, milk, nuts, seeds, and legumes (such as beans and lentils). Grains and some fat are important as well. No matter what your budget, healthy food options are available. Food supplements and vitamins may help when there is little fresh produce. *The key is always balance.*

EXERCISE

There is appropriate exercise for everyone's level of fitness. The simplest thing you can do is walk. It is not unusual for those who live in large cities to walk at least a mile or two a day. In most cities and towns, though, walking to work or school is not a viable option and a car is essential. This is why gyms and local sports clubs are so popular.

Today many forms of exercise are available that work with the mind as well as the body. Some of the most effective forms of exercise and techniques for singers are these:

- Alexander Technique, a way of balancing mind and body through developing efficient habits for daily living
- Feldenkrais, a very effective way to correct your body through micro-movements
- Pilates, exercises for balancing the body and correcting physical problems, especially alignment and the abdominal muscles
- Tai Chi, a beautiful, flowing Eastern martial art form
- Qigong, a combination of movement, breathing, and meditation
- Dance in many forms such as jazz, ballroom, salsa, tap, ballet, circle dancing, and square dancing

Your school or community may offer many of these forms of exercise.

Active exercises that jar and shake the body or make you pant and gasp can be fun and use up lots of energy, but they may not be helpful just before you sing. Jogging in cold air just before a lesson is not a good idea. More is not always better. Be sensible.

HEALTHY VOCAL HABITS

Your vocal health will be enhanced or damaged on a daily basis depending on how you use your voice for speaking and singing. By paying attention to your posture and breathing you can keep yourself out of vocal trouble.

Part One included information on how to practice. Go back and remind yourself of that information now. Wisely spent rehearsal time is vital to your vocal health and learning. Short practice sessions are advisable for the beginning singer. Just as you would not go out and run a mile or run for an hour if you had not run before, you would not sing for an hour either. Being methodical and patient is the best way to learn to sing well.

Habits That Can Harm Your Voice

POOR VOICE USE

At the top of the list of vocal abuse is yelling at sports events. Prolonged yelling puts a lot of pressure on the vocal folds and causes them to swell. The resulting hoarseness is called laryngitis (inflammation of the larynx). It is analogous to spraining your ankle—except that it is your voice. Since you can't wrap it up and protect it, you have to be quiet until the swelling has subsided. Unbounded enthusiasm is commendable, but vocalizing it is not recommended for singers. Remind yourself that the team cannot hear you individually. Therefore let the rest of the crowd do your yelling for you. Ring a bell, blow a horn; just don't yell.

Talking over loud noise and dance music is another way to create vocal problems. There is a catch-22 situation here. There is music playing and people talk over it. Someone then can't hear the music so the volume is turned up. People talk even louder. The music is turned up again. And so it goes on until everyone is shouting. The next morning there are scores of people who are hoarse, have very tired throats, and are somewhat deafened.

Another source of vocal abuse is constant throat clearing. People who do this are often unaware of their habit. Clearing the throat makes the vocal folds virtually explode air out and can cause damage in the long term. This can be a nervous habit to call attention to yourself as well. Ask your friends to let you know if you are constantly clearing your throat. It is common for speakers to clear their throats just before they begin to speak and nervous singers to do this before they sing. Most of the time clearing the throat is not necessary. When you feel the urge to clear, it is best to swallow or drink water instead.

AIRBORNE SUBSTANCES THAT IMPAIR THE VOICE

The job of the vocal folds is to protect your lungs. These folds are so sensitive that inhaling anything larger than 3 microns (much smaller than a speck of dust) in diameter causes you to cough. As further protection, there are tiny hairs called *cilia* attached to the cells that line the windpipe and lungs. They beat upward to clear any debris from your lungs. Airborne or inhaled toxins that are tiny are able to pass by the vocal folds and inflict untold damage on the cells that line the respiratory tract and imbed themselves in the cellular structure of your lungs. Over time the cells lose their protective capacity and disease processes have a clear path. This is particularly true if you smoke anything.

The toxicity of cigarettes is well documented and new evidence regarding cannabis is frightening. Both smoking and passive or secondhand smoking are considered unhealthy. The message for singers is this: *Don't smoke!* It is not helpful to your health or vocal career.

Living in air pollution is not helpful either. We do not always have a choice about where we live and work—smoky nightclubs or toxic big cities may be unavoidable. Make it a point to live in the cleanest environment possible. Keep your personal environment free of smoke, fumes, dust, and damp. At least you will avoid compounding the problem by adding your own pollution.

INGESTION OF TOXIC SUBSTANCES

Your body is working constantly to maintain its chemical balance. When you introduce substances that alter that balance, the body works hard to get rid of them. The broad category of recreational drugs is considered destructive to the body in general—especially in large amounts.

ALCOHOL

Moderation is always a good rule to follow. Drinking six beers one night and none for the next six nights does not constitute moderation—even if the average is one. Your liver is the organ responsible for clearing toxins from your body, and six beers can create mass panic in your liver. You can read many studies about alcohol. Some of these recommend a glass of wine every night; others tell you it is deadly. However, all tend to agree that getting drunk kills brain cells, slows your responses for nearly twenty-four hours, and plays havoc with your liver. Too much alcohol makes it difficult to sing on pitch or respond easily to your music.

Alcohol has a drying effect on the mucous membranes that line the throat and larynx. Over a period of time the dryness can become chronic and the husky, "drinker's voice" emerges. For those serious about their singing, heavy drinking is not an option. Contrary to thought, it does not help you sing better. It can cause you to perceive that you are singing better, but it is more likely to relax the muscles enough to create pitch problems.

NARCOTICS

There are times when we all want to escape the unpleasantness of life in some way. However, drugs like cocaine, opium derivatives, ecstasy, and any other variations will only defer our problems; they don't solve them. A performer, like an athlete, needs all senses and facilities available for the best performance.

Common Problems That Need Professional Help

The following section includes a general discussion of some common issues and typical problems encountered by singers. It is not intended to be a definitive medical statement or a tool for diagnosis, but is purely intended for information. For more specific knowledge, consult a specialist, refer to materials such as those listed in *Further Reading,* or search the Internet. When you have any doubts about the way you are feeling or singing, it is best to consult a health professional.

HOARSENESS

Hoarseness is a catch-all term that can cover a multitude of vocal problems. It occurs when there is any kind of swelling on the vocal folds that causes them to touch with uneven surfaces. It becomes a problem only when it does not go away. Then you have to begin to search for possible causes.

The following can cause temporary hoarseness:

- Poor speech habits
- Over-singing or singing too loudly
- Air conditioning
- Air travel
- Central heating with low humidity

- Singing for too long
- Constant throat clearing
- Drinking too much alcohol
- Medications such as antihistamines that dry the throat
- Medications like aspirin and ibuprofen that cause local bleeding
- Smoking
- Fatigue
- Your menstrual period
- Sore throat
- Cold or flu

Attending to vocal technique, drinking plenty of water, getting a good night's sleep, and humidifying your environment can help most of those problems. If you experience hoarseness after practicing or a choral rehearsal, it will normally go away after a few hours. It is not unusual to over-sing in a choral situation. However, if there is hoarseness after every rehearsal, you would do well to go to your teacher and look at what you might be doing vocally to cause this.

AIR TRAVEL

The incredible dryness experienced during flying can cause all kinds of respiratory symptoms. You are advised to drink lots of water. It is wise to breathe through a wet cloth or mask during the flight as well. This can make all the difference in the way you feel when you land.

EXCESS FLUID DURING MENSTRUAL CYCLES

During the menstrual period it is common for excess fluid to be present in many of the tissues of the body. This includes the vocal folds as well. This swelling makes you feel heavy and dull. You may even sound hoarse from the swelling on the vocal folds. It is best to sing gently on those days and take easy physical exercise when you can. Often singing makes you feel better.

MORE THAN HOARSENESS

As a general rule, when you are hoarse for more than two weeks, you need to seek professional advice. There can be any number of benign causes for this, so it is best not to be your own diagnostician. The problem can be systemic or localized in the vocal or respiratory tracts.

ALLERGIES

We seem to be living in an allergy-filled environment most of the time. There are so many types of allergies—from dust, pollen, perfume, and smoke to food intolerances and reactions to medicines—that determining the ones that you are sensitive to is not always easy. It is not fun to live with streaming eyes and stuffy noses, or with gallons of phlegm. If the allergy is seasonal, then you can get some relief in the off season. When your symptoms continue unabated, it is time to see a doctor or other health practitioner.

LARYNGITIS

Laryngitis is inflammation of the vocal folds and surrounding tissue. It can be viral or bacterial. You can tell the difference by the color of what you are coughing up. If it is greenish and foul-looking, it is usually bacterial and some medication might be in order. You can help yourself by keeping the throat moist at all times. Drinking lots of water and keeping your room humidified is important for your comfort. (Make sure you clean your humidifier periodically. That dampness can harbor all kinds of bugs and bacteria.) Inhaling steam is suggested by many doctors as a treatment for laryngitis and is highly effective in the healing process.

SINUSITIS

The sinuses may be too small to act as resonators and affect our singing positively, but they can certainly cause a lot of discomfort when they are infected. A sinus infection can cause headaches, make you feel heavy-headed, and create a postnasal drip that also causes you to be hoarse. Again, bringing up foul-colored mucus implies infection and indicates the need for professional help. Decongestants can allay the symptoms but may cause excessive drying of the throat. It is unwise to take decongestants over a long period of time.

PERSISTENT SORE THROAT

Like hoarseness, sore throats can stem from a variety of problems. They can be symptomatic of viral or bacterial infection, tonsillitis, sinusitis, and postnasal drip. When you have a sore throat, it is wise to maintain short rehearsals and take good care of your voice. If you overwork your voice while you have a sore throat, you run the risk of developing hoarseness.

VOCAL NODULES

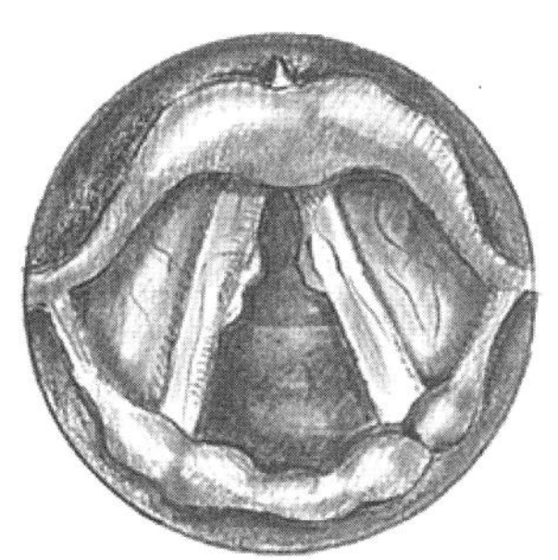

Figure 12.1
Vocal nodules

When people sing or speak with excessive tension or poor vocal technique, they abuse the vocal folds. The vocal folds bang together and create a swelling like a callus or a corn on the inner edges (see Figure 12.1). This may begin as a blood clot and slowly develop into something firmer and larger. The swelling or nodule prevents the vocal folds from touching cleanly and allows excess air through the resulting chink. The symptom is constant hoarseness or breathiness in the speaking and singing voice. There is loss of vocal range and a tendency for the voice to sound breathy, weak, and tired.

When nodules are discovered early enough, they can be corrected by voice and/or speech therapy. The ear, nose, and throat specialist will probably suggest that they be surgically removed if they are large and hard. Good vocal technique is the way to prevent and correct for vocal nodules. Removing the nodules surgically will only remove the symptoms and may leave scar tissue. Vocal nodules will return if you continue the same vocal habits. Many a budding singing career has been ruined by poor technique—no matter what the singing style.

Hoarseness will usually be the first symptom of vocal abuse. There are very few pain fibers in the larynx and it has no obvious way of letting you know you are in trouble. If you are having constant throat pain and vocal fatigue, you need to do something immediately.

VOCAL FATIGUE

Your voice can be overworked over a long period of time to the point of muscle fatigue. Tired vocal muscles, like any other muscle of the body, simply refuse to do what you want. One symptom of vocal fatigue is a wobble in the sound. By the time vocal fatigue sets in, the vocal folds are usually very damaged. This is a serious symptom and is not easily corrected. It is not a likely problem for you at the beginning of your vocal studies, but it is important for you to remember that your voice will not stand constant abuse without eventually rebelling. Classroom teachers yelling over noisy students and anyone shouting over constant noise are prone to this problem. Changing your work environment may be necessary if you want your voice to last your lifetime.

ACID REFLUX

Acid reflux is more common in older than younger people. However, it can happen to anyone at any age. Reflux typically happens during sleep when stomach acids are regurgitated. The acid secreted is a very potent hydrochloric acid that irritates and burns everything it touches. If you have ever wondered what the burning sensation was when you have vomited, it was this acid. It is not pleasant and is very harmful to the larynx. The symptoms of acid reflux include waking up with a burning sensation in the throat that goes away during the day, foul breath (more than your normal bad breath), and hoarseness. People with this problem are usually given special diets, instructed not to eat a heavy meal late at night, advised to keep the head more elevated than the feet at night, and given medication to neutralize the acid. If you think you have reflux, see your doctor.

DEAFNESS

Many people live in noisy environments—with busy streets, traffic, loud TVs and stereos, personal stereos and headphones, slamming doors, and loud concerts. We have become almost immune to the amount of loud noise that constantly surrounds us. It is slowly making us deaf.

The eardrum functions to protect the ear and transmit sound signals to your brain, and its protective capacity is damaged every time you overload it with loud sustained noise. After a rock concert, it takes the ear several days to recover from the trauma. You may notice that you hear poorly the day after attending such concerts. Wearing earplugs to these concerts is worth your consideration.

Loud noise is causing people to develop partial hearing impairment because of exposure to the excessive decibel levels of dance clubs, personal stereos, TVs, and other sources of noise. Some clubs are known to have sound at the decibel levels of a jet plane. Sound is considered harmful when it reaches ninety decibels. A jet plane takes off at 120 decibels. That is approximately thirty decibels over the hearing health limit. (Decibels go up by the power of ten, so you can work out just how loud 120 decibels might be.) The ears are an important part of singing. They are traumatized by long sessions of loud music. If your hearing is impaired, your singing could be affected because sensitivity to language, vocal feedback, and pitch perception will be reduced.

ALTERNATIVE HEALTH TREATMENTS

A number of options are available for treating some of the health problems discussed above. In addition to standard medical treatment, many people find help in homeopathy, naturopathy, acupuncture, nutrition, and other therapies. If you find you are taking medication on a long-term basis, it would be wise to seek further answers from a wider range of therapies regarding your problem. Some very useful healing is coming from areas of energy medicine such as EFT, Quantum Touch, and Integrative Quantum Medicine. (See the useful websites listed in the back of this book.)

Summary

This chapter has been devoted to the prevention of vocal ill health. Your voice is a precious and important aspect of your communication. Trying to communicate without sound is an extremely frustrating and slow process. There are few if any jobs in which no talking is involved. Singing or speaking while under vocal duress is counterproductive and vocally risky.

A positive spirit and a healthy lifestyle are the two most important things you can do for yourself and your voice. Paying attention to your attitudes, general health and fitness, and practice habits will enhance your vocal health and give you the confidence to use your voice and your body wisely for the rest of your life.

Epilogue

Now that you have finished *singing* this book, you are ready to explore more refined areas of vocal performance. You have been given the basic knowledge and repertoire for establishing an easily produced sound and a musically intelligent interpretation. You can use the principles in this book to sing in any musical style that interests you.

You have also been given the tools to discover things about your voice for yourself. While your singing teacher is very important for guidance and advice, learning to sing is a shared responsibility. In the end, only you can feel what is happening inside your body. Do not neglect its messages.

Ask for clarification when you have a question; it is not a sign of stupidity. Intelligent people ask questions and strive for understanding. While there is not an answer to every question, there are at the same time few mysteries. If we can let go of preconceptions and dogma and be open to new information and have the courage to explore, there is usually some logic at work. Where there is mystery, enjoy it and revel in the wonder of it all. Music and singing have space for magic and the mysterious.

The spirit that you bring to your singing will add huge amounts to the physical and musical skills you already have. It brings that little bit extra, and anyone can have spirit.

Singing is a joyful thing to do and it does not need to be classed as a skill for the specially gifted. It is part of the spirit of being human—and you have every right to "sound your spirit."

APPENDIX A

What's Your Singing IQ?

Whether you are just beginning to sing or you have sung for years, it is worth taking stock every now and then to find out what you know about your art. This little questionnaire is for your own fun and information. You don't have to get every answer right. There are no official Singing-IQ standards.

Mark each statement as *true* or *false*.

1. I want to sing because it expresses who I am. _______
2. Singing lessons are mainly for "classical" singers. _______
3. Knowing how to read music is mainly important for "classical" singing. _______
4. I feel I need to be perfect when I sing. _______
5. The way I use my speaking voice is important to my singing. _______
6. I might lose control of my voice if I allow my imagination to take over in a performance. _______
7. I am afraid to video my lessons or performances. _______
8. My voice is the most important aspect of my communication. _______
9. I let my emotions rule my performance. _______
10. I get hoarse each time I sing. _______
11. My throat hurts when I sing. _______
12. Singing off pitch or out of tune is OK as long as I communicate. _______
13. My posture contributes to the quality of my voice. _______
14. Good singers don't need to learn to act. _______
15. I don't have to worry about my sound; the microphone and sound engineer take care of that. _______
16. The lyrics are secondary to my sound. _______
17. A lot of physical movement while I am singing means I am really involved with the emotions of the text and music. _______
18. I get so nervous before a performance that I have to take something to get through the event. _______
19. Regular physical exercise is important for singers. _______
20. Energy Medicine is a helpful way of improving performance. _______

ANSWERS

Give yourself one point for every answer you match. A discussion of each statement follows. There is no such thing as failure on this questionnaire—only an opportunity for further learning.

1. True
2. False
3. False
4. False
5. True
6. False
7. False
8. False
9. False
10. False
11. False
12. False
13. True
14. False
15. False
16. False
17. False
18. False
19. True
20. True

DISCUSSION

1. *I want to sing because it expresses who I am.*

Then, of course, follow your passion. Expressing who you are through singing is the commencement of a journey. Singing classes and lessons are just the beginning, but without your interest and dedication, you will never know the joy it brings, whether for your own pleasure or for public performance. Nearly all singers who make it professionally are driven to sing and have an unremitting determination, passion, and focus. That is what keeps them working hard and persevering no matter what obstacles they face. Look at what singers have to go through to win any of the reality shows such as American Idol, Star Academy or X-Factor, first to get on the show and then to win it. While there may be fame and wealth at the end of the road, it is not a guarantee. Determination, drive, patience, guts, musical talent, and presence—or something compelling about your performance—are all needed on an ongoing basis for success in the performing arts industry.

2. *Singing lessons are mainly for "classical" singers.*

Every singer benefits from learning a healthy and reliable vocal technique including coordination of physical balance, breath, and phonation. This keeps singers healthy vocally and prolongs careers. Studying with teachers of all styles who can help you achieve a healthy vocal technique is important. (See Introduction: Getting Started)

3. *Knowing how to read music is mainly important for "classical" singing.*

Learning to read music is necessary for any performer. Professional musicians and singers are expected to learn quickly and come to practice or sessions prepared. If you have to have someone teach you the notes and rhythm, you are at a big disadvantage, and it will take you too long to learn your music. It is difficult to focus on performance when you are busy trying to remember the notes or rhythm. This leads to loss of confidence and vocal insecurity. (See Chapter Four: Learning Music Efficiently and Appendix E: Making Sense of a Music Manuscript)

4. *I feel I need to be perfect when I sing.*

Accuracy is important, but not to the detriment of musicality, presence, or spontaneity in performance. It takes more than one or two small errors to produce a failed performance. Some of the most famous performers in the world will admit to making quite a number of what they consider to be errors in a performance—and yet the audience may never know it, so their appreciation is not dulled. The audience is there for entertainment, not to look for your errors. Sometimes it is necessary to improvise on the spot, and needing to get it perfect will prevent this from happening. The need to get it right every time can come from several sources: the self-critic, someone in your life who told you that if it wasn't exactly right it was terrible, or one of the outdated teachers who bully pupils into doing well by constantly berating them. You do not need any of these things or people in your artistic life. (See Chapter Six: Performing)

5. *The way I use my speaking voice is important to my singing.*

You are using the same instrument for speech and singing, and we talk much more than we sing. The more you can practice healthy voice use when you are speaking, the less you will have to relearn for singing. For example, if you are speaking using a lot of throat tension, then you are going to have to work very hard to sing with freedom. (See Chapter Eleven: Articulation and Expression)

6. *I might lose control of my voice if I allow my imagination to take over in a performance.*

Maybe, but this isn't necessarily a bad thing. Imagination plays a crucial role in the communication of meaning, and even though you may feel as though you are "losing control" of your voice, you are actually freeing your voice to communicate your meaning more clearly. (See Introduction, "Technique Serves the Message")

Taking a risk does not mean walking onstage without adequate preparation such as knowing the music and the words. In fact, the more work you have done in advance, the more freedom you have to be creative in performance. It means you can dare to be totally committed to the present and the performance and allow your intuition and spontaneity to carry the moment.

7. *I am afraid to video my lessons or performances.*

One of the most important things you can do for yourself is observe your own practice, lessons, and performances. Unless you do, you will never truly know how you have done. While it may seem a bit uncomfortable at first, it will cut your learning time in half and change your performance drastically for the better. Don't cheat yourself or delude yourself into thinking you have achieved what you wanted without checking your performance and forming your own opinions.

8. *My voice is the most important aspect of my communication.*

Of course your voice is important and you want it to be wonderful. However, it is known that the voice comprises about 35–40% of your communication, the visible aspects 55%, and the words 7%. The complete agreement and balance of all of these factors creates superb communication. So without your body, presence, and imagination you do not have enough for an excellent and compelling performance.

9. *I let my emotions rule my performance.*

When you pay attention to the text and meaning you want to give to your performance, the emotion will be there without further action from you. It is far better when you allow your *imagination* to rule your performance. Many singers substitute excessive physical movement and exaggerated or inappropriate facial expressions for emotion. Inappropriate physical activity simply gets in the way of the voice and diminishes the vocal quality. Exaggeration of movement and expression on your part will make it difficult for the audience to get involved and share the emotion of the song; they will be too distracted by your physical excess. After all, they came to be part of it.

10. *I get hoarse each time I sing.*

Hoarseness means that the membrane covering the vocal folds (cords) becomes swollen and allows excess air to escape with the sound. This can signal a number of problems: singing for too long at a time, singing loudly and forcefully, singing in smoke-filled rooms over time, smoking, singing with too much tension, or environmental allergies that affect the respiratory tract. When you are hoarse after singing, it is a sign that you need to look at the effort with which you sing. (See Chapter Twelve: Maintaining a Healthy Voice)

11. *My throat hurts when I sing.*

This is an indication of poor vocal technique and tension. Find a good teacher. Singing should never hurt! Pain is the way your body tells you something is wrong. To sing with pain is to risk not reaching your singing aspirations, shortening your career, developing vocal pathology such as nodules, and possibly creating permanent vocal disability. (See Chapter Twelve: Maintaining a Healthy Voice)

12. *Singing off pitch or out of tune is OK as long as I communicate.*

Judging from a lot of singing today, this would appear to be true. However, it is not. Even well-known singers with raspy voices can sing with true pitch. If you sing off pitch deliberately for effect, that is one thing; however, it is not possible to have real vocal presence when you sing off pitch all the time. Singing consistently off pitch is usually a sign of faulty vocal technique. On very rare occasions, it could be due to a hearing problem.

13. *My posture contributes to the quality of my voice.*

It certainly does! Your vocal instrument—you—needs to be physically balanced so it can respond to your technique and imagination. Even though you may be in many different physical positions during performance, it is important to "set up your instrument" first. Give it a chance to develop efficient vocal reflexes before distorting it. No instrumentalist would play with a distorted instrument, and it is not to your advantage to do so either. If nothing else, your ears need to be aligned with the points of your shoulders so your vocal tract is in optimal position to respond to your vocal demands and give you a chance to sing with your best quality. (See Chapter One: Healthy Singing, and Chapter Seven: Physical Alignment)

14. *Good singers don't need to learn to act.*

While it is true that some well-known singers are poor actors, you do not want it to be true of you. Compelling performance requires heightened awareness and a wonderful imagination. This feeds your vocal quality and enables complete communication on stage. When singers neglect areas such as acting and mime as part of their training, they run the risk of diminishing communication onstage and keeping their audience from sharing the moment.

15. *I don't have to worry about my sound; the microphone and sound engineer take care of that.*

Wouldn't it be nice for the microphone and sound engineer to have that much ability to give you the voice you want? Sadly, whatever you put into the microphone is what is amplified. The microphone is a tool to help you be heard by a large audience, make a recording, or play with the sounds you make. The engineer can do some amazing things, but the final responsibility for your sound is on you.

16. *The lyrics are secondary to my sound.*

This is true only when you are vocalizing and not using words. Why sing words if the audience cannot understand them? While you want the best possible sound, the words demand equal emphasis and help you achieve the sounds you want. Expressive text is the product of your imagination and emotional experience, and gives credence to your performance.

17. *A lot of physical movement while I am singing means I am really involved with the emotions of the text and music.*

A lot of excess physical movement means that your brain is busy with the movement and that your voice is getting less energy—and is less effective. Unless your movement is appropriate to the text or the music, it will detract from the message of the song and compromise your performance. Inappropriate movement is rife in performance today and although it is often thought to mean wholehearted involvement in the music, you do not need to fall into that trap. Substitute quality for quantity. Compel your audience to listen because of your use of imagination and vocal color.

18. *I get so nervous before a performance that I have to take something to get through the event.*

If you fear you will not be perfect, relax. You will not be perfect. We are human, and an audience prefers to see a human in front of them. Of course, you want to sing as well as you can. However, unreal expectations set up an impossible task and create horrendous nerves. You have to ask yourself: "If I am this nervous, why am I performing?" When performers get this anxious, it is worth taking the time to question their practice habits, learning style, or teaching. There are many mind/body techniques like meditation and visualization that can transform those nerves into positive energy for performance. Taking medication or other drugs, including alcohol, only masks the symptom and does not solve the problem. You can also be tricked into thinking that you have done well when you have not. Look into healthier ways of dealing with your nerves.

19. *Regular physical exercise is important for singers.*

Your energy and health are vital to your voice and your performance. Singing in public takes stamina—much like the athlete who competes in front of thousands of people. It is not easy for the professional singer to get enough exercise when he or she has late nights, constant travel, and long practice sessions. Ten minutes of appropriate exercise twice a day is better than nothing. Surely you can find ten minutes and the discipline to use them well. Exercise is part of your general well being and vocal health. Try Qigong. It is gentle, moves a lot of your body, and gives you great energy, stamina, and flexibility. (See Chapter Twelve: Maintaining a Healthy Voice)

20. *Energy Medicine is a helpful way of improving performance.*

The fastest growing area of alternative therapy today is Energy Medicine. Energy medicine focuses on healing the human energy field and includes physical, metaphysical, mental, emotional, psychological, psychic, and spiritual aspects. It uses and combines a variety of techniques, including traditional Chinese medicine, Western medicine, kinesiology, and quantum physics. Many of these energy techniques are immediately useful to performers: EFT (Emotional Freedom Technique) uses affirmations and tapping on the end points of acupuncture meridians to great effect; Quantum Touch uses breathing and visualization techniques to produce excellent results; and IQM (Integrative Quantum Medicine) uses a combination of many of these to produce incredibly successful results. (See Some Recommended Websites)

APPENDIX B

Worksheet for Preparing the Text of Your Song

You will have to use your own imagination to answer many of these questions. Fill in each one of them before memorizing the text. This applies to every song you sing, independent of the style. Remember that you choose the characters, their costumes, colors, and materials; you design the set down to the last detail. By making a chart for each character in your song and filling in this worksheet, you will find that you really know the words and the song. The more imagination you use, the more compelling your singing will be.

1. How many characters are there? (This includes the narrator.)
2. Name each character and describe the following:
   a. What color are the eyes and hair? What is the height, weight, and age?
   b. What is the skin like to touch? Is the woman wearing perfume?
   c. Is the hair long, short, straight, or curly? Is it silky, thick, or thin? Is the man bald? Does he have a beard or moustache? If so, what color?
   d. Describe in great detail the clothes each character is wearing—the colors, specific materials, type of shoes, and any accessories.
   e. What is the personality like? Is the character sweet, mean, kind, loving?
3. What is the setting? Describe in detail the scenery around the character(s):
   a. Describe the type of house or interior, including curtains, wallpaper, and furniture. What can you see out the windows?
   b. If outside, describe the ground, the sights, smells, sounds, types of trees and flowers, colors, and depths of colors.
   c. Are there mountains, the sea, desert, streams and rivers? If so, give *full* descriptions. For example, is it on a beach? If so, what is the sand like? Are there sea grasses blowing in the breeze? How does the sea smell? sound? look? Is it calm or rough?
   d. Which season is it? What is the air like? Is it soft, a spring breeze, or stormy? Are there any smells in the air such as flowers, the sea, or cooking?

4. What is the main message of each character?
5. What is the message of the whole song *in one sentence?*
6. What is the one thing you want your audience to take away from hearing you sing this song?

Appendix C

Introduction to IPA: Pronunciation of Vowels and Consonants

The *International Phonetic Alphabet,* or IPA, was created in the late 1880s by a group of French language teachers who wanted to help students learn the sounds of unfamiliar languages. IPA is a series of symbols that represent individual sounds (or phonemes) that are used in languages. IPA is not tied to a specific language, and those who familiarize themselves with the symbols can learn to pronounce any language on earth. The International Phonetic Alphabet is a valuable tool for singers because you must first learn to speak a word before you can sing it. IPA has been widely adopted by singers and singing teachers, language teachers, and publishers of dictionaries. This partial list of IPA symbols includes those most commonly used by singers.

Many of the symbols such as [t] [p] [d] [k] [o] are already familiar to Americans while others like [æ] [ə] [ŋ] [θ] will look rather strange at first. Let's begin by looking at some basic *vowel sounds.*

VOWELS

closed [i]	long ee	"ee" as in bee, receive, green, jeans
open [ɪ]	short ih	"ih" as in sit, pretty, list, busy
closed [e]	pure ay	"ay" as in dictate, day, weigh, filet
open [ɛ]	open eh	"eh" as in bed, air, when, friend
broad [æ]	short a	"a" as in has, plaid, act, plant
bright [a]	bright ah	*Spanish:* madre; *French:* parle; *German:* Halle
dark [ɑ]	tall ah	"ah" as in father, dark, hot, pasta; *Italian:* caro, alma
closed [o]	pure oh	"oh" as in stone, moat, go, hotel
open [ɔ]	open oh	"aw" as in haughty, dog, saw, cause
open [ʊ]	open oo	"oo" as in hook, should, put, book
closed [u]	pure oo	"oo" as in pool, blue, noon, you
short [ʌ]	short uh	"uh" as in cup, shut, rough, flood
schwa [ə]	neutral uh	"uh" as in second syllable of little, even; *German:* blume; *French:* jeune

closed [y]	long umlaut u	"oo" + "ee," *German:* für; *French:* pur
open [ʏ]	short umlaut u	"oo" + "ee," *German:* mütter
closed [ø]	long mixed [e] - [ɛ]	"ay" + "oh," *German:* schön; *French:* adieu
open [œ]	mixed [ɔ] - [ɛ]	"aw" + "eh," similar to bird, earth, her; *German:* möchte; *French:* fleur
glide [j]	y	"yuh" as in yellow, union, punitive; *Italian:* piu; *German:* jah; *French:* bien
glide [w]	w	"wuh" as in water, we, quick, one; *Spanish:* bueno; *French:* oui; *Italian:* qui
glide [ɥ]	quick[ɯ]	*French:* lui, nuit

Many *consonants* in IPA are pronounced just as we pronounce them in American English: [b] [d] [f] [g] [h] [k] [l] [m] [n] [p] [s] [t] [v] [y] [z].

Other consonants merit their own unique symbols.

CONSONANTS

unvoiced [ʃ]	sh	"sh" as in shadow, shine, machine; *German:* schön; *French*: riche; *Italian:* lasciatemi
combined [tʃ]	ch	"ch" as in church, chili, itch; *Spanish:* mucho; *Italian:* cielo; *German:* deutsch
voiced [ʒ]	soft zh	as in treasure, leisure, azure; *French:* jeune, je, gymnopedi
combined [dʒ]	hard j	"juh" as in jelly, huge; *Italian:* giuro
soft [ç]	ichlaut	soft blown "ch" as in human; *German:* ich
hard [x]	achlaut	hard blown "ch," *German:* ach, Bach
unvoiced [θ]	soft "th"	"th" as in Thanksgiving, theater, with; *Castillian Spanish:* corazon
voiced [ð]	hard "th"	"th" as in these, writhe, then
liquid [ŋ]	ng	"ng" as in sing; *Italian:* ancora; *German:* bang
retroflexive [r]	er	American "er" as in red, year, car, court
n tilde [ɲ]	ñ	"en-yah" as in onion; *Italian:* sogno; *French*: cigne
liquid [ʎ]	[lj]	"el-yah" as in million; *Italian:* voglio, egli; *Castillian Spanish:* ballena

flipped [ɾ]	single flip	"r" flipped as in British: very; *Italian:* caro; *Spanish:* Maria; *German:* sehren; *French*: repos
rolled [rr]	rolled or trilled "r"	"rrrr" as in *Italian:* crudele, amor, terra; *French*: horrible; *Spanish:* rojo
voiced [β]	voiced "b"	*Castillian Spanish:* verlaba

Italian

A rule of thumb in Italian is to flip the [ɾ] when it is between two vowels: *cara, Figaro.* Roll the [rr] when it is before or after a consonant, or at the beginning or ending of a word: *amor, pronto, morte, ruggiadose.* Some words contain both rolled and flipped "r"s: *brillare.* Prolong the trilled [rr] in words spelled with "rr": *verra, sorriso.*

Some consonants that are aspirated and rather noisy in English—[t], [k], [p]—are very soft in Italian. They implode rather than explode. Also, in Italian be aware of double consonants, such as *sebben, fuggite, donzelle, batti.* Take a little time to "stick" on the double consonants, without stopping the flow of the musical phrase. Differentiation between single consonants and double consonants will make your pronunciation more authentic and fun.

Latin and Spanish

The Latin rounds and group songs in *The Singing Book* are pronounced very much like Italian. One major exception is that the [t], [k], and [p] are aspirated. Spanish also has a lot in common with Italian pronunciation, including many similar vowels and soft [t], [k], and [p]. Differences in Spanish pronunciation between Latin America and Spain (Castillian) are noted in the IPA for the individual songs.

French

In the French language there are special vowels called *nasal vowels.* These vowels resonate in both your mouth and your nose, and are sung with a slightly lowered soft palate. The "m" and "n" in nasal vowels are not pronounced: *enfante, tombe.* There are no English language equivalents to these nasal vowels, so you will need to experiment with the new sounds.

[ã]	nasal [a]	as in blanc, enfante
[ɛ̃]	nasal [ɛ]	as in main, Sainte
[ɔ̃]	nasal [ɔ]	as in bon, tombe
[œ̃]	nasal [œ]	as in parfum, un

To practice saying all four French nasal vowels, speak "A fine white wine" in French: "Un bon vin blanc." It is helpful to think of French as a very "round" language. Most American singers don't use their lips enough when singing French. Pucker up and also remember to keep the [t], [k], [p] consonants soft.

German

In contrast, the German language is full of noisy, aspirated consonants. When singing in German, go ahead and explode the [t], [k], [p], [ts], [x], and [ç]. Especially when singing words like *nicht* and *nacht,* you will need to shorten the vowels to allow plenty of time to blow air through the "ch." For singing, be sure that you don't gargle the [x] and [ç] in your throat. It's more like a cat's hiss or the way we say "huge" or "human" in English. The [x] is a bit farther back in your mouth than the [ç].

Also, be aware of "glottal" stops (places where the vowels begin with a popping sound) in German. Usually when a word begins with a vowel you will need to precede it with a slight pause for clarity, for example, "und ich." Americans are quite familiar with the gentle "grunt" of a glottal stop. Say "Oh, my!" and notice the percussive sound of the [o].

The more familiar you become with the symbols and sounds of the International Phonetic Alphabet, the easier and more enjoyable it will become to sing in foreign languages. You can also use the symbols to remind you of vowels you want to sing in English. For example, if you tend to sing "binch" instead of "bench," you can simply jot [ɛ] above the word.

IPA is a very practical language tool and can help you sing languages accurately. Practice speaking your texts aloud, and do your best to avoid a monotonous, robotic delivery. Once you have translated your text and learned your IPA pronunciation, speak the poetry with emotion and facial expression. When you know exactly *what* you are saying and *how* to say it, then the melody and accompaniment will add the final threads to your musical tapestry.

Appendix D

Additional Vocal Exercises

Just as athletes do specific warm-ups, stretches, and exercises to strengthen certain muscle groups, singers can choose specific exercises to target vocal technique. Some target areas for singers are *body, breath, resonance, flexibility,* and *range.*

Body For full-body exercises, refer to the alignment and physical stretching exercises in Part One.

Breath The vocal sighs, buzzes, raspberries, and trills introduced in Part One are excellent exercises for improving your breathing technique.

EXERCISE 1

Place the backs of your hands at the back of your lower ribs. With your best body alignment, inhale deeply and release the breath without deliberately pulling in your abs as you "chant" the alphabet from A to Z (or as far as you comfortably get). Think of chanting as fluid speaking—somewhere between speech and song. As you chant, be aware of a full body stretch. Avoid holding your breath between the inhalation and exhalation.

Resonance Any exercise that uses hums [m][n][ŋ] and glides [j] is helpful for creating a more resonant vibrant tone. Start with this very gentle [m] hum. Lips are lightly closed, top and bottom teeth are apart, tip of the tongue is forward, with a slight lift of the soft palate. Hum very softly on this descending pattern and notice the vibrations throughout your face and head. If you hum too loudly, you will feel vibrations mainly in your mouth. This soothing exercise is also a great "cool down" after you have finished your daily vocal practice time or a choral rehearsal.

EXERCISE 2

Once you have found an easy "ringing" sound, experiment with this simple 5-note descending pattern on a variety of texts, rhythms, dynamics, and moods. Be creative and have fun. You can sing words from your textbook, from your songs, from anywhere.

EXERCISE 3

mf
etc.
ma - ma - ma ma - ma - ma ma - ma - ma

EXERCISE 4

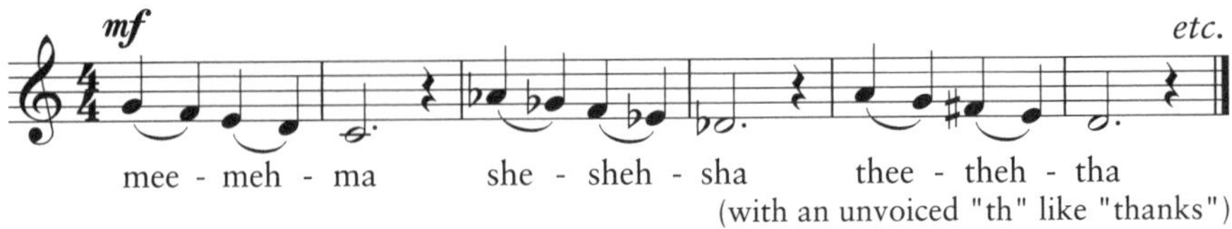
mf
etc.
mee - meh - ma she - sheh - sha thee - theh - tha
(with an unvoiced "th" like "thanks")

EXERCISE 5

mf
etc.
I love to sing! This is real-ly weird. Piz-za's great for lunch.

EXERCISE 6

mf
Hur - ry, you'll be late! Would you like to
dance? rol - ler coas-ters make me sick.
etc.

Range Now experiment with various vowels, words, dynamics, and moods on a descending octave *arpeggio*. Remember to modify or open the vowels on higher pitches.

EXERCISE 7

mf
etc.
Ah [a]
Oh [o]
Oo [u]

EXERCISE 8

Sing some ascending arpeggios now, both *legato* (smooth and connected) and *staccato* (light and detached). Take it as low and as high as you are comfortable.

EXERCISE 9

EXERCISE 10

Flexibility Start these vocal aerobics slowly, then gradually increase your speed. Have a friend watch (or use a mirror or video) to make sure that you aren't bobbing your chin and head as the pitches rise and fall.

EXERCISE 11

EXERCISE 12

Choosing different exercises every day will keep your vocalizing fresh. The goal is to apply the vocal skills (breath management, resonance, smooth registers, flexibility) to your songs. You can even create exercises from problem spots in your songs:

Example from "He Shall Feed His Flock," Handel

Spending a few minutes daily to exercise target areas in your vocal technique will make a big difference in how easily and healthily you sing your songs.

Appendix E

Making Sense of a Music Manuscript

The language of music has its own special symbols or alphabet. While they may look like hieroglyphics to the uninitiated, each symbol has very specific meanings to musicians. Following are some basic guidelines for looking at a musical score and beginning to make sense of it. We can do this by looking at the way a songwriter might approach notating a song. Where would the composer begin? The answer is with some manuscript paper. (For the purposes of this exercise, we will pretend this composer has no music writing facilities on his computer.)

Notation Manuscript paper is full of horizontal lines that are grouped into patterns of five. Each of these five-line and four space groups is called a *staff* or *stave*.

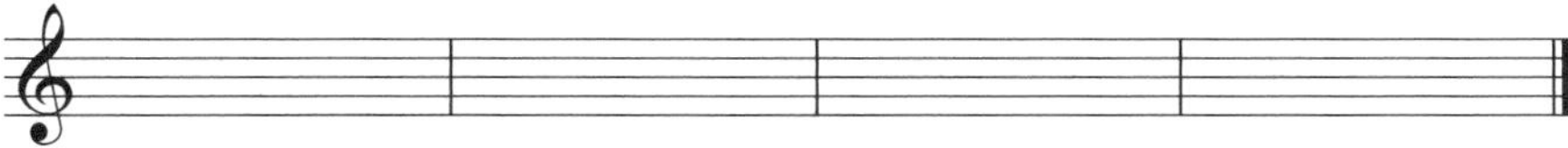

Several staffs joined to each other, as they are in the songs in this text, form a *system*.

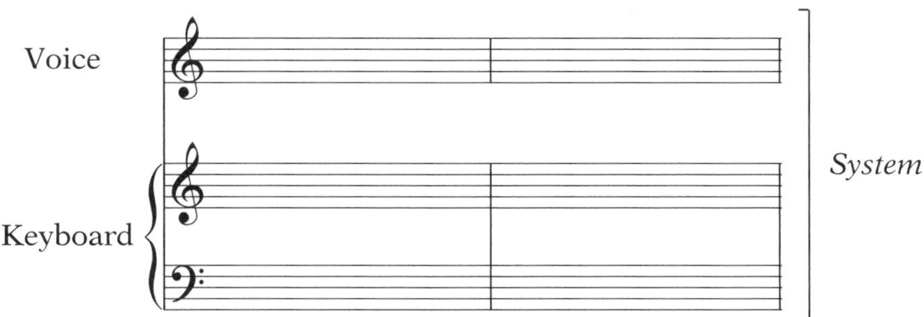

The staff is the scaffolding for the notes, or pitches, of the song. Each line and space represents a different note. Our system of notation uses the letters A, B, C, D, E, F, G as the names of the notes. They are repeated over and over again in different pitch ranges in units called octaves.

Staves are divided by vertical lines, or *bar lines,* into sections, called *measures:*

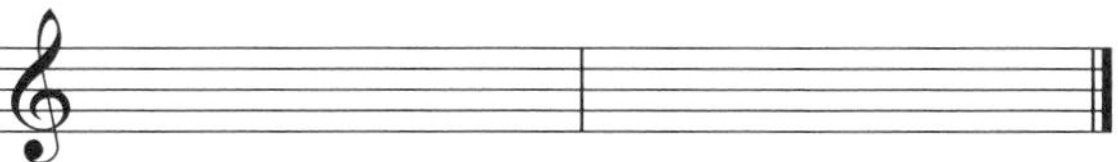

Their purpose is to group units of musical time. This ensures a regular accent or beat throughout the song. The value of these units is indicated by a *time signature* (see below) at the beginning of the composition.

However, before a composer puts the time signature on the lines, he has to denote whether the staff is designated for higher or lower pitches. Marking the staff with *clef signs* does this. The treble, or G clef, looks like 𝄞 and the bass, or F clef, looks like 𝄢

Note that the curled part of the treble clef is around the second line from the bottom of the staff. This tells you that the second line is the G above Middle C (C_4). Once you know the location of this single note, you can then figure out the rest of the notes.

The bass clef has one dot above and one below the second line from the top. This tells you the location of the F below Middle C.

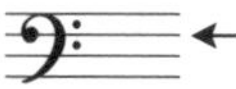

Notes are placed on the staff to tell you their duration and the correct pitches to sing or play. Below is an illustration of a piano keyboard, the names of the notes on it, and their relationship to the musical staff.

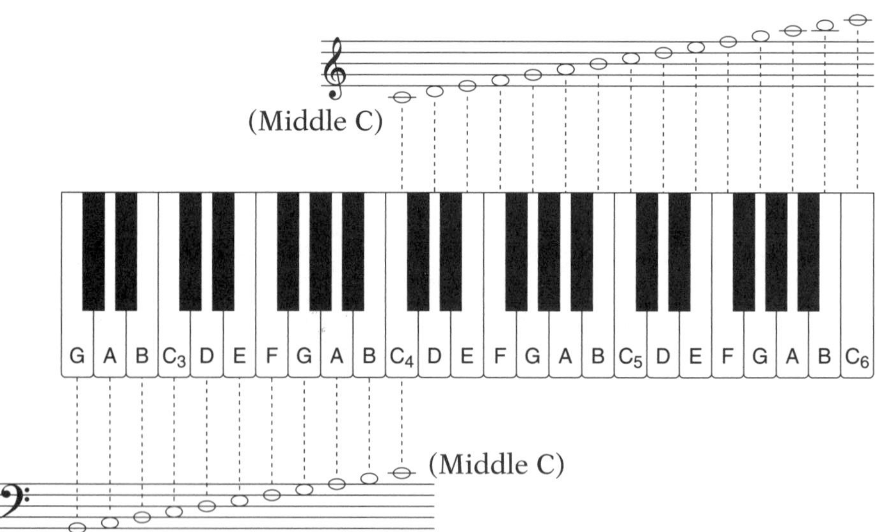

Rhythm The *time signature* tells us the meter of the song—

whether it is a waltz,

a march,

or a lullaby.

Time signatures can be thought of as a form of musical math. If you have a time signature of $\frac{3}{4}$ it means that in each measure there must be the equivalent of 3 one-quarter notes or beats. Mathematically, you may have any combination of musical notes or rests in each measure as long as they add up to three quarter notes. You will know the value of a note or rest by its appearance. (See table below.)

Note values		Rest values
𝅝	Whole	𝄻
𝅗𝅥	Half	𝄼
♩	Quarter	𝄽
♪	Eighth	𝄾
𝅘𝅥𝅯	Sixteenth	𝄿
𝅘𝅥𝅰	Thirty-second	𝅀
𝅘𝅥𝅱	Sixty-fourth	𝅁

A dot after a note increases the value by one half of its original value. For example, a dotted half note (𝅗𝅥.) is the equivalent of 3 quarter notes (♩♩♩).

EXERCISE

Look at two or three folksongs in Part Two.

1. Notice that the solo vocal part has its own staff, and it is connected by a line to the two staffs of the accompaniment. There is a treble clef sign for the singer and both treble and bass for the accompanist. Often the treble clef is used for both male and female singers. The male is expected to sing an octave lower than the music is written.
2. Look at several measures and notice how many different ways the value of the notes adds up to the amount indicated by the time signature. For example, in measures of $\frac{3}{4}$ time, you might have the following combinations that all add up to three quarters:
   a. Three quarter notes (♩♩♩)
   b. One quarter note, two eighth notes, and one quarter rest (♩ ♫ 𝄽) (Rests are an integral part of a composition, not a very quick holiday.)
   c. One half note and one quarter note (𝅗𝅥 ♩)

Pitch, Scales, and Key

Look at the illustration of the keyboard again. You will see that the same pattern of white and black keys is repeated many times. Each of these patterns is grouped into 7 white keys and 5 black keys making up 12 equal semitones or half steps. This is because the Western musical systems use a tuning system that is called *equal temperament*. Without this system, playing an instrument like the piano would be very cacophonic.

Acoustically what this means is that each pitch exhibits a certain frequency of vibrations. Find Middle C: 256 Hertz (cycles per second) is the frequency of vibrations that gives us the sound of Middle C. The C an octave below is half that frequency, or 128 Hertz; the C above is double, or 512. Every octave the frequency is doubled. This provides the basis for Western harmony.

Different scales have been used throughout music history. However, we will confine this discussion to those that you will commonly encounter. The twelve semitones or half steps become very important when we start to build a scale. They are combined with whole steps to create scale patterns. A whole step is the distance of two half steps between any two pitches. The *chromatic* scale uses all twelve semitones. For the music in Part Two, major and minor scales are used. A major scale is identified by a pattern of eight whole and half steps in specific places. The song "Do-re-mi" from *The Sound of Music* is based on the major scale and musical solfège, or singing names given to the notes. You know them as do, re, mi, fa, sol, la, ti, and do. If we use numbers, rather than names for the notes from 1 to 8, you will find the half steps fall between 3 and 4, and 7 and 8. Knowing this you can construct a major scale beginning with any note by keeping this pattern of whole and half steps.

C MAJOR SCALE: Half steps between 3–4 and 7–8

There are several versions of minor scales in use. Each of these versions has a particular pattern of whole and half steps as well. Composers use minor keys to add a different tonal color or to create melancholic moods in a song. Minor patterns look like this:

C NATURAL MINOR SCALE: Half steps between 2–3 and 5–6

C HARMONIC MINOR SCALE: Half steps between 2–3, 5–6, and 7–8

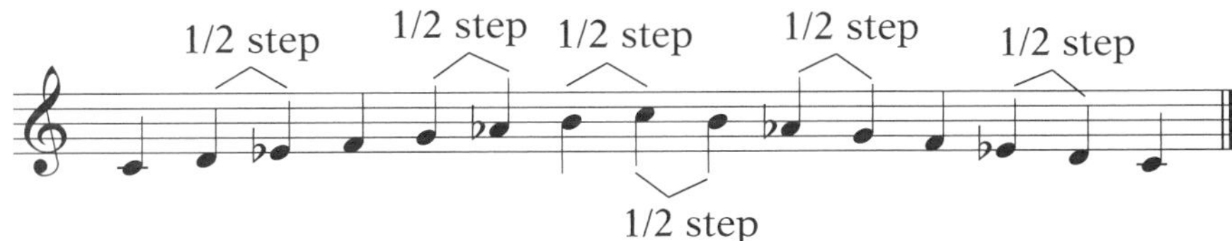

C MELODIC MINOR SCALE: Half steps between 2–3 and 7–8 ascending, and between 2–3 and 5–6 descending

BLUES SCALE: A variation of the minor *pentatonic* scale (all 5 black notes). See "Swingin' in Minor Blues," Part Two, p. 38.

Finding out for yourself . . .

- Use a real piano or the drawing on page 346 to construct a major scale. First find Middle C.
- Now add up whole and half steps to match the scale pattern of half steps between 3–4 and 7–8. Remember that each key of the piano is separated by a semitone or half step. So you need to move from C to the next black key, then to the next white key, and so on.
- What happens when you get to the note marked E? There is no black key next. So the half step is to a white key.
- Now you know that the C major scale uses only white keys.
- Now repeat the exercise beginning on the note G. How is it different?
- Now try your hand at constructing a natural minor scale from the note E.
- You can work with these concepts creating scales on any pitches of your choice.

You have found that the C major scale can be played without using any black keys. However, any other major scale is going to require the use of black keys in order to maintain the pattern. You found that in the key of G major there is a half step between F and the black key above it. That note would be called F-sharp. So that you would not have to keep writing a sharp sign in front of all the F's in the song, it is easier to give it a *key signature* next to the clef sign. That way, the musician would know that every F was to be played as an F-sharp unless otherwise directed.

Note: In general, the black note just above the white key takes its name and adds to it the word *sharp*. The note below the white key takes the name of *flat*. So what's the difference between F-sharp and G-flat? On the keyboard there is no difference. It has the same sound. However, in a song written in sharps, you would confuse things by calling F-sharp G-flat. For instrumentalists, there can be slight differences between F-sharp and G-flat. Most instruments have more leeway with pitches than the piano.

Key signatures use these two sets of symbols, sharps (♯) and flats (♭). A shortcut to knowing what major key the composition is written in is to look at the last sharp on the staff and go up to the next note name. For example, if there are four sharps, the last sharp is D-sharp. The next note up is E. The key is then E major. For major flat keys there is a different shortcut; the key will be that of the next-to-last flat. For example, if there are five flats—B, E, A, D, G—the next-to-last flat is D-flat and the key is D-flat major.

Common key signatures found in this book:

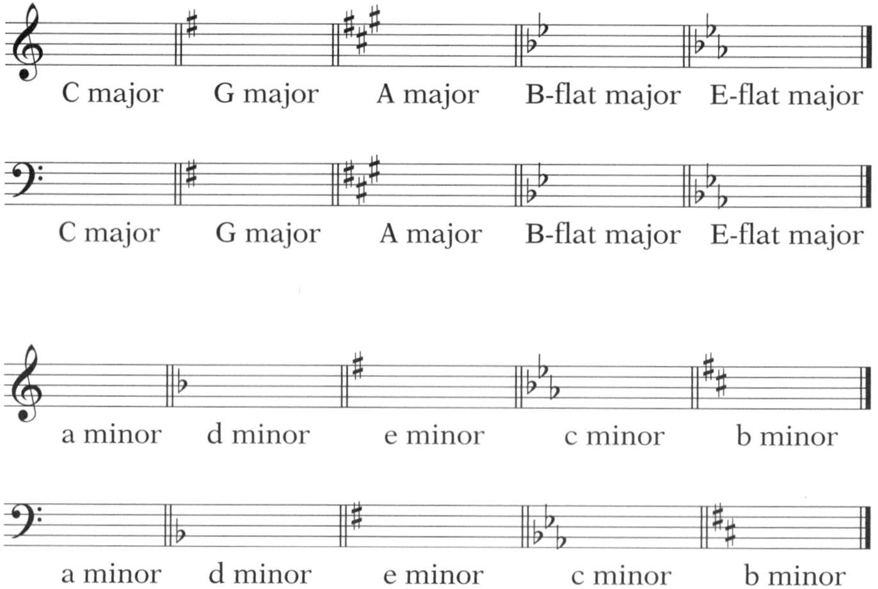

> **Finding out for yourself . . .**
>
> **Look at the key signatures of three or four songs in Part Two. In which keys are they written?**
>
> ***Hint:* Look at the beginning and ending bass notes.**

The key of a song is chosen by the composer for its ease or difficulty of playing or of singing, and sometimes for mood. Keys are consistent musical patterns that tend to center around one main note. For example, when a song is written in the key of C, its "home base" or *tonic note* is considered C. With C as the tonic it will feel uncomfortable or unresolved if the song ends on another sound. Contemporary and modern music tends to be less restricted by these patterns, and there is often less feeling of "key."

With the information you have now, it is possible to compose your own melody. What if you want to add harmony or chords to that melody? More information is necessary. What follows is some general information, not a complete scholarly description. For that, you need a course in music theory or a good book on the subject. You can also find information on the Internet.

Harmony

Harmony is created by combining several notes at once to make chords. Melody usually refers to a single musical line and harmony to multiple notes being heard at the same time.

> **Finding out for yourself . . .**
>
> **Now that you are somewhat familiar with the keyboard, you can create chords for yourself. We have numbered the notes of a scale from 1 to 8.**
>
> 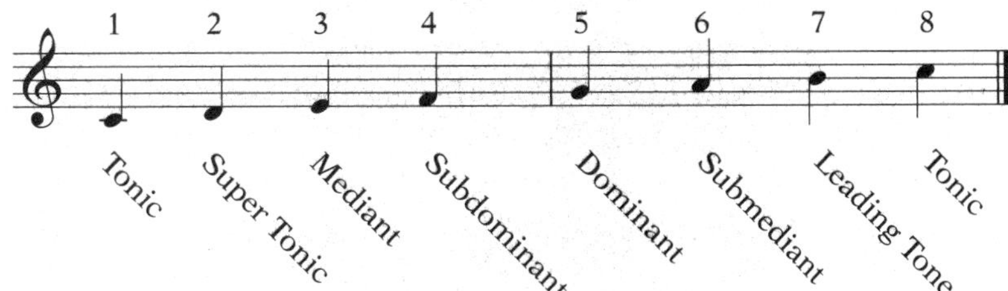
>
>
> **Beginning with Middle C, play notes 1, 3, and 5 together. You will find you have a chord.**
>
> **Now play notes 2, 4, and 6 together. This is a chord with a different sound.**

Play the following notes, and say the specific name of each chord while playing:

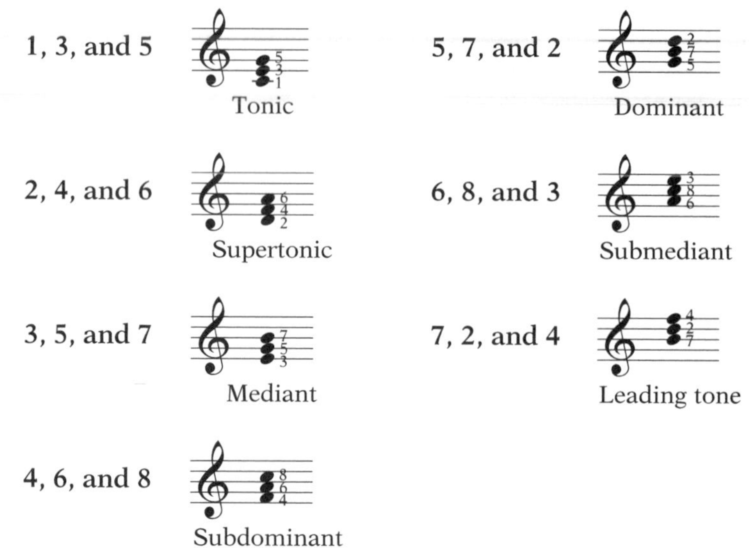

Which chords sound the same? Which ones sound different?

Now play chords with four notes together. For example, play 1, 3, 5, 7, or 5, 7, 2, 4.

Congratulations! You are almost playing jazz.

You can build a chord on any note of the scale. However, for our purposes, it is important to stick with the "correct" notes of the scale. For example, if you are in the key of G major, you must remember that there is an F-sharp in that key.

I hope you noticed that all the chords you composed had different qualities of sound. Each chord that you played was made up of intervals of a third. Some of those chords had a "major" quality and some of them had a "minor" quality. Every key has a variety of chord qualities. However, it is the predominant sound of the key that determines whether it is called major or minor. If the chord built on the first note of the key or scale has a major quality, the key is then determined to be major. A minor chord built on the first note of a scale implies that the key will be minor. Play a variety of chords at the keyboard and you will soon develop a sense of major and minor.

Look at the beginning of a song. Determine the key and then look at the chords. Notice the beginning and ending chords of the song. Usually you will find that they are both the tonic. The lowest bass note at the end of the song will usually be the tonic note of the key. You may notice also that the notes of any given chord can be placed in a variety of ways. For example, rather than playing 1, 3, and 5, play 3, 5, and 8 or 5, 8, and 3. These are all still the tonic chord, but in rearranged positions, or *inversions*. Find some time to play around with chords on a keyboard or at the piano.

The Internet has many music theory links. The music department at your school may have a list of links they find helpful. Music programs for computers (e.g., Finale or Sibelius) will write melodies, play and write chords, create an orchestra, and do many other wonderful musical things for you. In fact, there are programs that allow a pianist to play the music and the computer will turn it into a musical score.

However, it is important to know what you are doing. Knowledge stops panic in its tracks. The more you know about music, rhythm, and notes, the more confidently you can perform. It is easy to lose your confidence and trust if you are dependent on rote memory. "Fake it until you make it" is not particularly useful where musicianship is concerned.

Further Reading and Print Resources

BOOKS

Adams, David. *A Handbook of Diction for Singers: Italian, German, French.* New York: Oxford University Press, 1999.

Bunch, M. *Dynamics of the Singing Voice.* New York/Vienna: Springer-Verlag, 1997.

Bunch Dayme, M. *The Performer's Voice.* New York: W. W. Norton, 2005.

Dayme, M. *Creating Confidence.* e-book www.fccake.com, 2005.

Dayme, M. *The Little Book about Singing.* e-book www.fccake.com, 2006.

Calais-Germain, B. *Anatomy of Movement.* Seattle, WA: Eastland Press, 1993.

Conable, Barbara. *The Structures and Movement of Breathing.* Chicago: GIA Publications, 2000.

Craig, David. *A Performer Prepares: A Guide to Song Preparation for Actors, Singers and Dancers.* New York: Applause Theatre Book Publishers, 1999.

Dennison, P. *Brain-Gym.* Ventura, CA: Edu-Kinesthetics, 1986.

Emmons, S., and Thomas A. *Power Performance for Singers: Transcending the Barriers.* New York: Oxford University Press, 1998.

Goldsmith, Joan Oliver. *How Can We Keep from Singing: Music and the Passionate Life.* New York: W. W. Norton, 2001.

Kimball, Carol. *Song: A Guide to Art Style and Literature.* Revised Edition, Hal Leonard Corp., 2007.

Macdonald, Glynn. *Illustrated Elements of Alexander Technique.* London: Element, 2002.

Nelson, S., and Blades-Zeller, E. *Singing with Your Whole Self: The Feldenkrais Method and Voice.* Rochester, NY: Inspiration Press, 2000.

Ristad, E. *A Soprano on Her Head.* Moab, UT: Real People Press, 1982.

Sataloff, R. *Vocal Health and Pedagogy.* San Diego, CA: Plural Publishing Group, 2006.

Zander, R., and B. Zander. *The Art of Possibility: Transforming Professional and Personal Life.* Boston, MA: Harvard Business School Press, 2000.

SONGBOOKS

26 Italian Songs and Arias. Ed. John Glenn Paton. Alfred Publishing, 1991. Medium high and Medium low voice editions with accompaniment CDs.

The Definitive Jazz Collection. Indianapolis, IN: Hal Leonard Corp., 1989.

Singer's Library of Song: A Vocal Anthology of Masterworks and Folk Songs from the Medieval Era through the Twentieth Century. Ed. Patrick Liebergen. Alfred Publishing, 2005. High, Medium, and Low voice editions.

Some Recommended Websites

THE SINGING BOOK STUDENT WEBSITE

wwnorton.com/web/singing

Using the registration code provided with *The Singing Book,* students and teachers can access music in additional keys for all public-domain songs in the anthology. Users can listen to songs in various keys and print them as performance-ready sheet music.

VOICE-TEACHER WEBSITES

NATIONAL ASSOCIATION OF TEACHERS OF SINGING
www.nats.org

The site includes student message boards, NATS CHATS, and a Find-A-Teacher directory. Several websites listed in this book can be accessed through links on the NATS website.

MUSIC TEACHERS NATIONAL ASSOCIATION
www. mtna.org

Another good source for finding qualified voice teachers in your area.

LYRICS, TRANSLATIONS, AND DICTION

THE LIED AND ART SONG TEXTS
www.recmusic.org/lieder/

An extensive database of thousands of foreign and English song texts and translations. You can also find this page from the *Related Links* section of the NATS website.

THE DICTION DOMAIN
www.scaredofthat.com/dictiondomain

"From Catalan to Klingon," everything you always wanted to know about the International Phonetic Alphabet and singing in foreign languages.

VOCAL HEALTH

NATIONAL CENTER FOR VOICE AND SPEECH
www.ncvs.org/ncvs/info/singers

Information and articles for singers, including *Dr. Titze's Favorite Five Vocal Warmups for Singers.*

DIGITAL SHEET MUSIC

Commercial websites for purchasing, downloading, and printing vocal sheet music:

www.sheetmusicdirect.com

www.musicnotes.com

www.everynote.com

ONLINE LISTENING

Commercial websites for listening to and downloading recorded music:

www.apple.com/itunes

www.rhapsody.com

www.calabashmusic.com (world music)

PANDORA, CREATED BY THE MUSIC GENOME PROJECT

www.pandora.com

Musicians and music-loving technologists came together with the idea of creating the most comprehensive analysis of music ever. Type in a song title or artist you like and Pandora will find similar music to create a free online radio station.

ALTERNATE THERAPIES

The therapies below can be done with a practitioner or for yourself once you have learned the technique.

Emotional Freedom Techniques

www.emofree.com

Emotional Freedom Techniques (EFT) uses affirmations and tapping on end points of acupuncture meridians with great success for physical and psychological problems.

Quantum Touch

www.quantumtouch.com

Uses gentle breathing patterns and hands to balance and correct problems from spinal alignment to psychological issues.

Integrative Quantum Medicine

www.taoenergy.com

A very successful healing method integrating Chinese medicine, Western medicine, and quantum physics. Deals with any issue—physical, mental, or emotional.

Qigong and Tai Chi

www.taichihealthways.com

Features the work of Jesse Tsao. He has some of the best CDs and DVDs available for Qigong and Tai Chi. These are great for home practice if you cannot get to a class.

Index

Recordings to Accompany The Singing Book

The 2-CD set gives you three listening options for learning and practicing all of the songs in *The Singing Book*. Tracks 17 to 42 on CD 1 and all of the tracks on CD 2 are recorded in split-track stereo, with melody and guide rhythm on the right track and piano accompaniment on the left track. Using a computer or any CD player equipped with balance controls, you can adjust the speaker balance to hear either the melody/rhythm or piano accompaniment alone, or to hear both tracks played together. Stereos without balance controls will play both tracks simultaneously.

CD 1

1. Dance Your Dream Come True
2. Circle of Friends
3. Ballad (Major Key)
4. Swingin' in Minor Blues
5. There's Music in the Air
6. My Country 'Tis of Thee
7. Music Alone Shall Live
8. Oh, How Lovely Is the Evening
9. Babylon
10. Dona nobis pacem
11. Ah, Poor Bird
12. Shalom, chaverim
13. Ah, Poor Bird/Shalom
14. Alleluia I
15. Alleluia II
16. Alleluia III
17. Shenandoah
18. The House of the Rising Sun
19. Scarborough Fair
20. Danny Boy
21. The Water Is Wide
22. Salley Gardens
23. Suo-gân
24. Red Is the Rose
25. Flor, blanca flor
26. Niño precioso
27. Santa Lucia
28. L'hirondelle messagère
29. Dubinushka
30. Dance of Youth
31. Ev'ry Time I Feel the Spirit
32. Amazing Grace
33. Wayfaring Stranger
34. I've Got Peace Like a River
35. How Can I Keep from Singing?
36. Someone Like You
37. I Move On
38. Anything You Can Do

CD 2

1. Wand'rin' Star
2. Goodnight, My Someone
3. Ten Minutes Ago
4. Where is Love?
5. Over the Rainbow
6. Sing!
7. Somewhere Out There
8. A Time for Us/Un giorno per noi
9. You Raise Me Up
10. Be Who You Were Born to Be
11. True Colors
12. Don't Get Around Much Anymore
13. Blue Skies
14. When I Fall in Love
15. They Can't Take That Away from Me
16. Skylark
17. Come Again, Sweet Love
18. The Angler's Song
19. Donzelle, fuggite
20. Selve amiche, ombrose piante
21. Star vicino
22. Lungi
23. He Shall Feed His Flock
24. Ich liebe dich
25. If You've Only Got a Moustache
26. O Mistress Mine
27. El majo timido
28. Evening Prayer
29. Summertime
30. Oh, better far to live and die
31. The sun, whose rays are all ablaze
32. Toi, le coeur de la rose
33. The Hippopotamus
34. Come Ready and See Me